DARING NEW ADVENTURES OF
SUPERGIRL
VOLUME 1

JULIUS SCHWARTZ Editor – Original Series
JEB WOODARD Group Editor – Collected Editions
ROBIN WILDMAN Editor – Collected Edition
STEVE COOK Design Director – Books
SARABETH KETT Publication Design

BOB HARRAS Senior VP – Editor-in-Chief, DC Comics

DIANE NELSON President
DAN DIDIO and JIM LEE Co-Publishers
GEOFF JOHNS Chief Creative Officer
AMIT DESAI Senior VP – Marketing & Global Franchise Management
NAIRI GARDINER Senior VP – Finance
SAM ADES VP – Digital Marketing
BOBBIE CHASE VP – Talent Development
MARK CHIARELLO Senior VP – Art, Design & Collected Editions
JOHN CUNNINGHAM VP – Content Strategy
ANNE DEPIES VP – Strategy Planning & Reporting
DON FALLETTI VP – Manufacturing Operations
LAWRENCE GANEM VP – Editorial Administration & Talent Relations
ALISON GILL Senior VP – Manufacturing & Operations
HANK KANALZ Senior VP – Editorial Strategy & Administration
JAY KOGAN VP – Legal Affairs
DEREK MADDALENA Senior VP – Sales & Business Development
JACK MAHAN VP – Business Affairs
DAN MIRON VP – Sales Planning & Trade Development
NICK NAPOLITANO VP – Manufacturing Administration
CAROL ROEDER VP – Marketing
EDDIE SCANNELL VP – Mass Account & Digital Sales
COURTNEY SIMMONS Senior VP – Publicity & Communications
JIM (SKI) SOKOLOWSKI VP – Comic Book Specialty & Newsstand Sales
SANDY YI Senior VP – Global Franchise Management

DARING NEW ADVENTURES OF SUPERGIRL VOLUME 1

Published by DC Comics. Compilation and all new material Copyright © 2016 DC Comics. All Rights Reserved. Originally published in single magazine form in DARING NEW ADVENTURES OF SUPERGIRL 1-12. Copyright © 1982, 1983 DC Comics. All Rights Reserved. All characters, their distinctive likenesses and related elements featured in this publication are trademarks of DC Comics. The stories, characters and incidents featured in this publication are entirely fictional. DC Comics does not read or accept unsolicited submissions of ideas, stories or artwork.

DC Comics, 2900 West Alameda Ave., Burbank, CA 91505
Printed by RR Donnelley, Owensville, MO, USA. 6/10/16. First Printing.
ISBN: 978-1-4012-6346-1

Interior color reconstruction by Digikore.
Collection cover color by Allen Passalaqua.

Library of Congress Cataloging-in-Publication Data

Names: Kupperberg, Paul. | Infantino, Carmine, illustrator. | Oksner, Bob, illustrator.
Title: Daring Adventures of Supergirl vol. 1 / Paul Kupperberg ; illustrated by Carmine Infantino, Bob Oksner.
Description: Burbank, CA : DC Comics, [2016]
Identifiers: LCCN 2016018857 | ISBN 9781401263461 (paperback)
Subjects: LCSH: Comic books, strips, etc. | BISAC: COMICS & GRAPHIC NOVELS / Superheroes.
Classification: LCC PN6728.S89 K87 2016 | DDC 741.5/973—dc23
LC record available at https://lccn.loc.gov/2016018857

DARING NEW ADVENTURES OF
SUPERGIRL
VOLUME 1

PAUL KUPPERBERG writer **CARMINE INFANTINO** penciller

BOB OKSNER inker **TOM ZIUKO** colorist

BEN ODA ANDY KUBERT JOHN COSTANZA
ADAM KUBERT PHIL FELIX MILT SNAPINN
letterers

RICH BUCKLER & DICK GIORDANO
collection cover artists

SUPERGIRL BASED ON CHARACTERS CREATED BY
JERRY SIEGEL AND **JOE SHUSTER**
BY SPECIAL ARRANGEMENT WITH THE JERRY SIEGEL FAMILY

Cover by **Rich Buckler & Dick Giordano**

THE DARING NEW ADVENTURES OF

SUPERGIRL

BEGINNING A NEW CHAPTER IN THE LIFE AND TIMES OF THE MIGHTY MAID OF STEEL!

SHE WAS BORN IN A SOLAR SYSTEM FAR FROM THE FAMILIAR CONFINES OF OUR PLANETARY HOME... A REFUGEE FROM DISASTER ON A COSMIC SCALE.

YET FROM THE DEBRIS OF THIS CATASTROPHE ROSE HOPE, LIKE THE PHOENIX FROM THE FLAME -- HOPE FOR THE MYRIAD BEINGS OF THE UNIVERSE... AND A BLESSING FOR THE PLANET EARTH.

FOR IT WAS HERE THAT THIS DAUGHTER OF THE STARS FOUND A NEW HOME, WHERE SHE HAS BEEN TAKEN TO THE HEARTS OF ITS PEOPLE... AND IT IS SHE WHO HAS REPAID THIS KINDNESS OVER AND OVER AGAIN, DEDICATING HER LIFE TO THE WELL-BEING OF HER ADOPTED WORLD.

'A VERY STRANGE AND SPECIAL GIRL!'

PAUL KUPPERBERG
WRITER

CARMINE INFANTINO • BOB OKSNER
PENCILLER — INKER

BEN ODA — LETTERER
ZIUKO — COLORIST

JULIUS SCHWARTZ — EDITOR

NOT MANY PEOPLE TAKE THE TRAIN THESE DAYS. IT'S TOO *SLOW*, THEY SAY. TOO UNCOMFORTABLE. WHY GO BY RAIL WHEN AIRPLANES ARE SO MUCH *FASTER*?

TAKE, FOR EXAMPLE, THE *LAKE SHORE LIMITED* FROM NEW YORK TO CHICAGO. IT'S A TWENTY-HOUR TRIP, SNAKING COMPARATIVELY *LAZILY* THROUGH PENNSYLVANIA AND INDIANA, WHILE THE SAME JOURNEY BY *PLANE* IS A MERE 90 MINUTES.

BUT THE AGE OF *RAIL* TRAVEL IS NOT, THANKFULLY, QUITE OVER. OH, PERHAPS THESE *MODERN* TRAINS LACK THE *GLORY* OF EARLIER DAYS AND FAMED RUNS LIKE THE 20TH-CENTURY LIMITED AND THE ORIENT EXPRESS --

-- YET RUN THEY STILL DO, CATERING TO THOSE WITH A *FEAR* OF FLYING... OR WHO STILL PREFER TO ACTUALLY *SEE* WHERE THEY'RE HEADED --

-- OR THOSE FORTUNATE FEW WHO ARE IN ABSOLUTELY *NO* HURRY TO GET WHERE THEY'RE GOING.

AND NUMBERED AMONG THAT PARTICULAR GROUP ARE EVEN SOME WITH MUCH FASTER MEANS OF TRANSPORTATION AT THEIR DISPOSAL.

YES... IT'S *AMAZING* THE THINGS YOU MISS SEEING BY *FLYING* OVER THIS COUNTRY.

I KNOW WHAT YOU MEAN, MS. DANVERS. I *NEVER* TAKE A PLANE IF I CAN AVOID IT. HAVE *YOU* FLOWN VERY MUCH?

MMMM... A *BIT*, YES.

ROSSER GETS SAVED!!

LINDA DANVERS IS ONE OF THAT NUMBER --

-- AND A MOST *SPECIAL* ONE AT THAT.

OH, MR. WAINWRIGHT... IF ONLY YOU *KNEW*!

2

WELL, I THINK I'LL HEAD BACK TO THE DINING CAR. IS THERE ANYTHING I CAN BRING YOU, MR. WAINWRIGHT?

NOTHING FOR ME, THANKS. I'M SAVING MY APPETITE FOR WHEN WE HIT CHICAGO!

I'M GLAD HE DIDN'T DECIDE TO JOIN ME FOR LUNCH. NOT THAT HE ISN'T A NICE MAN--

--BUT FRANKLY, THE LAST THING I NEED RIGHT NOW IS A COMPANION FOR WHERE I'M HEADING--

--ESPECIALLY A COMPANION WHO DOESN'T CARE FOR FLYING!

≈SIGH≈ AND HERE I THOUGHT I'D BE ABLE TO TAKE IT EASY ON MY WAY TO MY NEW HOME. I GUESS IT JUST PROVES ONCE AGAIN THERE'S NO REST FOR THE WEARY--

--WHEN THE WEARY ONE HAPPENS TO BE SUPERGIRL!

I SUPPOSE THAT'S WHAT I GET FOR KEEPING MY SUPER-SENSES TUNED FOR TROUBLE WHEN I'D RATHER NOT DEAL WITH THESE THINGS--!

AHHH, WHO DO YOU THINK YOU'RE KIDDING, LADY? YOU KNOW PERFECTLY WELL YOU'D INTERRUPT A DATE WITH ROBERT REDFORD TO RESCUE A KITTEN FROM A TREE--

--AND THIS BEATS A KITTY ANY DAY OF THE WEEK!

3

PAY CLOSE ATTENTION TO THIS YOUNG WOMAN!

THAT SHE IS UNLIKE ANY OTHER IS BEYOND QUESTION -- HER VERY ACTIONS SPEAK LOUDER THAN ANY WORDS COULD EVER HOPE TO CONVEY --

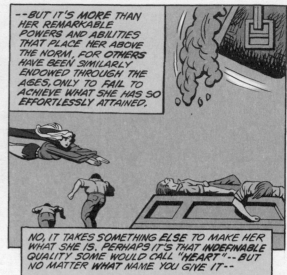

--BUT IT'S MORE THAN HER REMARKABLE POWERS AND ABILITIES THAT PLACE HER ABOVE THE NORM, FOR OTHERS HAVE BEEN SIMILARLY ENDOWED THROUGH THE AGES, ONLY TO FAIL TO ACHIEVE WHAT SHE HAS SO EFFORTLESSLY ATTAINED.

NO, IT TAKES SOMETHING ELSE TO MAKE HER WHAT SHE IS. PERHAPS IT'S THAT INDEFINABLE QUALITY SOME WOULD CALL "HEART"-- BUT NO MATTER WHAT NAME YOU GIVE IT--

--IT ALL BOILS DOWN TO THE FACT THAT SHE IS SUPERGIRL!

THANK RAO I WAS PASSING THROUGH WHEN I WAS! I SHUDDER TO THINK WHAT WOULD'VE HAPPENED TO THOSE MEN IF I WEREN'T AROUND TO SAVE THEM FROM THIS SHOWER OF MOLTEN STEEL!

BUT WE'RE NOT OUT OF THE WOODS YET-- NOT UNTIL I USE MY SUPER-BREATH--

WHOOOSH

--TO PUT THE DANGER ON ICE ...ER, SO TO SPEAK!

MAN, THAT WAS SOMETHIN' ELSE, SUPERGIRL! WHEN THE BUCKET'S GUIDE-CHAIN SNAPPED, WE FIGURED THOSE TWO WERE GONERS!

THE PLEASURE WAS ALL MINE! AFTER ALL, THAT'S WHAT I'M HERE FOR, ISN'T IT?

4

Y-YEAH, SUPERGIRL... BUT IF YOU *HADN'T* BEEN IN THE NEIGHBORHOOD, MY *LUCK* WOULD'VE RUN OUT! *THANK* YOU!

IF THERE'S *ONE* THING I'VE LEARNED IN MY LINE OF BUSINESS -- IT'S THAT *LUCK* SELDOM HAS ANYTHING TO DO WITH IT!

NOW, IF YOU GENTLEMEN WILL *EXCUSE* ME, I'VE GOT TO *FLY!* I HAVE A *TRAIN* TO CATCH...

--*LITERALLY!*

THEY BLINK AND SHE IS GONE --

--ONLY TO REAPPEAR MOMENTS LATER...ALBEIT IN A SLIGHTLY *DIFFERENT* GUISE... MANY MILES TO THE WEST...

LOOKS LIKE MY SEAT-MATE DIDN'T WAIT UP FOR ME TO GET BACK. JUST AS WELL, I *SUPPOSE.* I COULD DO *WITHOUT* HIS ASKING WHY I'M BACK SO FAST FROM LUNCH--

--AND I DOUBT HE'D BELIEVE ME IF I *TOLD* HIM!

BESIDES, I COULD DO WITH THE TIME TO *MYSELF*... TO SIT BACK AND *THINK.* IT'S SELFISH, I KNOW, BUT I *DESERVE* ...*WHOA!*

THERE YOU GO *AGAIN,* LINDA!

THERE'S *NOTHING SELFISH* ABOUT WANTING TO GET INTO *YOURSELF* FOR A WHILE INSTEAD OF THINKING ABOUT THE WHOLE BLASTED *WORLD!* I DO ENOUGH OF *THAT* AS SUPERGIRL--

-- AND WASN'T THE WHOLE *REASON* FOR THIS MOVE... TO GIVE MYSELF *SPACE* TO BE JUST PLAIN LINDA DANVERS?

I'VE BEEN SUPERGIRL FOR SUCH A *LONG* TIME, IT SEEMS. NOT THAT I'D GIVE THAT UP FOR *ANYTHING* ...BUT I FEEL LIKE I'VE TOTALLY *LOST* HOLD OF THE PART OF ME THAT DOESN'T SCOOT AROUND THE UNIVERSE IN SHORTS AND A CAPE!

I'VE FORGOTTEN WHAT IT *FEELS* LIKE TO BE JUST A *PERSON*... INSTEAD OF A *SYMBOL!*

5

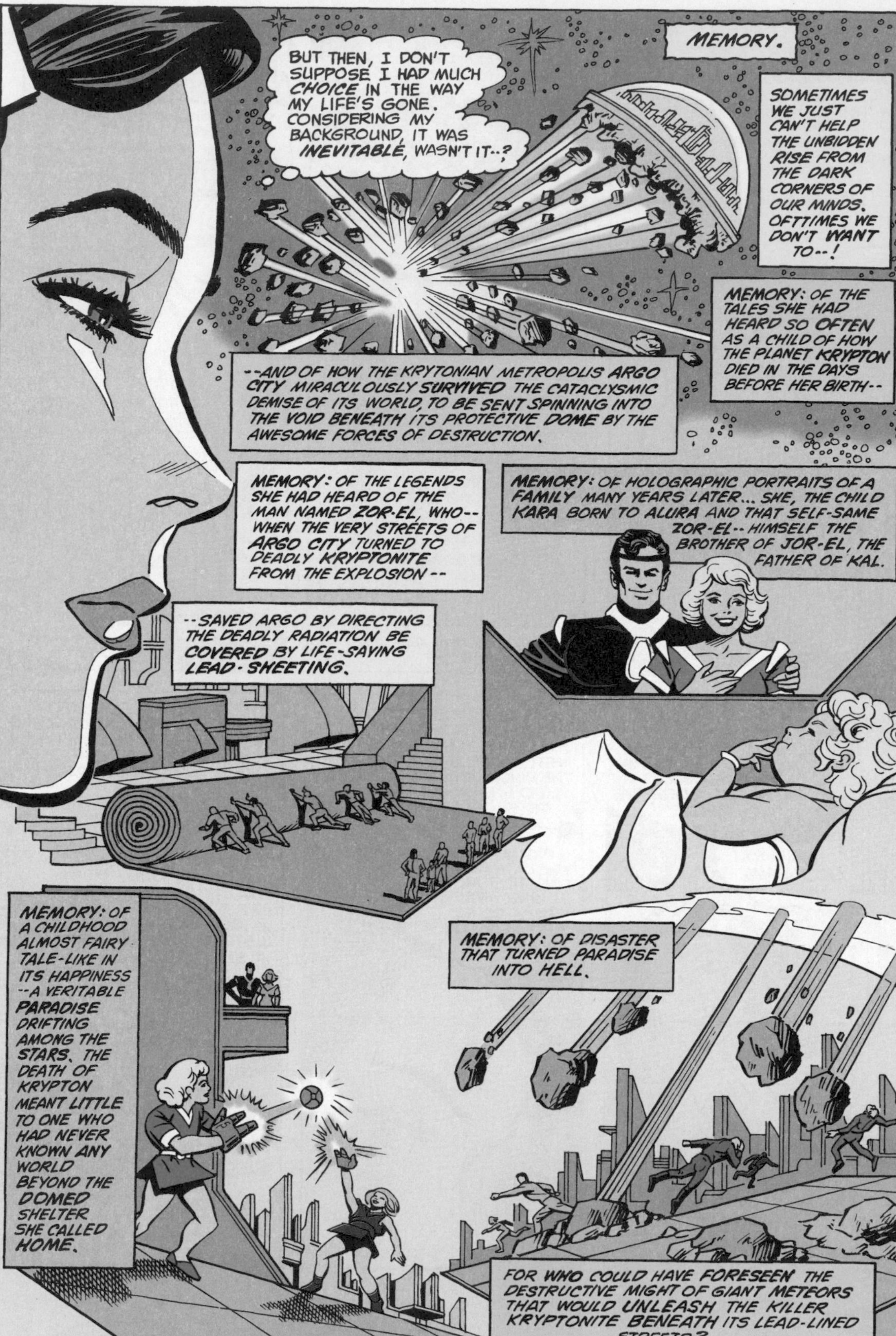
MEMORY.
BUT THEN, I DON'T SUPPOSE I HAD MUCH CHOICE IN THE WAY MY LIFE'S GONE. CONSIDERING MY BACKGROUND, IT WAS INEVITABLE, WASN'T IT..?
SOMETIMES WE JUST CAN'T HELP THE UNBIDDEN RISE FROM THE DARK CORNERS OF OUR MINDS. OFTTIMES WE DON'T WANT TO--!
MEMORY: OF THE TALES SHE HAD HEARD SO OFTEN AS A CHILD OF HOW THE PLANET KRYPTON DIED IN THE DAYS BEFORE HER BIRTH--
--AND OF HOW THE KRYTONIAN METROPOLIS ARGO CITY MIRACULOUSLY SURVIVED THE CATACLYSMIC DEMISE OF ITS WORLD, TO BE SENT SPINNING INTO THE VOID BENEATH ITS PROTECTIVE DOME BY THE AWESOME FORCES OF DESTRUCTION.
MEMORY: OF THE LEGENDS SHE HAD HEARD OF THE MAN NAMED ZOR-EL, WHO--WHEN THE VERY STREETS OF ARGO CITY TURNED TO DEADLY KRYPTONITE FROM THE EXPLOSION--
--SAVED ARGO BY DIRECTING THE DEADLY RADIATION BE COVERED BY LIFE-SAVING LEAD-SHEETING.
MEMORY: OF HOLOGRAPHIC PORTRAITS OF A FAMILY MANY YEARS LATER... SHE, THE CHILD KARA BORN TO ALURA AND THAT SELF-SAME ZOR-EL--HIMSELF THE BROTHER OF JOR-EL, THE FATHER OF KAL.
MEMORY: OF A CHILDHOOD ALMOST FAIRY TALE-LIKE IN ITS HAPPINESS --A VERITABLE PARADISE DRIFTING AMONG THE STARS. THE DEATH OF KRYPTON MEANT LITTLE TO ONE WHO HAD NEVER KNOWN ANY WORLD BEYOND THE DOMED SHELTER SHE CALLED HOME.
MEMORY: OF DISASTER THAT TURNED PARADISE INTO HELL.
FOR WHO COULD HAVE FORESEEN THE DESTRUCTIVE MIGHT OF GIANT METEORS THAT WOULD UNLEASH THE KILLER KRYPTONITE BENEATH ITS LEAD-LINED STREETS?

MEMORY: OF DESPERATION AS SOLUTIONS WERE TRIED... AND DISCARDED AS USELESS.

MEMORY: OF HER FATHER'S WORDS -- OF THE SON OF HIS LATE BROTHER JOR, GROWN NOW TO MANHOOD ON A DISTANT WORLD WHOSE EXISTENCE WAS GLIMPSED THROUGH A SUB-SPACE TELESCOPE.

IT WAS THERE YOUNG KARA WOULD GO... ALONE.

IT SEEMED ALL THE PEOPLE OF ARGO CITY WERE SOON TO JOIN THEIR KRYPTONIAN BRETHREN IN DEATH -- SAVE FOR ONE OF THE FAMILY OF ZOR-EL.

MEMORY: OF A SORROW THAT WOULD NEVER DIE.

MEMORY: OF ARRIVAL ON HER NEW HOME AND THE MEETING OF A FRIEND.

MEMORY: OF THE GIRL'S LAST VIEW OF ARGO CITY AS IT SPUN AWAY TO BE LOST FOR ALL TIME TO THE STARS.

HER WORLD WAS GONE -- AND A WHOLE NEW ONE WAS TO OPEN BEFORE HER... ONE SHE WOULD NOT NEED TO FACE ALONE.

MEMORY: IT'S FUNNY HOW THE SAME EXPERIENCES ELICIT SUCH VERY DIFFERENT EMOTIONS WHEN SEEN THROUGH THE EYES OF TIME.

WHEW! YOU'VE COME A LONG WAY, BABY! BUT THEN, YOU'RE NOT THE SAME LITTLE GIRL OF FIFTEEN THESE DAYS --

... EXCEPT, MAYBE, FOR THE PAIN OF LOSS...!

LINDA DANVERS SIGHS DEEPLY TO HERSELF AND THEN LOOKS OUT THE WINDOW. PERHAPS THIS ISN'T THE BEST TIME TO LOSE HERSELF IN THE PAST, SHE THINKS WITH A SMILE.

BECAUSE SHE'S ARRIVED!

7

MEANWHILE, SEVERAL MILES TO THE NORTH OF LINDA'S POINT OF ARRIVAL, IN ONE OF THE MANY *LUXURY CO-OPS* THAT LINE THE *NORTH SHORE* OF *LAKE MICHIGAN...*

--AND IN LOCAL NEWS AT NOON, A *THREE-ALARM* BLAZE SWEPT THROUGH A *SOUTH-SIDE* TENEMENT THIS MORNING, KILLING *THREE*--

--AND *GANG-WAR* ACTIVITIES *ESCALATE* AT THE *CABRINI-GREEN HOUSING PROJECT.* ALSO, POLICE ARREST EIGHT MEN CHARGED WITH RUNNING THE CITY'S *BIGGEST DOPE RING.* DETAILS AFTER THESE COMMERCIAL MESSAGES...

SPLENDID. POSITIVELY SPLENDID!

I-I WISH YOU WOULDN'T *DO* THAT, *MR. PENDERGAST!* IT SEEMS SO... SO...

GHOULISH, MY DEAR?

IN A WAY, I SUPPOSE IT *IS* AT THAT. ON THE OTHER HAND, IT'S MERELY *MORE* SIGNS OF THE *DECAY*--

--AND ISN'T THAT, AFTER ALL, WHAT WE'VE WORKED SO LONG AND SO *DILIGENTLY* ALL THESE YEARS TO BRING ABOUT, DEAR *GAYLE?*

I SUPPOSE. BUT THOSE PEOPLE... DYING-- *KILLING* EACH OTHER-- *ROTTING* THEIR BODIES WITH DRUGS--!

SOMETIMES I'M NOT SURE I CAN *HANDLE* IT, MR. PENDERGAST! I MEAN I CAN ALMOST *FEEL* IT-- LIKE IT WAS A *REAL, PHYSICAL* THING!

EVERY TIME SOMEONE *DIES* OR *HATES* OR *DESTROYS... I* KNOW IT-- LIKE IT WAS *ME* DOING THOSE THINGS!

I DUNNO... MAYBE YOU'VE BEEN *WRONG* ALL ALONG. MAYBE I *AM* CRAZY!

NO, GAYLE-- MERELY *DIFFERENT!* I'VE TOLD YOU -- YOU ARE *SPECIAL... UNIQUE* TO THIS DYING WORLD. *YOU* ARE A *"SENSITIVE,"* YES --

--BUT ALSO ARE YOU SO MUCH *MORE!*

8

YOU ARE THE *FORERUNNER* OF A *NEW WORLD!* IMAGINE, SIMPLE LITTLE *GAYLE MARSH* FROM SKOKIE, ILLINOIS-- AND FROM YOU SHALL COME THE *NEW WAY!*

WE'VE WATCHED THE *DECAY* OVERCOME US FROM *AGES.* YOU'VE SEEN HOW IT'S TAKEN OVER HUMANITY, MARCHING IT *SLOWLY* TOWARD THE INEVITABLE *BRINK--*

--TAKING WITH IT ANY *CHANCE* FOR THE SURVIVAL OF MANKIND AS WE KNOW IT! BUT THAT CAN *ONLY* HAPPEN IF WE *ALLOW* IT TO FOLLOW ITS *NATURAL* PROGRESSION!

THINK OF IT, DEAR GAYLE -- *THROUGH YOU,* MANKIND HAS A *CHANCE!* YET, AS IN *ALL* GREAT THINGS, THERE *WILL* BE A *PRICE* TO PAY!

BUT DESPITE THAT, WE *ARE* FORTUNATE INDEED! WE'VE *ISOLATED* THE *DECAY* AND KNOW NOW WHAT WE MUST DO TO TURN BACK ITS PUTREFYING WAVE!

OH, YES, GAYLE, WE *ARE* LUCKY--

--FOR *WHAT* ARE A FEW PALTRY *MILLION* LIVES WHEN BALANCED AGAINST THE WEIGHT OF *HUMANITY!*

I *KNOW* ALL THAT, MR. PENDERGAST. *REALLY* I DO! YET... WHENEVER I *THINK* ABOUT WHAT I'M GOING TO HAVE TO *DO,* I GET SO AFRAID--! WH-*WHAT'S* IT GOING TO *FEEL* LIKE...?

THEN YOU *SHOULDN'T* THINK ABOUT IT, GIRL! WHEN THE TIME COMES FOR US TO *ACT,* I SHALL THINK FOR US *BOTH--*

--WHILE ALL *YOU* NEED DO IS *DESTROY* THIS FETID CESSPOOL OF *DECAY* CALLED *CHICAGO!*

GAYLE MARSH SHUDDERS EVER SO *SLIGHTLY* AT THE MAN'S WORDS, YET STRANGELY, SHE FINDS COMFORT IN HIS TOUCH.

BUT SHE IS A *SENSITIVE,* THUS DOES SHE ACCEPT THE SENSUAL OVER HER FEARS... AND RELIEF FLOODS THROUGH HER BEING.

9

EVEN AS GAYLE MARSH MAKES HER FATEFUL DECISION, LINDA DANVERS IS COMING TO FACE THE RESULTS OF ONE OF HERS...

I CAN'T BELIEVE HOW EXCITED I'M GETTING!

IT'S NOT LIKE I'VE NEVER BEEN TO CHICAGO BEFORE...BUT I GUESS THIS IS DIFFERENT!

ALL THOSE OTHER TIMES, I WAS JUST PASSING THROUGH OR VISITING, BUT NOW I'M DOING A LOT MORE THAN VISITING--

--I'M COMING HOME!

CHICAGO! IT IS KNOWN BY OTHER NAMES AS WELL--THE WINDY CITY...A DERISIVE TERM COINED BY A VISITING NEW YORK JOURNALIST, HAVING TO DO MORE WITH THE TOWN'S POLITICS THAN THE WEATHER.

"HOG BUTCHER TO THE WORLD"...THE POET'S JAB AT THE STINK AND SQUALOR OF THE LONG-GONE CHICAGO STOCK-YARDS.

THE SECOND CITY...A NOT-SO-FRIENDLY REFERENCE TO THE ILLINOIS CITY'S PERPETUAL RUNNER-UP STATUS TO NEW YORK.

YET CHICAGOANS SEEM TO EMBRACE THESE EPITHETS, MAKING THEM INSTEAD NAMES TO BE PROUD OF, AS IF TO SHOW THE WORLD IT CAN DO NOTHING TO DAUNT THE FIERCE PRIDE OF THE CITY ON THE LAKE.

LINDA FEELS IT ALREADY, AND ANY DOUBTS SHE MAY HAVE HAD OVER BEGINNING HER LIFE ANEW IN THIS PLACE ARE SUDDENLY GONE.

IT'D BE SO MUST *FASTER* TO HEAD FOR THE COLLEGE *SUPERGIRL-STYLE*, BUT CONSIDERING I'VE GONE THROUGH THE HASSLE OF *TRAINING* IT THIS FAR...

TAXI!

THE *LAKE SHORE UNIVERSITY* ADMISSIONS BUILDING, CABBIE ...AND LET'S TAKE THE *SCENIC ROUTE.*

ONE *GUIDED TOUR,* COMIN' RIGHT UP, MISS!

RRW R/1

MUST BE *EXCITIN'* FOR YOU, MISS. I MEAN, LEAVIN' *HOME* AND COMIN' ALL THE WAY OUT HERE TO *CHICAGAH* FOR SCHOOL AND ALL!

YES, I SUPPOSE IT *IS.*

LAKE SHORE DRIVE SOUTH

NO NEED TO TELL THE MAN THIS IS *HARDLY* THE FIRST TIME I'VE LEFT ONE HOME TO TAKE UP IN ANOTHER-- AND AFTER MY TRIP FROM *ARGO CITY* TO *EARTH* --

--MOST OF THOSE'VE BEEN MORE LIKE *CROSSING THE STREET* IN COMPARISON! THAT'S NOT TO SAY THEY HAVEN'T ALL LEFT THEIR *MARK--*

"-- BUT SOMEHOW IT'S TOUGH TO TAKE ANY MOVE TOO HARD ONCE YOU'VE BEEN HALF-WAY ACROSS THE UNIVERSE!"

"I WAS A *REAL STRANGER* IN A VERY *STRANGE LAND!* WITH NOWHERE ELSE TO GO, *SUPERMAN* HAD NO CHOICE BUT TO PLACE ME IN *MIDVALE ORPHANAGE* UNDER THE NAME *LINDA LEE.*"

"EARTH WAS KIND OF DISAPPOINTING AT FIRST. ALL I COULD SEE WAS THAT IT WASN'T *ARGO CITY...* DIDN'T HAVE THE *SCIENTIFIC MAJESTY* OF MY HOME WORLD.

"AND MOST IMPORTANTLY, IT DIDN'T HAVE MY *PARENTS!*"

"I HATED IT!"

11

"I LEARNED A LOT ABOUTH EARTH DURING MY TIME IN MIDVALE... AND EVEN *MORE* ABOUT MYSELF. SURE, I WAS *DIFFERENT* FROM THE OTHER KIDS, BUT IN MY CASE, *DIFFERENT* WASN'T BAD--IT WAS *SPECIAL*.

"--AND GAVE HER A HOME... AND A NAME.

"AND EARTH WAS SPECIAL TOO--ESPECIALLY SINCE IT HAD PEOPLE LIKE *FRED* AND *EDNA DANVERS* LIVING ON IT. WHILE EVERYONE ELSE WANTED INFANTS TO ADOPT, THEY SAW THE LONELINESS AND *NEED* OF A TEEN-AGE GIRL--

"I CAN NEVER FORGET *ZOR-EL* AND *ALURA*, BUT THE *DANVERS* WERE MY PARENTS FROM THAT MOMENT ON. THEY THOUGHT I WAS PRETTY *SPECIAL*--

"MAN, WERE THEY SURPRISED TO FIND OUT JUST HOW *MUCH*!

"IF IT WEREN'T FOR THEM, I'D HAVE *NEVER* GOTTEN OVER THE *BITTERNESS* I FELT WHEN I THOUGHT MY NATURAL PARENTS HAD DIED--"

--AND I DOUBT I'D EVER BE ABLE TO REALLY *LOOK* AT MY NEW WORLD AND SEE IT AS IT *TRULY* IS... NOT JUST A WORLD THAT'S *NOT* ARGO CITY--

--BUT A BEAUTIFUL, SPECIAL PLACE IN THIS UNIVERSE!

... I SAID, WE'RE *HERE*, MISS! *MISS*--?

SO WE *ARE*! THANKS FOR THE RIDE AND *TOUR*.

MY PLEASURE! AND... *WELCOME* TO CHICAGAH!

FRIEND, I DON'T THINK I'VE EVER BEEN *HAPPIER* TO BE ANYWHERE!

LINDA DANVERS TAKES A DEEP BREATH AND TURNS TO GREET HER NEW LIFE. IT'S FITTING THAT IT SHOULD BEGIN HERE AT *LAKE SHORE UNIVERSITY*--

ADDISON HALL

--ITSELF JUST BEGINNING AS THE *WINDY CITY*'S NEWEST INSTITUTION OF HIGHER EDUCATION.

12

AND AS WITH ANYTHING BEGINNING, IT SHOULD COME AS NO SURPRISE THAT THINGS ARE, AT BEST, CONFUSING...

ER... EXCUSE ME--?

HI THERE... *HELLO!* CAN I GET SOME *HELP* HERE, PLEASE?

ADMISSION OFFICE

I, ER... SAID, I COULD USE SOME... *YOO-HOO!* DO YOU *HEAR ME--?!*

LOOK, I'M *NEW* HERE AND I COULD USE SOME *ASSISTANCE....!*

LINDA TO ANYBODY... LINDA TO *ANYBODY....!* IS EVERYBODY *DEAF!?*

EXCUSE ME, BUT I SAID I NEED--

--HELP!

EEEEK!

SHEESH! LISSEN, HONEY, IF YOU'RE HERE TO ENROLL IN *TRAFFIC COP SCHOOL*--FORGET IT! YOU'RE IN THE *WRONG* PLACE!

TRY THE *PSYCHOLOGY DEPARTMENT* AND YOU'LL BE GETTING *WARMER,* MISS!

HUH? WHAT'D YOU *SAY?*

OH, *BROTHER!*

I *SAID,* I'M *REGISTERING* IN THE *PSYCHOLOGY DEPART...*

WAITAMINNIT, WAITAMINNIT! YOU *DON'T* HAVE TO SHOUT-- *SEE?*

TO TELL YOU THE *TRUTH,* IT'S THE *ONLY* WAY TO KEEP YOUR *SANITY* AROUND HERE, IF YOU KNOW WHAT I *MEAN!*

C-COTTON BALLS--?! HA HA HA!

YOU THINK *THAT'S* FUNNY? YOU OUGHTA TRY *WORKING* HERE SOMETIME, KIDDO!

13

I THINK I'LL *PASS*, THANKS!

NOW *AS I WAS TRYING* TO SAY, I'M HERE TO *REGISTER*. MY NAME'S LINDA DANVERS AND...

PLEASED TO MEET'CHA, LINDA. I'M *JOAN RAYMOND*, *NEW* IN THESE PARTS, ARE YOU?

YEAH... BUT GETTING *LESS* SO BY THE SECOND. WHAT'S A GIRL GOTTA DO TO REGISTER AROUND HERE?

TRY ASKING *ME*, LIN! I KNOW ALL ABOUT *THAT* STUFF.

'GROAN!'- I'VE GOT TO BE AT THE *HOUSING OFFICE* IN TEN MINUTES AND *YOU'RE* TAKING A *GIGGLE-BREAK* AT MY EXPENSE!

YOU'RE RIGHT, LIN. SORRY. LOOK, LEMME MAKE IT UP TO YOU, OKAY? YOU LOOK LIKE A *DECENT* SORT-- AND I'D KINDA *HATE* TO SEE YOU GET *STUCK* WITH ONE OF THEM *DUMPS* THE HOUSING OFFICE USUALLY PASSES OFF ON UNSUSPECTING FRESHMEN! C'MON...!

HOLD IT, JOAN--! WHAT ABOUT REGISTRATION...?

NO *SWEAT*, KIDDO-- YOU CAN DO THAT *ANY TIME!* YOU JUST GOT YOURSELF A *FRIEND* IN THE REGISTRAR'S OFFICE!

BUT... BUT...

BUT ME *NO BUTS*, LINDA! IT JUST SO HAPPENS A *GREAT* APARTMENT'S OPENED UP IN MY BUILDING! DO YOU *WANT* IT OR DON'TCHA?

LEAD ON, MacDUFF!

WELL, IT LOOKS LIKE I'VE *FINALLY* MET AN *IRRESISTIBLE FORCE* THAT'S TOO MUCH EVEN FOR A *SUPERGIRL!*

LEMME TELL YOU, LIN... YOU'RE GONNA JUST *LOVE* THIS PLACE! GOT A *GREAT* BUNCH OF NEIGHBORS TOO--ER, BESIDES *ME*, THAT IS!

HMMM, *NICE* CLOTHES YOU GOT THERE. YOU WOULDN'T BY ANY CHANCE BE A *SIZE EIGHT*, WOULD YOU? YEAH, I'LL BET YOU *ARE!*

EH, HOW *LONG'VE* YOU HAD THIS *SHYNESS* PROBLEM, JOAN?

14

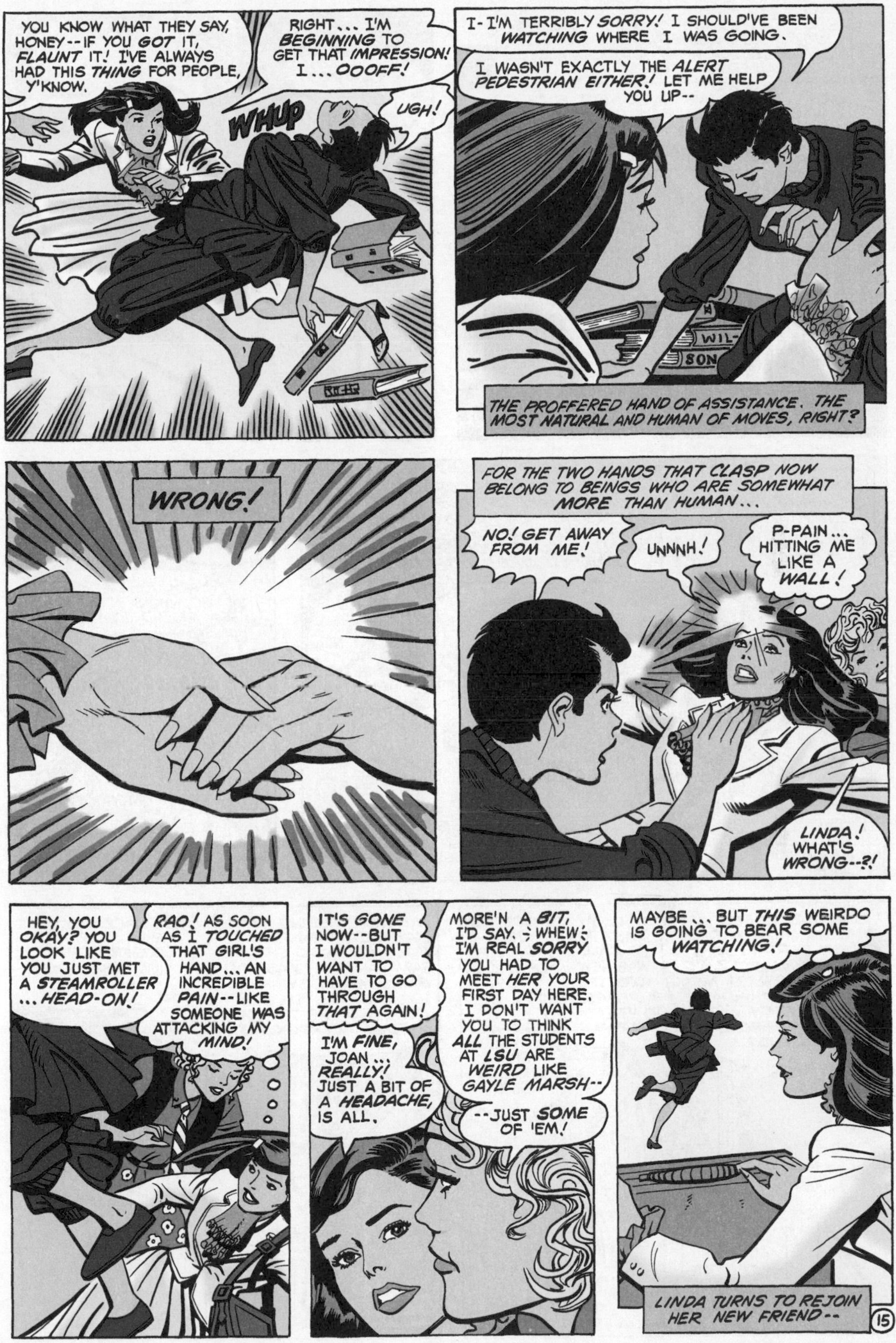
YOU KNOW WHAT THEY SAY, HONEY--IF YOU GOT IT, FLAUNT IT! I'VE ALWAYS HAD THIS THING FOR PEOPLE, Y'KNOW.
RIGHT... I'M BEGINNING TO GET THAT IMPRESSION! I... OOOFF!
WHUP
UGH!
I-I'M TERRIBLY SORRY! I SHOULD'VE BEEN WATCHING WHERE I WAS GOING.
I WASN'T EXACTLY THE ALERT PEDESTRIAN EITHER! LET ME HELP YOU UP--
WIL-SON
THE PROFFERED HAND OF ASSISTANCE. THE MOST NATURAL AND HUMAN OF MOVES, RIGHT?
WRONG!
FOR THE TWO HANDS THAT CLASP NOW BELONG TO BEINGS WHO ARE SOMEWHAT MORE THAN HUMAN...
NO! GET AWAY FROM ME!
UNNNH!
P-PAIN... HITTING ME LIKE A WALL!
LINDA! WHAT'S WRONG--?!
HEY, YOU OKAY? YOU LOOK LIKE YOU JUST MET A STEAMROLLER ...HEAD-ON!
RAO! AS SOON AS I TOUCHED THAT GIRL'S HAND... AN INCREDIBLE PAIN--LIKE SOMEONE WAS ATTACKING MY MIND!
IT'S GONE NOW--BUT I WOULDN'T WANT TO HAVE TO GO THROUGH THAT AGAIN!
I'M FINE, JOAN... REALLY! JUST A BIT OF A HEADACHE, IS ALL.
MORE'N A BIT, I'D SAY. -WHEW- I'M REAL SORRY YOU HAD TO MEET HER YOUR FIRST DAY HERE. I DON'T WANT YOU TO THINK ALL THE STUDENTS AT LSU ARE WEIRD LIKE GAYLE MARSH--
--JUST SOME OF 'EM!
MAYBE... BUT THIS WEIRDO IS GOING TO BEAR SOME WATCHING!
LINDA TURNS TO REJOIN HER NEW FRIEND--
15

-- LITTLE RECOGNIZING WHAT SHE HAS JUST ENCOUNTERED...AND COMPLETELY UNAWARE OF WHAT THAT CHANCE MEETING HERALDS--!

LORD... IT WAS TERRIBLE!

I'VE NEVER FELT SUCH... SUCH RAW POWER IN MY LIFE! WHY DIDN'T MR. PENDERGAST WARN ME--

--THEY'D BE COMING?!...

CHICAGO IS A CITY OF NEIGHBORHOODS ...EACH WITH ITS OWN DISTINCTIVE IDENTITY.

WHILE SOME ARE MOST DECIDEDLY ETHNIC IN MAKE-UP, OTHERS, LIKE ROGERS PARK ON THE NORTHEASTERN EDGE OF TOWN, ARE MIXED BAGS OF PEOPLE... YOUNG PROFESSIONALS -- ARTISTS -- AND STUDENTS...

COME IN, CHILDREN... COME IN! NO NEED TO STAND IN THE HALL--

--WHEN I'VE GOT A PERFECTLY GOOD APARTMENT FOR YOU TO SIT IN!

HIYA, MRS. BERKOWITZ. HOW YOU DOING TODAY, HONEY?

ACH, DON'T ASK! SO, WHO'S YOUR FRIEND, JOANIE--?

SOMEONE TO FILL THAT VACANT APARTMENT ON THE THIRD FLOOR, IDA BERKOWITZ, I'D LIKE YOU TO MEET MY GOOD FRIEND LINDA DANVERS FROM..., ER, WHERE YOU FROM, GOOD FRIEND?

WELL, MY LAST PORT OF CALL WAS NEW YORK. IT'S A PLEASURE TO MEET YOU, MA'AM.

OOH, NEW YORK! SUCH A PLACE THAT IS, MY HYMIE AND ME WERE THERE ONCE... IN 1933.

WE WERE VISITING MY BROTHER THEN FROM POLAND. RADIO CITY, WE SAW -- AND THEY WAS STILL BUILDING THE EMPIRE STATE BUILDING. SO, TELL ME -- THE DODGERS ARE STILL DOING GOOD IN BROOKLYN?

WELL, ACTUALLY, MA'AM, THE DODGERS LEFT NEW YORK MANY YEARS AGO.

16

NU? WITH THE *RENTS* LIKE THEY ARE IN NEW YORK, WHO CAN *BLAME* THEM?

BUT YOU DIDN'T COME TO LISTEN TO AN OLD WOMAN'S *BABBLINGS.* YOU NEED AN APARTMENT?

THAT I *DO,* MRS. BERKOWITZ.

THEN I'LL MAKE US ALL A NICE CUP OF TEA AND SPONGECAKE AND SEE WHAT WE CAN DO FOR YOU.

ISN'T SHE *WILD,* LINDA? MRS. B'S THE SWEETEST THING -- TREATS ALL THE TENANTS LIKE THEY WERE HER *KIDS!* NOT ONLY THAT, BUT SHE MAKES THE *BEST CHICKEN SOUP* WEST OF *TEL AVIV!*

SO, *DRINK UP,* GIRLS, AND LINDA, TELL ME *ALL* ABOUT YOURSELF. I LIKE TO KNOW *EVERYTHING* ABOUT MY TENANTS.

Y- YOU MEAN I'VE *GOT* THE APARTMENT? ALREADY?

WHAT! I'M NOT GOING TO TAKE JOANIE'S FRIEND IN?

SHORTLY...

I TAKE IT FROM THE SMILE YOU *LIKE,* LINDA?

MRS. BERKOWITZ-- I *LOVE* IT! IT'S *PERFECT!*

WELL, I *TRY* TO KEEP A NICE BUILDING.

CONSIDER THIS PLACE *RENTED,* MA'AM. I'M GOING TO GO RIGHT *NOW* AND CALL THE MOVING COMPANY AND HAVE THEM DELIVER MY STUFF TOMORROW.

TAKE YOUR *TIME,* DARLING. IT'LL *BE* HERE.

AND SO WILL I, ONCE I... HUH?!

YOU DON'T *KNOW* IT YET, MISS, BUT YOU'RE ONE *LUCKY* LADY! DO YOU *REALIZE* WHO YOU'VE JUST MOVED IN NEXT DOOR TO!?

ER... NO. BUT YOU'RE GOING TO *TELL* ME, AREN'T YOU?

GAD! SHE'S NOT ONLY *BEAUTIFUL,* SHE'S ALSO *WITTY!* AND YES, I AM INDEED!

17

JOHN OSTRANDER, ESQUIRE... AT YOUR SERVICE, MILADY! THRILLING, AIN'T IT?

SHEESH! IS THIS GUY BUGGIN' YOU, LINDA?

I DUNNO. I HAVEN'T DECIDED YET.

YOU CAN RUN, BUT YOU CAN'T HIDE FROM ME, WOMAN! I KNOW WHERE YOU LIVE!

IS THAT GUY FOR REAL?

JOHNNY O? NOBODY KNOWS FOR SURE-- BUT WE'VE BEEN TRYIN' TO GET HIM TO DONATE HIS BODY TO SCIENCE SO THEY COULD FIND OUT.

MEANWHILE...

BLAST IT, GIRL-- I ASKED IF YOU WERE CERTAIN!

I ONLY KNOW WHAT I FELT, MR. PENDERGAST. AND THAT GIRL I TOUCHED... SHE WAS ONE OF THEM... I KNOW IT! SHE'S GOT THE POWER TO STOP ME IF SHE WANTS.

IT CAN'T BE! HOW COULD ANYONE KNOW--?

AND WHAT AWESOME POWERS COULD SHE HAVE TO POSSIBLY MATCH THE MUTANT ABILITIES YOU WERE BORN WITH, GAYLE? YOU WERE GIVEN A MAGNIFICENT GIFT, GIRL... ONE UNEQUALED BY ANYONE ON THIS PLANET!

THE MOMENT I SAW YOU POSSESSED THAT POWER, I KNEW WHAT YOU WERE PUT ON THIS EARTH FOR--AND THAT ONLY I COULD LEAD YOU ON THIS MISSION OF SALVATION!

WE'VE TRAINED SINCE YOU WERE BUT A CHILD, GAYLE -- TRAINED YOU TO USE YOUR INCREDIBLE MENTAL ABILITIES FOR A SINGLE THING--

--TO WIPE OUT THE DECAY!

BUT... I TRUST YOUR INSTINCTS, DEAR GIRL-- AND YOUR POWER! AND IF YOU HAVE SENSED THERE IS ONE WHO HAS COME TO STOP YOU, THEN WE CAN AFFORD NO FURTHER DELAY!

WE MUST BEGIN OUR MISSION ...NOW!

I-I'M AFRAID, MR. PENDERGAST.

DON'T BE, MY DEAR--I AM WITH YOU. NOW, COME-- WE'VE STILL MANY PREPARATIONS TO MAKE!

GAYLE MARSH CAN ONLY NOD. EVENTS HAVE BEEN SET IN MOTION -- AND FOR ALL HER POWER, SHE CAN DO NOTHING TO HALT THEM.

18

AND THERE ARE MANY OTHERS IN THE CITY WHO WILL LIKEWISE FIND THEMSELVES CAUGHT UP IN THESE EVENTS... AMONG THEM, LINDA DANVERS.

BUT FOR THE MOMENT, AT LEAST, SHE STANDS IGNORANT OF WHAT IS SOON TO TRANSPIRE, REVELING INSTEAD IN THE PEACE THAT COMES WITH THE END OF A SIGNIFICANT DAY IN HER YOUNG LIFE.

LINDA IS HAPPY. SHE HAS FOUND A NEW PLACE FOR HERSELF IN THIS WORLD -- NEW FRIENDS TO SHARE IT WITH.

SHE HAS SEEN MANY PLACES AND DONE MANY THINGS WITH HER LIFE, YET NONE HAVE BROUGHT THIS AMOUNT OF CONTENTMENT TO HER SOUL.

MORE'S THE PITY THIS PEACE CANNOT *LAST!*

BRRR! STRANGE -- IT'S SUDDENLY GOTTEN SO *CHILLY*... AND *CLOUDY!* I WONDER WHAT --?

GREAT *KRYPTON!* WHERE'S MY MIND *BEEN* --? I SHOULDN'T FEEL THE COLD THIS WAY! WHAT...?

THE ANSWER --

-- *LIES TO THE WEST!*

WHAT IN THE NAME OF *RAO* IS THAT --?!

INCREDIBLE! WHAT -- OR *WHOEVER* -- IS ABLE TO *BLOCK* MY *SUPER-VISION* FROM SEEING IT WITH SOME SORT OF *AURA!* AND FROM THE *CHILL* I'M GETTING, THIS CAN'T BE GOOD NEWS!

IF MY SUPER-SENSES WON'T DO ME ANY GOOD FOR *LONG-DISTANCE* OBSERVATION --

-- THEN IT'S TIME FOR LINDA TO BOW OUT OF THE *PICTURE* --

-- AND *SUPERGIRL* TO TAKE A LOOK... *CLOSE* UP!

19

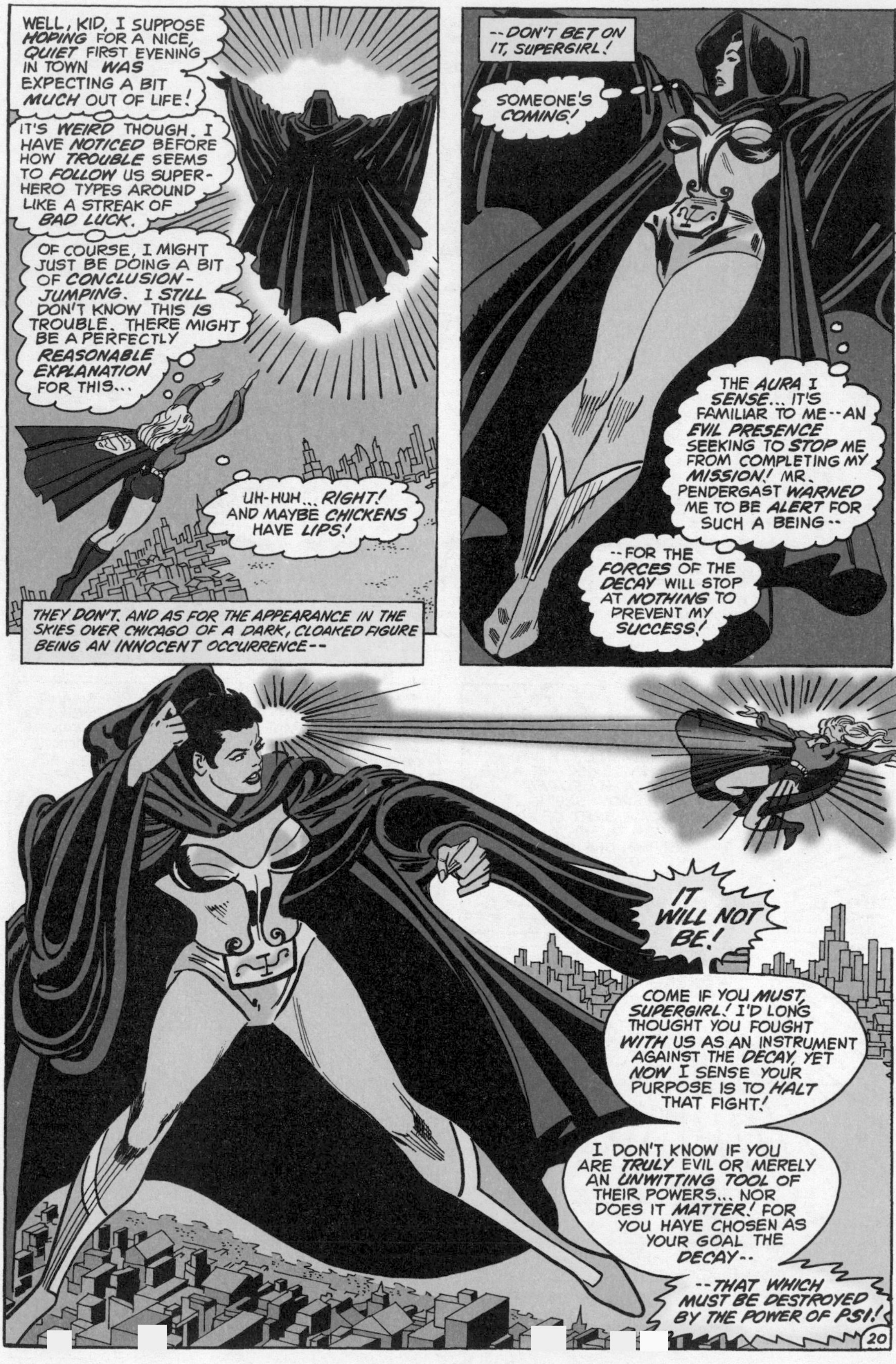

WELL, KID, I SUPPOSE HOPING FOR A NICE, QUIET FIRST EVENING IN TOWN WAS EXPECTING A BIT MUCH OUT OF LIFE!
IT'S WEIRD THOUGH. I HAVE NOTICED BEFORE HOW TROUBLE SEEMS TO FOLLOW US SUPER-HERO TYPES AROUND LIKE A STREAK OF BAD LUCK.
OF COURSE, I MIGHT JUST BE DOING A BIT OF CONCLUSION-JUMPING. I STILL DON'T KNOW THIS IS TROUBLE. THERE MIGHT BE A PERFECTLY REASONABLE EXPLANATION FOR THIS...
UH-HUH... RIGHT! AND MAYBE CHICKENS HAVE LIPS!
THEY DON'T. AND AS FOR THE APPEARANCE IN THE SKIES OVER CHICAGO OF A DARK, CLOAKED FIGURE BEING AN INNOCENT OCCURRENCE--
--DON'T BET ON IT, SUPERGIRL!
SOMEONE'S COMING!
THE AURA I SENSE... IT'S FAMILIAR TO ME--AN EVIL PRESENCE SEEKING TO STOP ME FROM COMPLETING MY MISSION! MR. PENDERGAST WARNED ME TO BE ALERT FOR SUCH A BEING--
--FOR THE FORCES OF THE DECAY WILL STOP AT NOTHING TO PREVENT MY SUCCESS!
IT WILL NOT BE!
COME IF YOU MUST, SUPERGIRL! I'D LONG THOUGHT YOU FOUGHT WITH US AS AN INSTRUMENT AGAINST THE DECAY, YET NOW I SENSE YOUR PURPOSE IS TO HALT THAT FIGHT!
I DON'T KNOW IF YOU ARE TRULY EVIL OR MERELY AN UNWITTING TOOL OF THEIR POWERS... NOR DOES IT MATTER! FOR YOU HAVE CHOSEN AS YOUR GOAL THE DECAY--
--THAT WHICH MUST BE DESTROYED BY THE POWER OF PSI!
20

IT IS PURE PSYCHIC ENERGY UNLEASHED... AND IT IS LIKE NOTHING THE GIRL OF STEEL HAS FELT BEFORE! SHE KNOWS A LESSER BEING WOULD NOT HAVE SURVIVED SUCH A BLAST!

BWAMM!

SHE, TO THE GOOD FORTUNE OF THE CITY BELOW, IS ANYTHING BUT--!

THAT ACTUALLY *HURT!* THIS *PSI* CHARACTER'S GOT A HEAP OF *EXPLAINING* TO DO, AND JUDGING FROM HER ATTITUDE, SHE'S *NOT* ABOUT TO DO MUCH *TALKING* JUST BECAUSE I ASK REAL NICE AND *POLITE!* I'M GOING TO HAVE TO BE A *BIT* MORE--

--FORCEFUL!

ALL RIGHT, LADY... I DON'T KNOW WHAT THIS *DECAY* GARBAGE YOU'RE GIVING ME IS ALL ABOUT, BUT I'VE GOT A DEFINITE *DISLIKE* OF BEING TOSSED AROUND LIKE A *RAGDOLL!*

OOOFFF! SUPERGIRL--?

WOULD YOU LIKE TO DO SOME EXPLAINING, OR DO YOU *PREFER* THE *ROUGH STUFF?*

SO, THE *DISCIPLE* OF *DECAY* IS FAR MORE *RESILIENT* THAN I'D *EXPECTED!* SO BE IT! IT IS A *MISTAKE--*

-- I'LL *NOT* MAKE *AGAIN!*

FAH-WHOOOM!

21

YOU PITIFUL **FOOL**--! I COULD ALMOST FEEL **SORRY** FOR YOU WERE I NOT YOUR **MASTER** THE FOUL BEING WHICH **HUNGERS** FOR THE **DEATH** OF OUR WORLD!

IN **ANOTHER** TIME, I MIGHT BE TEMPTED TO **SPARE** YOU... BUT I'LL **NOT** GIVE IN TO THE **DECAY'S** FETID **TEMPTATIONS**... **NOT** WITH SO MUCH AT **STAKE**!

~ WOOF! ~ ONE THING'S FOR **SURE**--I'M EITHER UP AGAINST ONE MIGHTY **POWERFUL LOONEY** OR **PSI** KNOWS SOMETHING **I** DON'T!

BUT SHE'S NOT GIVING ME MUCH SPACE TO FIND OUT! I'VE ALSO GROWN **ACCUSTOMED** OVER THE YEARS TO **NOT** FEELING PAIN LIKE THAT--

GUY MARTIN

--AND THAT'S A **HABIT** I'M NOT ABOUT TO **BREAK**!

THWAK!

CAN'T GIVE HER TIME TO **RECOVER**! I'VE GOTTA KEEP POUNDING AWAY AT HER BEFORE SHE GETS A **CHANCE** TO STRIKE **AGAIN**!

WHY... **WHY** DO YOU BATTLE AGAINST THE **INEVITABLE**? MUST I SEND YOU **BACK** TO YOUR MASTER AS THE **DECAY** HE SO FERVENTLY DESIRES BEFORE YOU RECOGNIZE THE **FUTILITY**?

SURRENDER, SUPERGIRL! MAKE YOUR PEACE WITH WHATEVER DEITY YOU CALL YOUR OWN... FOR YOU ARE TO **MEET** HIM **SOON**!

YOU'RE...UHHH... **WELCOME** TO **TRY**... BUT I WASN'T **PLANNING** ON TAKING ANY TRIPS JUST NOW!

THEN YOU ARE **MISTAKEN**--

--IF YOU **BELIEVE** YOU'VE ANY **CHOICE**!

NO, MR. PENDERGAST! P-PLEASE DON'T!

SILENCE, GAYLE! DID I NOT **TELL** YOU BEFORE... YOU NEEDN'T **CONCERN** YOURSELF WITH **THOUGHT**-- MERELY ALLOW **MY** BEING TO ENTER YOURS... MAKE YOUR POWER **MINE**!

22

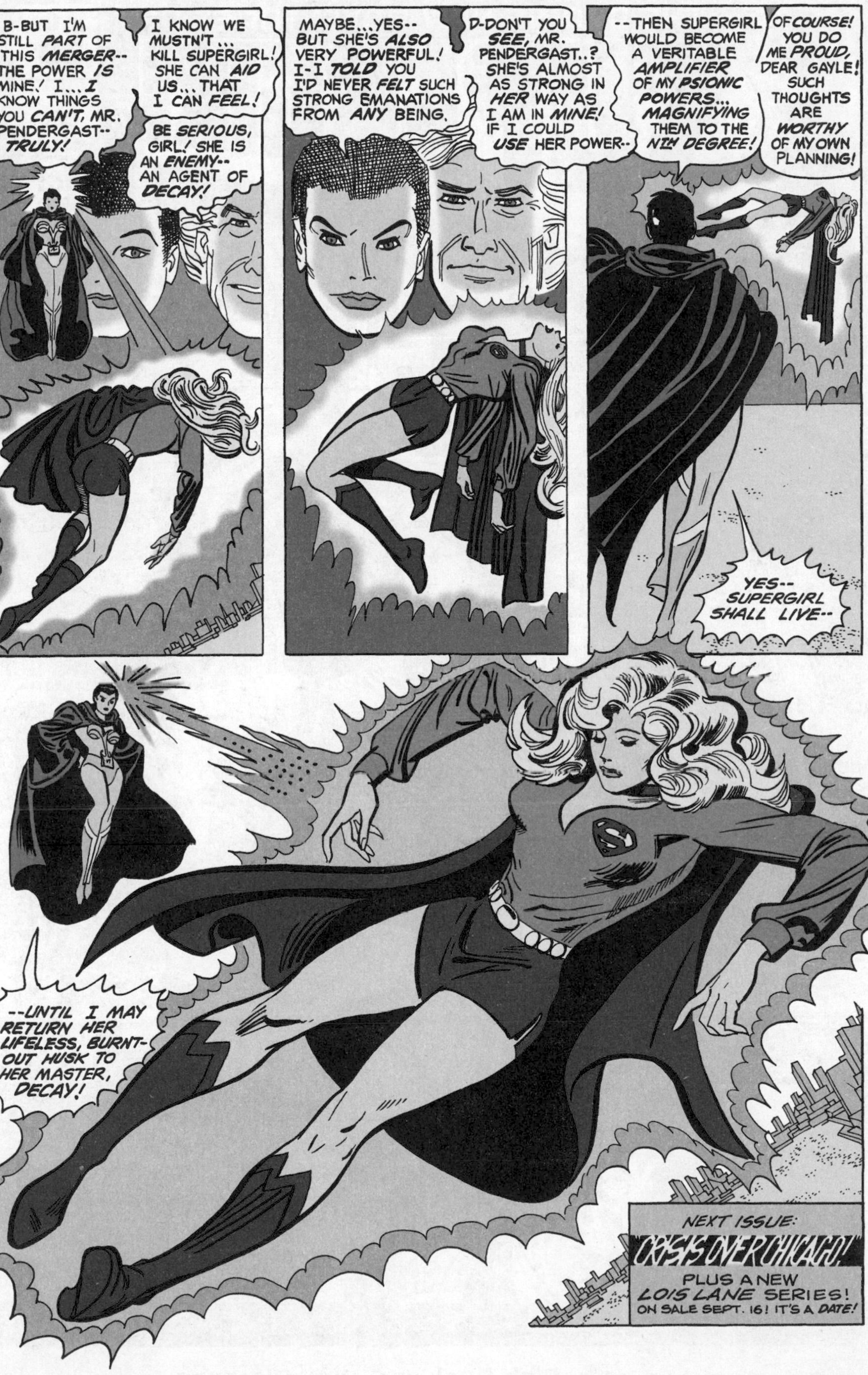
B-BUT I'M STILL PART OF THIS MERGER-- THE POWER IS MINE! I...I KNOW THINGS YOU CAN'T, MR. PENDERGAST-- TRULY!
I KNOW WE MUSTN'T... KILL SUPERGIRL! SHE CAN AID US...THAT I CAN FEEL!
BE SERIOUS, GIRL! SHE IS AN ENEMY-- AN AGENT OF DECAY!
MAYBE...YES-- BUT SHE'S ALSO VERY POWERFUL! I-I TOLD YOU I'D NEVER FELT SUCH STRONG EMANATIONS FROM ANY BEING.
D-DON'T YOU SEE, MR. PENDERGAST..? SHE'S ALMOST AS STRONG IN HER WAY AS I AM IN MINE! IF I COULD USE HER POWER--
--THEN SUPERGIRL WOULD BECOME A VERITABLE AMPLIFIER OF MY PSIONIC POWERS... MAGNIFYING THEM TO THE NTH DEGREE!
OF COURSE! YOU DO ME PROUD, DEAR GAYLE! SUCH THOUGHTS ARE WORTHY OF MY OWN PLANNING!
YES-- SUPERGIRL SHALL LIVE--
--UNTIL I MAY RETURN HER LIFELESS, BURNT-OUT HUSK TO HER MASTER, DECAY!
NEXT ISSUE:
CRISIS OVER CHICAGO!
PLUS A NEW LOIS LANE SERIES!
ON SALE SEPT. 16! IT'S A DATE!

Cover by **Rich Buckler** & **Dick Giordano**

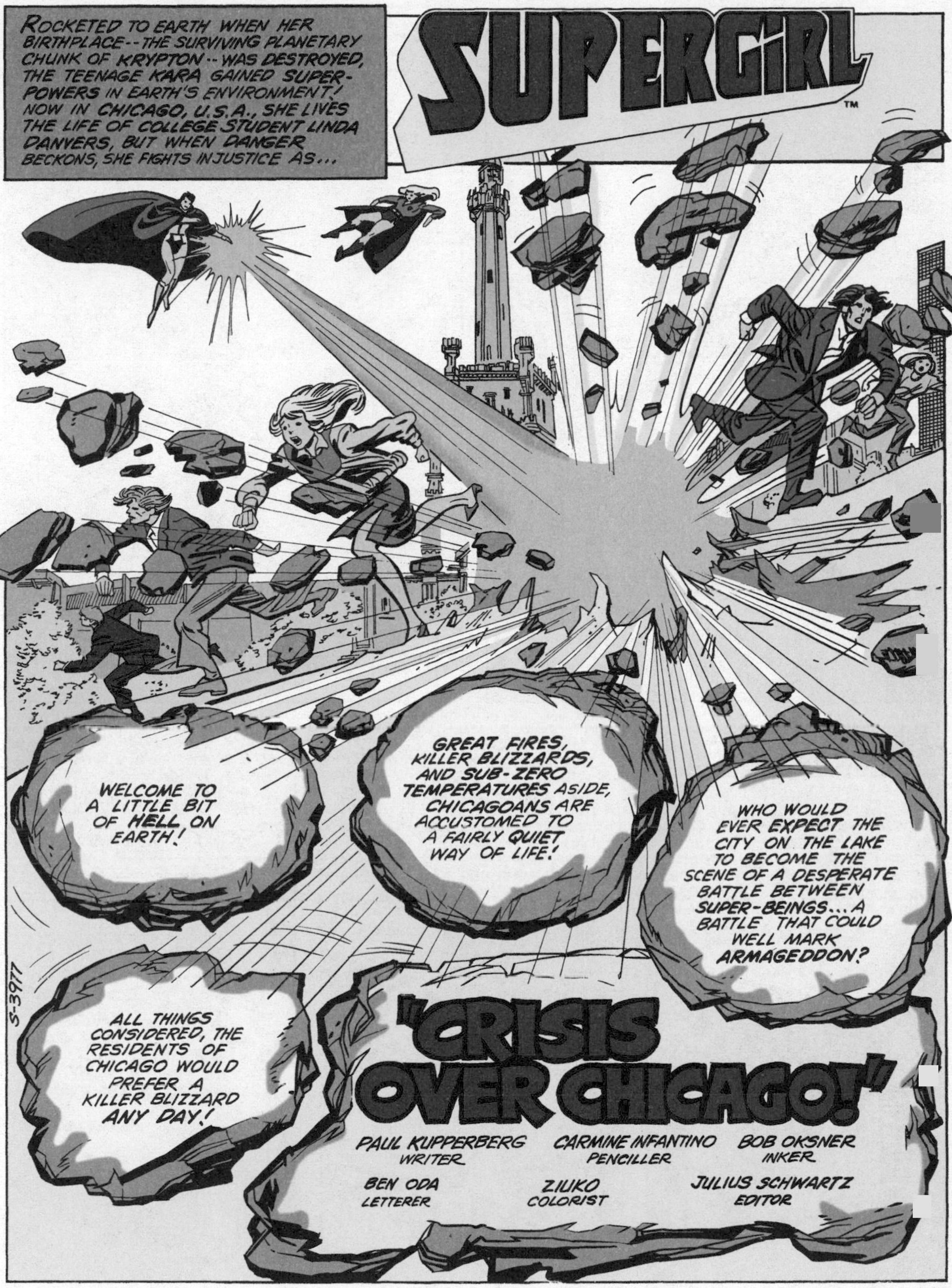
ROCKETED TO EARTH WHEN HER BIRTHPLACE--THE SURVIVING PLANETARY CHUNK OF KRYPTON--WAS DESTROYED, THE TEENAGE KARA GAINED SUPER-POWERS IN EARTH'S ENVIRONMENT! NOW IN CHICAGO, U.S.A., SHE LIVES THE LIFE OF COLLEGE STUDENT LINDA DANVERS, BUT WHEN DANGER BECKONS, SHE FIGHTS INJUSTICE AS...
SUPERGIRL™
WELCOME TO A LITTLE BIT OF HELL ON EARTH!
GREAT FIRES, KILLER BLIZZARDS, AND SUB-ZERO TEMPERATURES ASIDE, CHICAGOANS ARE ACCUSTOMED TO A FAIRLY QUIET WAY OF LIFE!
WHO WOULD EVER EXPECT THE CITY ON THE LAKE TO BECOME THE SCENE OF A DESPERATE BATTLE BETWEEN SUPER-BEINGS... A BATTLE THAT COULD WELL MARK ARMAGEDDON?
ALL THINGS CONSIDERED, THE RESIDENTS OF CHICAGO WOULD PREFER A KILLER BLIZZARD ANY DAY!
"CRISIS OVER CHICAGO!"
PAUL KUPPERBERG WRITER
CARMINE INFANTINO PENCILLER
BOB OKSNER INKER
BEN ODA LETTERER
ZIUKO COLORIST
JULIUS SCHWARTZ EDITOR
S-3977

THE LADY'S NAME IS PSI, AND SHE IS A WOMAN WITH A MISSION--

MORE POWER-- I MUST HAVE MORE!

HER MISSION, ALAS, IS THE DESTRUCTION OF THIS PROUD CITY THROUGH THE FORCE OF HER MUTANT-BORN ABILITIES...

THOUGH SHE HAS JUST BEGUN HER WORK, THERE SEEMS TO BE LITTLE DOUBT SHE WILL SUCCEED!

PSI IS ALSO A WOMAN POSSESSED--LITERALLY!

SUPERGIRL'S WILL IS POWERFUL INDEED, GAYLE! THOUGH WE HAVE HER PHYSICAL FORM IN OUR GRASP, STILL DOES SHE RESIST! YOU MUST FIGHT HER!

I-I'M TRYING, MR. PENDERGAST ...REALLY! I JUST CAN'T SEEM TO BREAK THROUGH--!

YOU'VE NO CHOICE! I HAVE TRAINED YOU IN THE USE OF YOUR PSIONIC POWERS EVER SINCE CHILDHOOD AS THE WEAPON AGAINST THE ENCROACHMENT OF THE DECAY!

B-BUT IT HURTS! I CAN FEEL THE AGONY OUR MENTAL STRUGGLE IS CAUSING SUPERGIRL!

BAH! YOUR EMPATHIC ABILITIES HAVE ALWAYS BEEN A WEAKNESS! CLOSE YOUR MIND TO IT... ALLOW ME TO BE YOUR THOUGHTS--

--ELSE WE'LL NEVER FIND THE OTHERS LIKE YOU,...AND THIS FETID CESSPOOL OF DECAY WILL SURVIVE TO SPREAD ITS SICKNESS!

CHICAGO MUST DIE... AND WE MUST BE ITS AGENTS OF DESTRUCTION!

2

‡UHH‡ F-FEEL SO... S-STRANGE! CAN BARELY THINK STRAIGHT... ALL I REMEMBER IS COMING UP AGAINST *PSI*... THEN -- *NOTHING!*

WHERE AM I...?

IT'S SHEER AGONY FOR THE *MAID OF MIGHT* TO SHIFT HER GLANCE *DOWNWARDS*...

IN THAT FIRST, HORRIFYING INSTANT, SHE ALMOST *WISHES* SHE *HADN'T!*

GREAT RAO! NO!

SHEER *PANDEMONIUM* BELOW! GOT TO *BREAK FREE* AND ‡ARRRHH!‡

'TIS *USELESS* TO *RESIST,* SUPERGIRL! THE *PSIONIC HOLD* YOU ARE CAUGHT IN IS A MATCH EVEN FOR YOUR MUCH-VAUNTED *KRYPTONIAN MIGHT!*

DON'T GO... ‡UHHH‡ BETTING ON THAT... ‡UHHH!‡

YOU CAUSE YOURSELF *NEEDLESS PAIN,* SUPERGIRL! *OPEN YOURSELF* TO ME... *PSI!* *SUBMIT* YOUR WILL TO THE *CLEANSING* OF YOURSELF-- AND THE *WORLD!*

MASS MURDER... YOU MEAN....!

I'M NOT ‡UHHH‡ ABOUT TO BE MADE PARTY TO *THAT, PSI!* ANY PLANS YOU'VE MADE ‡UHHH‡ TO THE *CONTRARY*...

...YOU CAN JUST ‡UHHH‡ TAKE...

...AND STICK... IN YOUR ‡UHHH‡ *EAR--*

3

--'CAUSE I'VE GOT POWER I HAVEN'T EVEN USED YET!

NO! IT'S NOT POSSIBLE--!

I-I'M SORRY, MR. PENDERGAST... I COULDN'T *HOLD* HER! I *REALLY* COULDN'T...!

THWOOOM!

THE EFFORT HAS COST HER FAR *MORE* THAN SHE SHOWS, YET THE GIRL OF STEEL KNOWS NOW WHAT SHE FACES, AND THOUGH EVERY FIBER OF HER BEING CRIES OUT FOR REST AND A RESPITE FROM THE PAIN--

--SHE IS *DETERMINED:* FOR THE SAKE OF THE CITY BELOW, SHE MUST *ENDURE!*

I'M *THROUGH* PLAYING WITH YOU, PSI! WHATEVER YOU HAD *PLANNED* FOR CHICAGO IS *FINISHED...* AND SO ARE YOU!

IF YOU KNOW WHAT'S *GOOD* FOR YOU, YOU'LL TELL ME WHAT IN THE NAME OF SANITY IS GO-ING ON HERE!

THE... *DECAY!* MUST FIGHT ITS SPREAD... *ROTTING* THE WORLD... DESTROYING US!

YOU CALL *THAT* SAVING THE WORLD--?!

WHAT KIND OF MONSTER *ARE* YOU? IF I HADN'T STOPPED YOU WHEN I DID, PEOPLE WOULD'VE BEEN *KILLED...HALF* THE CITY WIPED OUT!

YOU MAY SEE THAT AS SALVATION, LADY... BUT IT'S *SLAUGHTER,* PLAIN AND SIMPLE!

RAO, CAN'T YOU SEE YOU'RE *HURTING* PEOPLE!

I... I-- KNOW...

4

GAYLE!--DO NOT *LISTEN* TO HER *VILE* *LIES!* SHE IS AN *AGENT* OF THE *DECAY*...SHE WILL SAY *ANYTHING* TO SUBVERT OUR WORK! STRIKE OUT--

STRIKE NOW!

TWOOOM!

-OOFF!- *WHAT* IN THE NAME OF KRYPTON AM I *DEALING* WITH--?

ONE MINUTE SHE'S *DOCILE* LIKE A *LAMB*, AND THE *NEXT*...*BLAM*--I GET SENT FLYING INTO *NEXT WEEK!* MUCH AS I'D *LIKE* TO HANG AROUND AND FIGURE IT OUT--

KRASHH!

--*DUTY CALLS!*

YOU'VE HAD *ALL* THE *FREE SHOTS* YOU *GET* AT THIS GIRL OF STEEL, *PSI!*

I *WAS* INTERESTED IN HEARING YOUR STORY *BEFORE*, BUT *NOW* I'M JUST *MAD*--

BWAMPF!

--AND THAT'S A STATE OF AFFAIRS I *GUARANTEE* YOU'RE *NOT* GOING TO *LIKE!*

BOK!

KNOPF!

PITIFUL FOOL! YOUR *MASTER* HAS *DUPED* YOU INTO *BELIEVING* HIS *FOULNESS*...*TRICKED* YOU INTO *ACCEPTING* THE MORAL AND SPIRITUAL *DECAY* OF HUMANITY AS THE *WAY!*

YOU *SEE* HOW MANKIND *DESTROYS* ITSELF THROUGH HATE...THROUGH FILTH...THROUGH BODILY *CONTAMINATION*...AND YET YOU CAN *STILL* FIGHT ME--?

BOMPFF!

YOU'VE *GOT IT!* I'M NOT ALL THAT *THRILLED* WITH THE *WAY* THINGS ARE *EITHER*--BUT *WIPING* OUT THE CITY *ISN'T* THE ANSWER!

WE CAN ARGUE *PHILOSOPHY* FROM NOW UNTIL *DOOMSDAY!* ME, I'D RATHER *HEAT* THINGS UP FOR YOU WITH A BIT OF MY *VISION!*

5

My HEAT-BEAM... BACKFIRED!

How can you **REDUCE** this to a mere matter of **WORDS**, SUPERGIRL?

It is not **TALK** which has brought us to the **BRINK** of extinction... it was **ACTIONS**--

--THE ACTIONS of the INSIDIOUS WREAKER of **DECAY**! But he **CAN** be STOPPED--

--WHEN WE HAVE OBLITERATED HIS BASE OF OPERATIONS! AND FROM THE **ASHES** OF THAT DESTRUCTION SHALL RISE A **NEW WAY**-- A NEW **RACE** OF BEINGS OF WHICH I AM BUT THE **FIRST**!

WE ARE **HOMO SUPERIOR**... MUTANTS WHO WILL **RESIST** DECAY'S SPREAD AND LEAD IGNORANT MANKIND IN A **CLEANSING** OF THE WORLD!

HOO-BOY! ANOTHER **NUT** WITH A DREAM OF A **MASTER RACE**!

MORE OF **DECAY'S FILTH**! OTHERS HAVE TRIED WHAT WE SEEK-- BUT THEY DID SO FOR **POWER**, TO **FURTHER** THE **SPREAD** OF **DECAY**!

WE SEEK NOT TO **RULE**, BUT TO **GUIDE** MANKIND BACK TOWARD **PEACE**... AND LEAD THEM TO A NEW **DAWNING**!

RIIIGHT! AND WHAT'S A COUPLE OF HUNDRED THOUSAND **DEATHS** WHEN YOU'RE TRYING FOR THE **GARDEN OF EDEN**--?

LADY, THAT'S A **CROCK**! CALL IT WHATEVER YOU **WANT**, BUT **I'M NOT BUYING**! YOUR GAME IS **POWER**-- AND IF **ANYONE'S** SERVING THIS **DECAY**, IT'S **YOU**!

WHAMM!

LET'S TALK ABOUT THE **MORALITY OF MASS MURDER** IN THE NAME OF YOUR **CAUSE**--

--TELL ME ABOUT THE **LEVELING** OF AN ENTIRE CITY OF PEOPLE JUST BECAUSE THEY DON'T **HAPPEN** TO **FIT** INTO YOUR GRAND SCHEME--

BRIIIT!

--EXPLAIN THAT TO ME, PSI ...AND **THEN** YOU TELL ME WHICH ONE OF US **DESERVES** THE LABEL OF **FILTH**!

UGH! PLEASE... NO--!

BWLAM!

6

WHAT'S THE MATTER, PSI--? CAN'T *TAKE* IT? WHAT'S A LITTLE HURTING TO A BIG, BRAVE MEMBER OF THE *MASTER RACE*--!

I--I DIDN'T... DIDN'T KNOW ... PLEASE! LEAVE ME...

UH-UH, PSI! YOU *HAD* YOUR *CHANCE*-- BUT YOU DECIDED TO PLAY *HARDBALL* IN THE *BIG LEAGUE*... AND *OUR* RULES ARE *TOUGH!*

...PLEASE...

CEASE YOUR PITIFUL *WHINING*, GAYLE! SHE CANNOT HARM US-- *UNLESS* YOU LISTEN TO THE *DECEITFUL* WORDS OF HER *EVIL MASTER!*

YOU'VE COME TO THE *WRONG* PLACE FOR PITY! YOU TRIED TO *USE* ME IN THIS INSANITY! I DON'T *APPRECIATE* THAT IN THE *LEAST*--

--AND BEFORE I'M *THROUGH* WITH YOU, YOU'LL *WISH* YOU'D PICKED ON *ANOTHER PLANET* TO PLAY *GOD* WITH!

SHE IS THE *DECAY*, GAYLE-- SHE IS YOUR *ENEMY!* DO NOT *FORGET* THAT... DO NOT LET HER *SWAY* YOU FROM YOUR *MISSION!*

MAYBE EARTH *WON'T* MAKE IT PAST ITS OWN PROBLEMS... MAYBE IT *WILL!* BUT *WHICHEVER* WAY IT GOES, IT'S GOING *ALONE*, PSI--

--WITHOUT SOME *SUPER-POWERED MANIAC* TO *KILL* IT IN THE NAME OF *SALVATION!*

NOW, GAYLE... NOW! STRIKE THE WITCH *DEAD* BEFORE HER *EVIL* TAKES YOU!

AND SUDDENLY, PSI SCREAMS!

IT IS AN UNEARTHLY WAIL OF TORMENT, THE SHRIEK OF ONE TORN BETWEEN WHAT SHE BELIEVES... AND *TRUTH!*

IIAAAAEEEE

ITS MANIFESTATION IS *AWESOME*--

7

--FOR THERE IS NO SOUND. INDEED, THERE IS A SUDDEN, UNNATURAL SILENCE THAT GRIPS THE AIR, AS IF ALL SOUND HAS BEEN OBLITERATED BY THE GREATER URGENCY OF PSYCHIC PAIN UNBOUND--

--AND THEN, PSI IS GONE!

AND A MOMENT LATER, SO IS THE PAIN!

RAO! TALK ABOUT SPLASHY EXITS--!

FELT LIKE MY HEAD WAS GOING TO SPLIT WIDE OPEN FROM THAT ONE... BUT IT WASN'T AN ATTACK! WEIRD...LIKE PSI WAS REALLY HURTING--!

THWAMM

IT DOESN'T MAKE MUCH SENSE, I SUPPOSE-- BUT THEN, THIS WHOLE EPISODE'S BEEN BONKERS FROM THE START!

I PROBABLY HAVEN'T SEEN THE LAST OF PSI... BUT FAR BE IT FROM ME TO LOOK A GIFT HORSE IN THE MOUTH! THAT LITTLE FRACAS HAS JUST ABOUT LEFT ME BUSHED--

--AND THAT'S THE LAST THING I CAN AFFORD THE NEXT TIME SHE POPS UP! THANK GOODNESS--

"--I'VE GOT SOMEWHERE TO FALL OUT FOR THE NIGHT!"

I WAS LUCKY TO GET THIS APARTMENT MY FIRST DAY IN CHICAGO! EVEN WITHOUT FURNITURE, IT'S GOING TO BE NICE TO BE HOME! I... HUH--?!

EHH...EITHER MY BOUT WITH PSI'S LEFT ME MORE RATTLED THAN I REALIZED--

--OR THERE'S REALLY SOMEBODY IN MY APARTMENT! WELL, THERE'S GONNA BE ONE MIGHTY SORRY BURGLAR IN TOWN TONIGHT ...FOR TWO REASONS: ONE HE'S HITTING AN EMPTY APARTMENT--

8

--WHICH, PIECE OF *BAD LUCK NUMBER TWO,* HAPPENS TO BELONG TO *SUPERGIRL!* I'M... *HUH?!*

JOAN RAYMOND... AND MY FURNITURE--?!

HOWDY, NEIGHBOR! LISSEN, I HOPE YOU DON'T *MIND,* BUT THE MOVERS SHOWED UP WITH YOUR STUFF RIGHT AFTER YOU LEFT--

--SO I FIGGERED, WHAT THE HECK, WE MIGHT AS WELL *SURPRISE* YOU AND HAVE IT ALL SET UP FOR YOU WHEN YOU GOT BACK! SO--

SURPRISE!

DON'T JUST STAND THERE LIKE A *LOX!* C'MON IN AND MAKE YOURSELF AT HOME... MEET THE *UNPACKING PARTY!*

YOU'VE ALREADY MET *JOHNNY OSTRANDER,* OUR *WEIRD-O* RESIDENT ACTOR! AND THIS HERE'S MY *ROOMMATE CHERYL DELARYE* AND HER BEST BEAU, *DARYLL SIMMONS!*

SEEIN' AS HOW THIS IS YOUR VERY FIRST DAY IN TOWN, YOU DON'T HAVE TO DO ONE THING AROUND HERE! REST YOUR LITTLE TOOTSIES AND LEAVE THE UNPACKING TO *US!*

HEY, THE *LEAST* YOU CAN DO IS OFFER THE FAIR DAMSEL SOME *REFRESHMENTS...*

THANKS... *ALL* OF YOU! TO TELL THE *TRUTH,* I WASN'T LOOKING FORWARD TO DOING THIS ON MY OWN!

WHAT ARE NEIGHBORS FOR IF NOT TO TAKE *ADVANTAGE* OF ANYWAY, BEAUTIFUL?

BESIDES, YOU EVER TRY AND SAY *NO* TO JOAN?

NOW DON'T GO GIVING LINDA THE IMPRESSION I'M A *SLAVE DRIVER,* KIDDIES...OTHERWISE I'LL BE FORCED TO TAKE THE *WHIP* TO YA! *BACK* TO WORK!

PUH-LEASE, DON JUAN! GIVE THE POOR GIRL A *BREAK!*

≈SIGH!≈ I *HATE* WATCHING PEOPLE AT MANUAL LABOR. WHAT SAY YOU AND I LEAVE THESE *PLEBS* AND GO BE *NAUGHTY* TOGETHER...?

I AM, HONEY! I'M GIVIN' HER A *CRACK* AT *ME!*

9

Panel 1:

YOU KNOW, WHEN I *FIRST* MET YOU, JOHN, I THOUGHT YOU WERE SOME KIND OF *NUT!*

SHUCKS! THAT SHOWS YOU SOMETHING ABOUT *FIRST IMPRESSIONS*, DON'T IT?

UH-HUH...THAT THEY'RE *USUALLY RIGHT!*

Panel 2:

EXCUSE ME, I'M GOING TO HELP OUT A LITTLE!

:SHEESH!: I DON'T GET *NO* RESPECT....!

Panel 3:

HEY, NOW... YOU *HEARD* JOAN--YOU JUST HAUL YOURSELF BACK THERE AND SIT THIS ONE OUT! WE'RE ALMOST DONE ANY-WAY!

I KNOW, BUT I WAS FEELING KIND OF *GUILTY* WATCHING YOU FOLKS DO ALL THE WORK.

SO, YOU'RE JOAN'S *ROOMIE*, HUH?

Panel 4:

YEAH. OH, I KNOW WHAT YOU'RE *THINKIN'* --HOW'CUM AN *OLD LADY* LIKE ME'S SHARING A PLACE WITH A *COLLEGE KID*, RIGHT--?

UH, NOT *ACTUALLY.* I DIDN'T TAKE YOU FOR AN OLD LADY.

BLESS YOU, HONEY, BUT I'M *33*, AND COMPARED TO JOAN, SOMETIMES I *FEEL* THAT WAY!

Panel 5:

HMMM... I THINK I *SEE* WHAT YOU MEAN. SO, TO ASK YOUR *OWN* QUESTION... *HOW'CUM* AN "OLD LADY" LIKE YOU'S SHARING A PLACE WITH A COLLEGE KID?

'CAUSE IT JUST *SO HAPPENS* I'M A STUDENT *MYSELF* AT LAKE SHORE UNIVERSITY. I GUESS I'M WHAT YOU'D CALL A *LATE BLOOMER!*

Panel 6:

I KIND OF GET THE *FEELING* THERE'S *MORE* TO IT THAN *THAT!*

SAW RIGHT *THROUGH* MY PRETENSE, HUH? NAW, I WAS JUST... UH, *OTHERWISE ENGAGED*, LET'S SAY, FOR THE LAST FIFTEEN YEARS. FIGURED IT WAS ABOUT TIME I GOT ME AN EDUCATION.

YOU ABOUT THROUGH HERE, BABE? WE GOTTA BE RUNNING IF WE'RE GONNA CATCH THAT FILM DOWNTOWN.

DONE AND *DONE*, LOVER. JUST DON'T TRY TO KEEP ME OUT *LATE*... I GOT AN *EARLY* CLASS TOMORROW!

I CAN'T THANK YOU PEOPLE ENOUGH! AS SOON AS I GET SETTLED IN, YOU'RE ALL INVITED BACK-- EXCEPT *THIS* TIME FOR *PARTYING*!

WE GOTTA BE GOING TOO, LIN! *RIGHT*, JOHNNY-O?

ME? I'M IN NO *BIG* HURRY...

SURE, YOU ARE, JUNIOR! *MOVE IT*!

HEY... I DON'T NEED A *BOULDER* TO FALL ON ME TO TELL ME I AIN'T *WELCOME*--!

A BOULDER-- GEE, I NEVER THOUGHT OF *THAT* BEFORE.' NITEY-NITE, LIN, SEE YA TOMORROW!

¡WOOF! MUCH AS I APPRECIATE THEIR HELP, I THOUGHT THEY'D *NEVER* LEAVE!

PSI REALLY GAVE ME A RUN FOR MY MONEY, AND I'VE BEEN AT THIS GAME TOO *LONG* TO BELIEVE I'VE SEEN THE *LAST* OF HER! NOPE, I'D BET MY *CAPE* SHE'LL BE BACK--

--BUT UNTIL SHE SHOWS AGAIN--

--I THINK I'LL JUST *SLEEP*...

IT'S A WEARY LINDA DANVERS WHO FALLS ACROSS HER BED IN HER ROGERS PARK APARTMENT AND IS ASLEEP IN MOMENTS--

⑪

SHE SHOULD HAVE STAYED *AWAKE!*

FOR EVEN AS LINDA DRIFTS OFF INTO THE COMFORTING WARMTH OF SLEEP, THE SOURCE OF HER CONCERN IS JUST COMING AWAKE NOT THREE MILES TO THE SOUTH...

...I ASKED IF YOU COULD *HEAR* ME, GAYLE!

ANSWER ME, GAYLE, BLAST YOU!

UHH...OH, *MR. PENDERGAST...* WH-WHAT'S--

YOU LITTLE *IDIOT!* YOU CAME *LIMPING* BACK HERE LIKE AN INJURED *DOG* AFTER YOUR BOUT WITH SUPERGIRL, VIRTUALLY *INCOHERENT* WITH FEAR!

S-SUPERGIRL...? I DON'T... REMEMBER...

DON'T YOU? OR HAS YOUR *SUBCONSCIOUS* MERELY *BLOCKED* YOUR PITIFUL *FAILURE* FROM YOUR MIND?

BAH! I'M *DISGUSTED* WITH YOU! I'D HAD SUCH *HOPES* FOR YOUR INCREDIBLE *POTENTIAL*, YET TIME AFTER TIME HAVE YOU *DISAPPOINTED* ME--

--GIVING IN TO YOUR EVERY *WEAKNESS*, ALLOWING *NOT* THE FORCE OF *GOOD* WE REPRESENT TO RULE YOU... *RATHER* EMBRACING *DECAY'S* EVERY ATTEMPT AT *SUBVERSION!*

WE COULD HAVE HAD THE *WORLD*... BUT FOR *YOU!*

PLEASE, MR. PENDERGAST...

IT'S TOO *LATE,* GAYLE! YOU ARE NO LONGER OF ANY *USE* TO THE FIGHT! YOU HAVE *PROVEN* YOURSELF ...*UNWORTHY!*

YOU CAN'T *DO* THIS TO ME... NOT *WITHOUT* LETTING ME AT... AT LEAST *EXPLAIN!*

I *COULDN'T* GO THROUGH WITH IT... NOT AFTER *LISTENING* TO SUPERGIRL! SHE'S *RIGHT,* MR. PENDERGAST ...BUT SO ARE *YOU!* DECAY IS TAKING OVER THE WORLD... AND HE *SHOULD* BE STOPPED-- BUT *NOT* THIS WAY!

12

WHAT *OTHER* WAY *IS* THERE?

DECAY'S EVIL MUST BE *WIPED* FROM THE FACE OF THE EARTH AND ONLY THE *CLEANSING FIRES* OF YOUR MIND MAY DO THIS!

INSTEAD, YOU HAVE CHOSEN TO *ALLY* YOURSELF WITH THE *AGENT* OF *DECAY*... TO *ABANDON* THE FIGHT BEFORE IT HAD EVEN TRULY *BEGUN!*

NO... I SWEAR... I--I...

SILENCE, GIRL! YOU CAN SAY *NOTHING* THAT WILL SWAY ME NOW! ONLY THROUGH YOUR *ACTIONS* MIGHT YOU HAVE *PROVEN* YOURSELF...

BUT THEN, YOU *HAVE,* HAVEN'T YOU?

NO *MORE,* MR. PENDERGAST... *PLEASE*...

MY WORDS *STING* YOU, GIRL-- STING YOU BECAUSE THEY ARE *TRUE!*

N-NO....!

IT IS TOO *LATE* FOR PLEADING, GAYLE MARSH! YOUR *USEFULNESS* HAS COME TO AN *END--!*

NO...

13

OH YES, GIRL...*YES!*

AMONG HER MANY OTHER PSYCHIC SKILLS, GAYLE MARSH IS ALSO A SENSITIVE.

HER EMPATHIC ABILITIES MAKE THIS YOUNG WOMAN PREY TO THE EMOTIONS OF THOSE AROUND HER TO A *STARTLING* DEGREE.

THUS, WHEN SHE FEELS THE HATRED EMANATING LIKE A PHYSICAL THING FROM HER MENTOR, SHE CANNOT *HELP* BUT REACT--

--TO QUELL THE HATRED--

HI-YEEEEEE

--TO DESTROY ITS *SOURCE*--

--TO FIND SOME *PEACE* FOR HERSELF!

NOOOOOOOOO --SOB!-- *STOP* IT PLEASE....!

IT'S *TOO* MUCH...! YOU DON'T *REALIZE* WHAT YOU'RE DOING--

--THE FORCES INVOLVED--

--THE *POWER* YOU HAVE... *FOOL!*

YESSSS! I--I CAN *FEEL* IT NOW ...SUCH MIGHT NOW THAT--

14

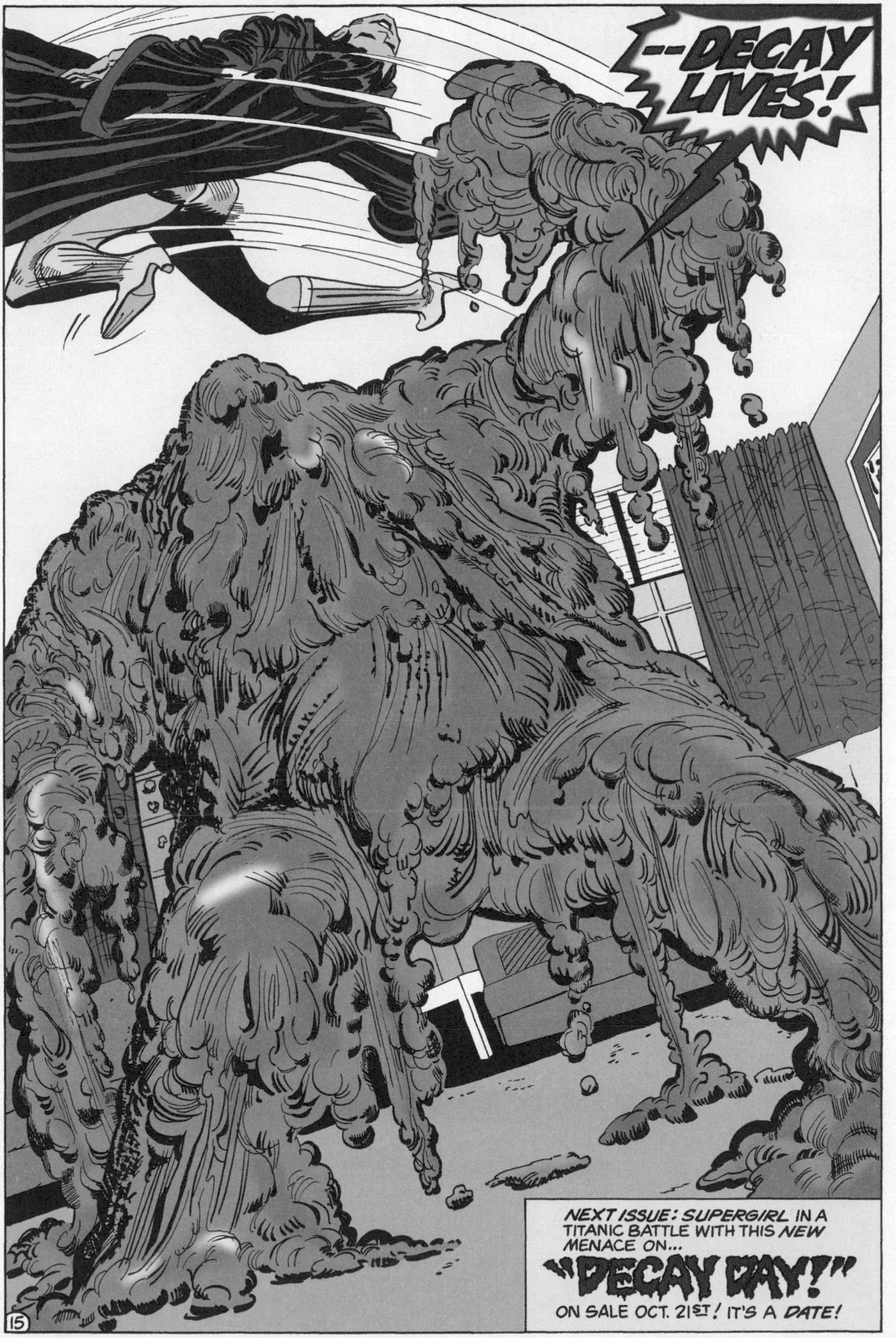
--DECAY LIVES!
NEXT ISSUE: SUPERGIRL IN A TITANIC BATTLE WITH THIS NEW MENACE ON...
"DECAY DAY!"
ON SALE OCT. 21ST! IT'S A DATE!
15

Cover by **Keith Giffen** & **Klaus Janson**

ROCKETED TO EARTH WHEN HER BIRTHPLACE--THE SURVIVING PLANETARY CHUNK OF KRYPTON--WAS DESTROYED, THE TEENAGE KARA GAINED SUPER-POWERS IN EARTH'S ENVIRONMENT! NOW IN CHICAGO, U.S.A., SHE LIVES THE LIFE OF COLLEGE STUDENT LINDA DANVERS, BUT WHEN DANGER BECKONS, SHE FIGHTS INJUSTICE AS...

SUPERGIRL

WHAT A *BUMMER!* MY *FIRST* FULL DAY AS A STUDENT AT *LAKE SHORE UNIVERSITY* AND WHAT'D I *DO...?* *OVERSLEEP* AND MISS MY *TRAIN!* TALK ABOUT *AUSPICIOUS* BEGINNINGS--!

I SUPPOSE I WAS MORE *POOPED* THAN I REALIZED AFTER THAT KNOCK-DOWN-DRAG-OUT I HAD WITH *PSI* YESTERDAY.* STILL, THERE HASN'T BEEN A PEEP OUT OF HER SINCE SHE *DISAPPEARED*, SO MAYBE I'VE SEEN THE *LAST* OF HER--

--WHICH WOULD MAKE MY *PREMIERE* *RUN-IN* WITH A SUPER-BADDY HERE IN MY NEW HOMETOWN AN *UNQUALIFIED* SUCCESS! *WAY TO GO*, KARA BABY!

*Which, for our purposes, translates to *LAST ISSUE* -- Julie

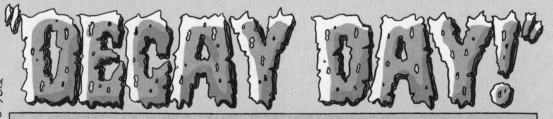

"DECAY DAY!"

| PAUL KUPPERBERG WRITER | CARMINE INFANTINO + BOB OKSNER ARTISTS | BEN ODA - LETTERER TOM ZIUKO - COLORIST | JULIUS SCHWARTZ EDITOR |

REALLY *BIZARRE* THOUGH--! I WONDER WHY IT IS THAT *TROUBLE* SEEMS TO FOLLOW US SUPER-HERO TYPES AROUND LIKE FLEAS ON A STRAY DOG?

I MEAN, I'D JUST *BARELY HIT* CHICAGO WHEN PSI POPPED UP, THREATENING TO *REALLY* HIT THE CITY... LIKE WITH A *SLEDGEHAMMER,* ALL IN THE NAME OF SOMETHING CALLED *"DECAY"!*

I SHOULD BE *THANKFUL* SHE'S GONE, CONSIDERING THE POWERS SHE DEMONSTRATED, BUT I CAN'T HELP WONDERING *WHO* SHE WAS... WHAT SHE WAS *AFTER.*

AND *WHY,* FOR CRYING OUT LOUD, SHE TOOK OFF IN A *SCREAMING FIT* LIKE SHE HAD A *HORNETS' NEST* UNDER HER HOOD!

THERE YOU GO, LOOKING A *GIFT-HORSE* IN THE TEETH AGAIN, KIDDO.

THE *LAST* THING I'D ASK SANTA FOR NEXT CHRISTMAS WOULD BE A *RETURN BOUT* WITH PSI ANYWAY--SO IF SHE'S GONE FOR GOOD, THAT'S *OKAY* WITH ME!

COUGHLIN HALL

BUT ENOUGH WITH THE SUPER-HEROING ALREADY! THINKING SUPERGIRL-TYPE THOUGHTS AFTER I'VE PUT ASIDE THE CAPE AND SHORTS IS A *BAD HABIT* I REALLY OUGHT TO *BREAK.*

IT'S TIME I GOT INTO THE SWING OF THINGS AS *LINDA DANVERS,* STUDENT... ESPECIALLY SINCE I'M *15 MINUTES LATE* FOR AN APPOINTMENT WITH MY NEW *FACULTY ADVISOR* IN THE *PSYCH* DEPARTMENT!

PSYCHOLOGY

MOMENTS LATER, DEEP WITHIN THE BOWELS OF L.S.U.'S COUGHLIN HALL...

DR. *BARRY METZNER*... DEPARTMENT OF PSYCHOLOGY... THIS MUST BE THE PLACE. ÷SHEESH÷ LOOKS LIKE A *HURRICANE'S* BEEN HERE-- BUT ONLY *AFTER* IT LET THE *TORNADO* PASS!

HELLO--? ANYBODY *ALIVE* IN HERE...?

HUH? WHAT...? YES? ER... CAN I, ER... *HELP* YOU, MISS?

DR. METZNER, I PRESUME?

2

THAT'S ME. EH, COME IN, WHY DON'T YOU? HMMM... WHERE'D IT GO...?

LOSE SOMETHING, SIR?

WHAT? OH, YES... UNDOUBTEDLY.

AWW WELL, I'M SURE IT'LL TURN UP *EVENTUALLY.* IT USUALLY DOES WHEN I LEAST *EXPECT* IT. SO PLEASE, HAVE A *SEAT,* YOUNG LADY.

A SEAT, HUH? *WHERE?*

KEE-RIPES! I'VE REALLY GOT TO GET THIS PLACE, ER... *TIDIED* UP ONE OF THESE YEARS! NOW, WHAT'D YOU SAY YOUR *NAME* WAS--?

LINDA DANVERS.

PLEASED TO MEET...AHHHH! *THERE* YOU ARE, YOU LITTLE BUGGER! I'VE BEEN LOOKING ALL *OVER* FOR YOU.

AND WHAT'S THE TROUBLE, MS. DANVERS?

THIS GUY'S *UNBELIEVABLE...* BUT KINDA *CUTE,* ACTUALLY. I DIDN'T KNOW COLLEGES STILL KEPT *ABSENT-MINDED PROFESSORS* ON THE PAYROLL.

NO TROUBLE. I'M AN *INCOMING FRESHMAN* AND I'D LIKE TO *MAJOR* IN YOUR *DEPARTMENT.* I WAS TOLD *YOU* WOULD BE MY *ADVISOR.*

GOOD, GOOD, MS. DANVERS, ER, *TELL* ME, THOUGH-- WHAT MADE YOU CHOOSE *PSYCH* OVER SAY, *PHYSICAL EDUCATION?*

THE WORKINGS OF THE HUMAN *MIND* HAVE AL- WAYS *INTRIGUED* ME. I SUPPOSE YOU COULD SAY I'VE DEALT WITH *LOTS* OF PEOPLE THE LAST FEW YEARS. I'M INTERESTED IN WHAT MAKES THEM *TICK...*

...ESPECIALLY THE PEOPLE I DEAL WITH AS SUPERGIRL!

SOUNDS LIKE A *HEALTHY* REASON TO ME. YOU'D BE *AMAZED* AT HOW MANY *NUT JOBS* WE GET IN THIS FIELD.

ER....RIGHT.

3

ANYWAY, WHY DON'T I GIVE YOU ALL THE NECESSARY INFORMATION TO *READ* AND THEN YOU CAN COME BACK AND DISCUSS YOUR SCHEDULE WITH ME...HMMM. WONDER WHERE THAT STUFF GOT OFF TO *NOW?*

WHOOPS!

WOULD *THIS*, BY ANY CHANCE, BE WHAT YOU'RE *LOOKING* FOR?

NO, NO, I'M LOOKING FOR...*THAT!* OH, YES, THAT'S THE CATALOG ALL RIGHT! *VERY GOOD,* MS. DANVERS!

THANKS A BUNCH, DR. METZNER. I'LL READ THROUGH THIS AND GET BACK TO YOU.

SWELL...ER, BY THE *WAY,* MS. DANVERS -- YOU WOULDN'T, ER... BY ANY *CHANCE* BE LOOKING FOR A *JOB,* WOULD YOU?

TRUTH TO TELL, I HADN'T REALLY *THOUGHT* ABOUT IT!

THE THING IS, I'VE BEEN TRYING TO FIND SOMEONE TO *REPLACE* MY SECRETARY FOR *WEEKS* NOW, NOT A BLESSED ONE OF THE PEOPLE THEY SEND ME SEEMS TO BE ABLE TO UNDERSTAND *MY FILING SYSTEM.*

WANNA GIVE IT A *TRY?* YOU FOUND THAT CATALOG PRETTY FAST.

WELLLL... I SUPPOSE I'D HAVE TO WORK *ONE* OF THESE DAYS TO HELP WITH THOSE LITTLE DAY-TO-DAY *EXTRAS*... LIKE FOOD AND *RENT.*

AND WORKING *ON* CAMPUS MAKES IT A LOT *EASIER* ON THE *SHOE LEATHER...* SO *WHY NOT?* DOC-- CONSIDER ME *HIRED!*

SWELL! WONDERFUL!

IF YOU CAN MAKE IT *TOMORROW,* THAT'LL BE *GREAT.* YOU, ER...*MAY* HAVE *NOTICED* THIS PLACE COULD *USE* A *BIT* OF STRAIGHTENING UP.

UMMM...YEAH, I KINDA *DID* NOTICE THAT.

...ALTHOUGH *THIS* JOB LOOKS LIKE IT MAY BE TOO TOUGH EVEN FOR *SUPERGIRL!*

4

NOW *THAT* WAS A STROKE OF *LUCK,* BARRY OL' SON, GOOD SECRETARIES ARE HARD TO *COME BY*-- ESPECIALLY SUCH AN *ATTRACTIVE* ONE AS *HER...* ER, SHE!

OF COURSE, THINKING LIKE *THAT* COULD GET ONE IN LOTS OF *TROUBLE* WITH THE ADMINISTRATION, BUT I...

YEE-OUCH! DUMPED *LIVE ASHES* IN MY HAND!

CHICAGO IS A CITY OF MORE THAN 3 MILLION PERSONS, MOST OF WHOM HAVE *SOME* MANNER OF DWELLING TO CALL HOME. BUT OF THESE MILLIONS, SEVERAL THOU-SAND *DON'T*--

--AND THEY, LIKE LOUIE TRUMBULL, AGE 56, ARE FORCED TO TAKE TO THE *STREETS.*

IT'S NOT SO BAD FOR A GOOD PART OF THE YEAR-- LIKE *NOW,* WITH THE AUTUMN AIR STILL WARM AND THE THREAT OF THOSE *LEGENDARY* CHICAGO SNOWS STILL MONTHS AWAY. LOUIE *COULD* DO *WORSE* THAN TAKING TO THIS ALLEYWAY FOR HIS SLEEP...

... HE COULD--BUT HE'D HAVE TO GO AN AWFUL *LONG* WAY TO DO IT.

WHEW! IT SURE DO *STINK* IN HERE...SMELLS LIKE SOMETHIN' JEST CURLED UP IN TH' CORNER AND WENT AN' *DIED!* *PHEW!*

BUT BEGGARS CAN'T BE *CHOOSERS,* I ALWAYS SAY...HECK, I AIN'T NO *ROSEBUSH* M'SELF. HEH HEH.

'SIDES, I AIN'T HAD MY *BEAUTY REST* YET TODAY. HEH HEH. *BEAUTY REST...*THET *SLAYS* ME, THET DOES... HEH HEH HEH.

NO, FOOL--

5

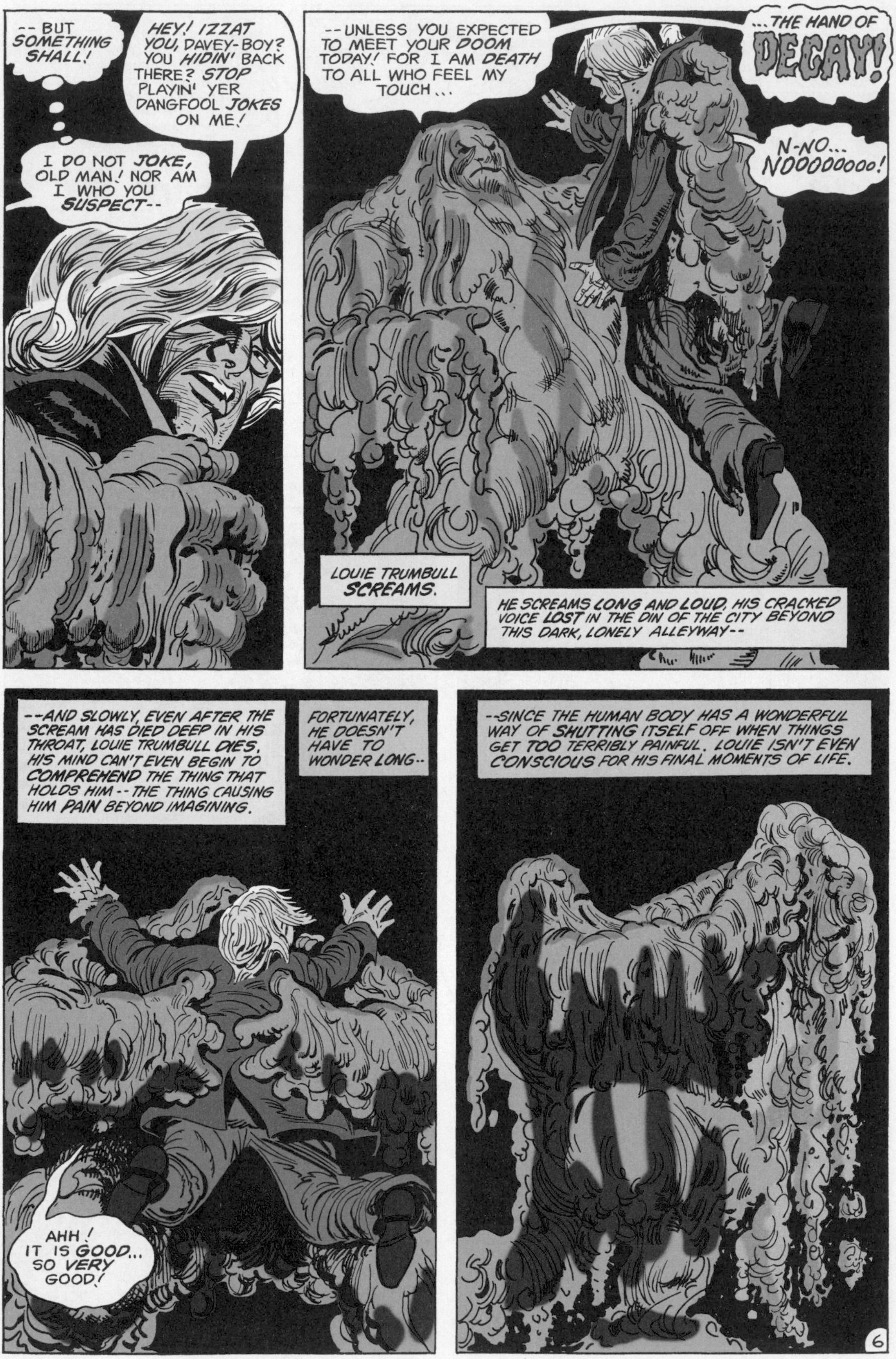
-- BUT SOMETHING SHALL!
HEY! IZZAT YOU, DAVEY-BOY? YOU HIDIN' BACK THERE? STOP PLAYIN' YER DANGFOOL JOKES ON ME!
I DO NOT JOKE, OLD MAN! NOR AM I WHO YOU SUSPECT--
--UNLESS YOU EXPECTED TO MEET YOUR DOOM TODAY! FOR I AM DEATH TO ALL WHO FEEL MY TOUCH...
...THE HAND OF DECAY!
N-NO... NOOOOOOOO!
LOUIE TRUMBULL SCREAMS.
HE SCREAMS LONG AND LOUD, HIS CRACKED VOICE LOST IN THE DIN OF THE CITY BEYOND THIS DARK, LONELY ALLEYWAY--
--AND SLOWLY, EVEN AFTER THE SCREAM HAS DIED DEEP IN HIS THROAT, LOUIE TRUMBULL DIES. HIS MIND CAN'T EVEN BEGIN TO COMPREHEND THE THING THAT HOLDS HIM -- THE THING CAUSING HIM PAIN BEYOND IMAGINING.
FORTUNATELY, HE DOESN'T HAVE TO WONDER LONG--
AHH! IT IS GOOD... SO VERY GOOD!
--SINCE THE HUMAN BODY HAS A WONDERFUL WAY OF SHUTTING ITSELF OFF WHEN THINGS GET TOO TERRIBLY PAINFUL. LOUIE ISN'T EVEN CONSCIOUS FOR HIS FINAL MOMENTS OF LIFE.
6

IT'S NOT THAT ANYONE WILL PARTICULARLY *MISS* HIM-- THERE WEREN'T THAT MANY WHO KNEW HE EXISTED IN THE *FIRST PLACE.*

STILL IN ALL, IT'S *NOT A VERY NICE WAY TO DIE.*

I AM... FULFILLED.

YET THIS SHALL NOT *LAST.* SOON I WILL BE IN NEED OF *MORE* DECAY TO SUSTAIN ME...

THUS IS IT *FORTUNATE* THERE ARE SO MANY *OTHERS* ABOUT... JUST *WAITING* TO FEEL THE *HAND OF DECAY!*

MEANWHILE, ACROSS TOWN, IN *CHICAGO'S LOOP...*

...FURTHERMORE, MR. OSTRANDER, YOU'LL HAVE TO KEEP IN MIND WE DEAL IN MATTERS OF THE UTMOST *SECRECY* HERE AT *ADAMS, KYLE,* AND *WASHBURN ASSOCIATES*--

--SECURITIES, BONDS... MATTERS OF *THAT* SORT. IT *REQUIRES* THAT YOU SAY AS *LITTLE* ABOUT YOUR WORK HERE AS *POSSIBLE* TO ANYONE OUTSIDE THE FIRM.

OH, HEY, I *UNDERSTAND,* MR. *ADAMS,* YOU CAN *COUNT* ON ME KEEPIN' MY CARDS *CLOSE* TO THE CHEST.

LET'S *HOPE* SO, MR. OSTRANDER.

NO *SWEAT,* SIR... *HONEST.* LISTEN, UNTIL I GET SOME *ACTING GIGS,* I NEED THIS JOB. YOU WON'T BE *SORRY* YOU HIRED ME.

7

THEN LET'S GET *STARTED!*

YOUR FIRST JOB IS TO DELIVER THIS *PACKAGE* TO A *MR. WILSON* AT THE *DRAKE HOTEL,* ROOM 756. HE'S EXPECTING YOU. IT'S *IMPORTANT* YOU'RE *PROMPT.*

DELIVERING PACKAGES TO HOTELS, HUH? JUST LIKE THEM OLD *HITCHCOCK* MOVIES. THIS WILSON GUY A *SPY* OR SOMETHING?

AYE-AYE, CAPTAIN.

NEVER MIND THE LEVITY, MR. OSTRANDER. HAVEN'T YOU A *JOB* TO DO?

THE BOY'S A *BUFFOON*--!

WHICH FITS OUR NEEDS TO A "*T*"! HE'LL PERFORM HIS TASKS AS ORDERED TO, AND IF HE'S *CAUGHT*--

--HE'S THE *PERFECT SPECIMEN* TO TAKE THE *RAP!*

ADAMS TO ONE.! IT'S ON ITS *WAY!*

EXCELLENT, ADAMS. THANK YOU.

MORE OF THESE GENTLEMEN-- AND SOME ASSOCIATES OF THEIRS WE'VE YET TO MEET-- IN *FUTURE ISSUES.* FOR NOW--

-- WE TURN OUR ATTENTION TO *NORTH OF THE LOOP,* WHERE SCHOOL IS LETTING OUT FOR THE DAY...

WELL, LIN--WHAT'VE YOU GOT TO SAY ABOUT YOUR *FIRST DAY* AT GOOD OL' *LAKE SHORE U.?*

HEAVY!

HEAVY? WHAT'S WITH THE CALIFORNIA-TYPE TALK, KEEDO?

I MEANT THE BOOKS, JOAN--THEY'RE HEAVY! I CAN'T BELIEVE THESE'RE *ALL* FOR JUST *ONE* SEMESTER!

THAT'S THE *PRICE* OF HIGHER EDUCATION, LIN.... *SORE MUSCLES.* YOU OUGHTTA DO WHAT *I* DO-- *FORGET* THE BOOKS AND USE THE CASH TO *PARTY.*

UH-HUH. SO HOW'CUM IF YOU SPEND ALL YOUR TIME *PARTYING*-- AND FROM WHAT I'VE SEEN OF YOU IN *ACTION,* NEIGHBOR, I DO *BELIEVE* YOU DO--

--YOU END UP PULLING *STRAIGHT-A'S?*

WELL, I *DID* GET A B+ IN *PHYS ED* LAST TERM, BUT DON'T TELL. YOU'LL *SPOIL* MY REPUTATION.

YOUR *SECRET'S SAFE* WITH ME, I...HUH?! WHAT'S ALL THE *RACKET?*

WHEEE!!

8

AREN'T *I* THE LUCKY ONE--! I GET TO *SEE* WHERE THE COPS ARE RUSHING OFF TO EVEN *BEFORE* THE *SIX O'CLOCK NEWS!*

LOOKS LIKE IT'S NOT ALL FUN AND *GAMES* IN THE LOOP--AND *NOT* JUST BECAUSE IT HAPPENS TO BE *RUSH-HOUR.* I DON'T KNOW *WHAT* THAT SHAMBLING MON-STROSITY'S *SUPPOSED* TO BE--

--BUT I *DO* KNOW WHAT HIS *APPEARANCE* IN CHICAGO MEANS TO A CERTAIN *BLONDE SUPER-HEROINE!*

JOANIE-- YOU HEADING BACK HOME NOW?

I *GUESS* SO. I THOUGHT WE WERE GONNA RIDE THE TRAIN THERE *TOGETHER...?*

GEE WHIZ, I'D *LOVE* TO, BUT I *JUST* REMEMBERED SOMETHING I'VE *GOT* TO DO! WOULD YOU DO ME A *BIG* FAVOR?

NAME IT, HONEY, AND IT'S *YOURS!*

GREAT! COULD YOU DROP THESE OFF AT MY APARTMENT ON YOUR WAY UP-STAIRS? *THANKS,* JOANIE, YOU'RE A *REAL SWEETHEART!*

WOOOF!

BUT... BUT...

BY GEORGE... I THINK I'VE BEEN *DUPED!*

THANKS *AGAIN!* SEE YOU *LATER!*

JOAN RAYMOND CAN ONLY SIGH AS SHE TURNS TOWARD HOME. LINDA DANVERS DEFINITELY HAS OTHER PLANS... PLANS THAT INCLUDE *NOT* THE YOUNG STUDENT HERSELF--

--BUT *SUPERGIRL...*

9

...AND FROM THE LOOKS OF THINGS, THE MAID OF MIGHT'S APPEARANCE HERE COULDN'T BE MORE TIMELY...

KEEP BACK, MEN! WE DON'T WANT TO *RUSH* THAT....THAT *THING* TILL WE KNOW WHAT IT CAN DO!

YES-- *COWER* BEHIND YOUR PROTECTIVE ARMAMENTS, HUMANS! YOU HAVE YET TO WIT-NESS THE *POWER* OF DECAY--

--POWER TO MAKE ALL OF MANKIND *COWER* AND TREMBLE....POWER TO *FEED* OFF THE MORAL AND PHYSICAL *ROT* THEY HAVE SO *THOUGHTFULLY* PROVIDED ME--

--POWER TO LIVE AND DESTROY WITH BUT A TOUCH!

BRO-*THER!* DON'T TELL ME YOU'RE *ANOTHER* WEIRDO OUT TO SMASH THE WORLD ALL BY HIS *LONESOME?*

AND HERE I THOUGHT ONLY NEW YORK HAD A *NONSTOP SUPPLY* OF *UGLIES* AND CREEPS TO MENACE IT!

SUPERGIRL!

SO YOU'VE COME *BACK* TO DISRUPT MY PLANS, HAVE YOU--?

YOU MUST BE MISTAKING ME FOR *ANOTHER* SUPER-PERSON! I DON'T BELIEVE WE'VE HAD THE *PLEASURE*-- ALTHOUGH I *HAVE* HEARD YOUR NAME *MENTIONED* BEFORE.

ALL THINGS CONSIDERED, I'LL TRY TO MAKE OUR FIRST MEETING THE *LAST* AS WELL-- NOT TO MENTION *PAINFULLY SHORT*... FOR *YOU*, THAT IS!

FWHAAAM!

10

YOU ARE *LAUGHABLE!* THOUGH YOU HAVE DEDICATED YOUR LIFE TO BATTLING MY *UNWITTING* MINIONS OF THE DECAY, YOU HAVE NEVER YET HAD TO FACE THEIR *MASTER*--

--THE LORD OF DECAY!

:*UGH!*: WHAT'S WITH THIS BOZO, ANYWAY? HE *MUST* BE THE GUY *PSI* WAS RAMBLING ON ABOUT YESTERDAY*--

*LAST ISSUE --Julie

--BUT I *STILL* HAVEN'T FIGURED OUT *EITHER* OF THEIR *ANGLES!*

I'LL ADMIT YOU'RE *STRONG*...BUT I BLEW YOUR FRIEND *PSI* OUT OF THE POOL--AND I CAN DO THE *SAME* TO YOU!

DO NOT MENTION THAT NAME TO ME! SHE IS A *TRAITOR* AND LIKE *YOU,* SHALL *DIE* FOR OPPOSING ME!

AND SPEAKING OF A CERTAIN PSIONICALLY-POWERED LADY....! ACROSS TOWN, IN THE APARTMENT OF THE MAN NAMED PENDERGAST...

:*SOB!*: OH MY GOD....IT....IT *HURTS!* I DON'T KNOW HOW MUCH *LONGER* I CAN *ENDURE* IT!

NOOOOOO...

THE HURT SLICES THROUGH HER LIKE A *KNIFE*--BUT IT IS NO PAIN BORN OF *PHYSICAL* INJURY, FOR *GAYLE MARSH* IS A MUTANT....POSSESSING TELEKINETIC POWERS BEYOND EQUAL--

--AND AN *EMPATHETIC* ABILITY THAT IS HER CURSE. SHE REMEMBERS THE YEARS MR. PENDERGAST TRAINED HER IN THESE SKILLS TO FIGHT THE EVIL OF THE *DECAY*--

--REMEMBERS TOO HER *FAILURE* AT DESTROYING THIS EVIL WHEN FACED WITH THE CHALLENGE OF *SUPERGIRL,* AND PENDERGAST'S HATRED OF HER BECAUSE OF THIS--

--AND, LORD HELP HER, HOW SHE LASHED OUT IN THE FACE OF THE OVERWHELMING PSYCHIC PAIN FROM THIS HATE--

--CREATING IN HOWARD PENDERGAST THE LIVING EMBODIMENT OF THE VERY THING HE'D DEDICATED HIS MADNESS TO DESTROYING--

-- *DECAY!*

11

BUT THE PAIN IN GAYLE MARSH DID NOT *END* THERE. IF ANYTHING, IT IS *WORSE* NOW... FOR THERE IS A *LINK* BETWEEN WHO SHE *IS* AND WHAT SHE HAS *CREATED*--

--AND SHE MUST FIND IT AND END IT--

--LEST IT TEAR HER APART FROM WITHIN.

MEANWHILE...

BEAR *WITNESS* TO MY POWER, SUPERGIRL, AND KNOW YOU THAT I WAS BORN TO *POWER*-- CREATED TO DE-STROY THE LAST VESTIGES OF ALL THAT IS PURE AND *CLEAN* IN THIS WORLD--

--AND THOSE WHO STAND IN THE WAY OF MY *DESTINY!*

I DON'T MEAN TO SOUND *HOSTILE*... BUT YOU'RE ABOUT AS *CRAZY* AS YOU ARE *UGLY*-- AND *THAT'S* MAJOR INSANITY!

...BUT CRAZY DOESN'T MEAN *HARMLESS*, FAR FROM IT! AND JUDGING BY WHAT HE DID TO THAT CAR WITH JUST A *TOUCH*--

KREE-WAKP!

12

--THE *LAST* THING I WANT TO DO IS LET HIM GET HIS GRUBBY PAWS ON ME! I MAY BE *INVULNERABLE* TO JUST ABOUT *EVERYTHING*, BUT I'D *HATE* TO FIND HE'S ONE OF THE *FEW* THINGS CAPABLE OF HURTING ME!

MAYBE SOME *OTHER* TIME, BIG GUY, BUT I JUST GOT THIS SUIT BACK FROM THE *CLEANERS* AND I DON'T NEED YOUR GRIMY *MUCK* DIRTYING IT UP AGAIN!

WHAP!

LAUGH, GIRL.... *MOCK* DECAY IF YOU WILL--

KREEE-EEEEEK!

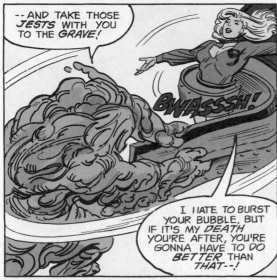

--AND TAKE THOSE *JESTS* WITH YOU TO THE *GRAVE!*

BWASSSH!

I HATE TO BURST YOUR BUBBLE, BUT IF IT'S MY *DEATH* YOU'RE AFTER, YOU'RE GONNA HAVE TO DO *BETTER* THAN THAT--!

MAYBE YOU WANT TO TRY SOMETHING LIKE *THIS*--

KNOPF!

--AND THEN FOLLOW IT UP WITH SOME REAL *GLITZY* MOVE--

--LIKE *GIFT-WRAPPING* ME .... SO!

FOOL!

KRWHAM!

I AM NO WEAK BUFFOON LIKE *PSI!* I AM *DECAY*... AND *NOTHING* THAT IS CAN WITHSTAND MY *TOUCH!*

13

OH-- THIS CITY WILL BE BUT THE *BEGINNING,* SUPERGIRL--AND *YOU* THE FIRST *CASUALTY* OF MY WAR!

LISTEN, IF THAT'S THE WAY YOU *WANT* IT, BUDDY....! BUT *UNTIL* YOU'VE MANAGED TO DESTROY ME LIKE YOU KEEP *PROMISING,* WOULD YOU *MIND* NOT DOING SO MUCH *DAMAGE!* THESE BUILDINGS AREN'T *CHEAP,* YOU KNOW!

HEY-- I'VE GOT A *GREAT* IDEA--

--WHY DON'T WE TAKE THIS FIGHT SOMEWHERE WE CAN BE *ALONE?*

RELEASE ME, SUPERGIRL!

OKAY--*OKAY!* YOU *DON'T* HAVE TO GET *VIOLENT* ABOUT IT! HOW'S *THIS?*

THUMP!

¡*ARRRRGGH!* ENOUGH! DECAY IS NO HUMAN'S *FOOL!* I... WILL... NOT... HAVE... IT!

HEY! I *ASKED* YOU TO CUT THAT OUT! SEE WHAT HAPPENS WHEN I TRY TO BE *MS. NICE-PERSON?* JUST FOR THAT, FELLA, I'M GOING TO HAVE TO *PUNCH OUT YOUR LIGHTS!*

YOU ARE FREE TO *TRY!*

MMMPHFFF

R-RAO! DECAY'S POWER... INCREDIBLE... H-HURTING ME....?!

14

NEXT ISSUE: "HAIL, HAIL, THE GANG'S ALL HERE!" ON SALE NOV. 18! IT'S A DATE!

Cover by **Keith Giffen & Mike DeCarlo**

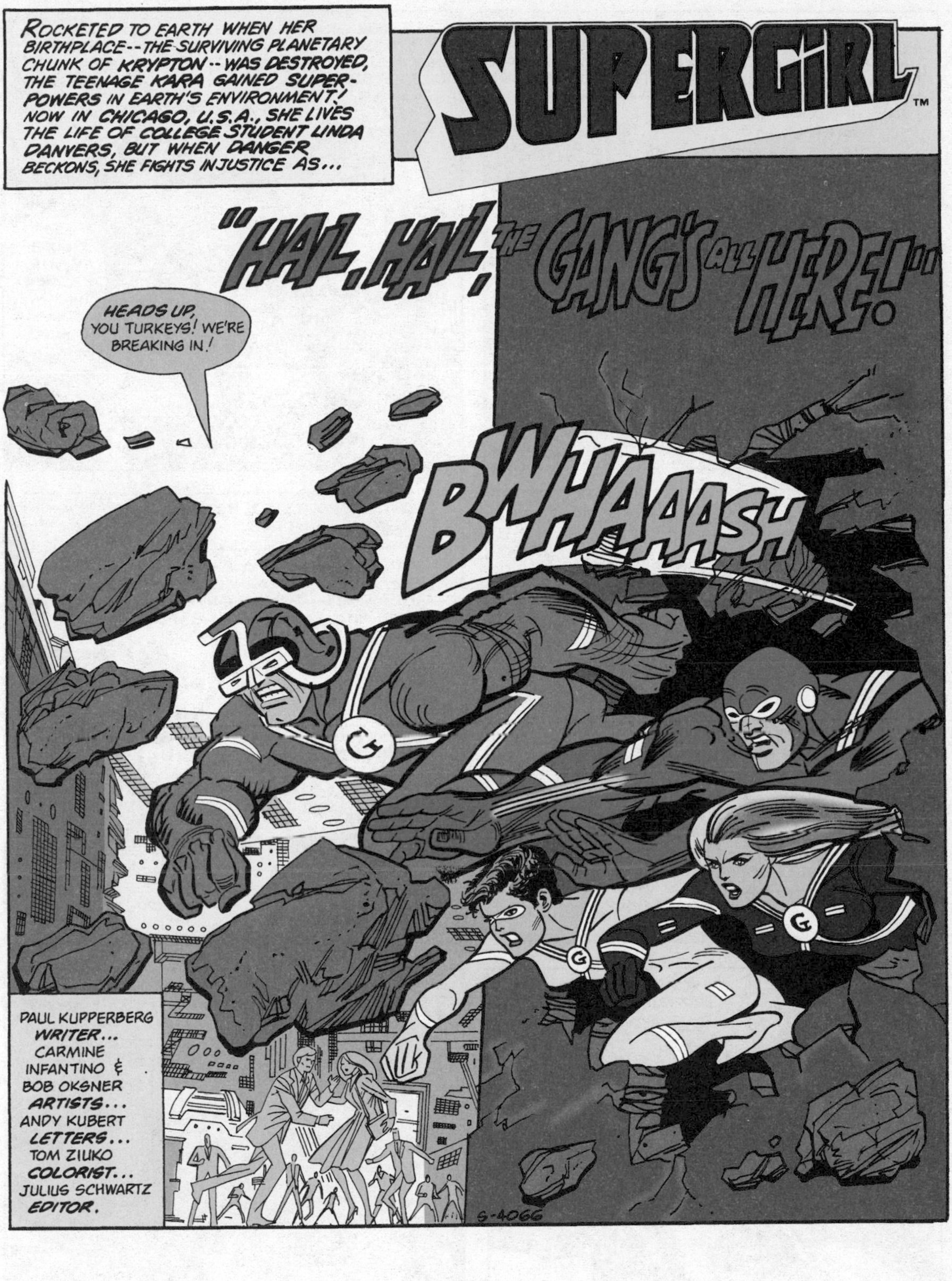
ROCKETED TO EARTH WHEN HER BIRTHPLACE--THE SURVIVING PLANETARY CHUNK OF KRYPTON--WAS DESTROYED, THE TEENAGE KARA GAINED SUPER-POWERS IN EARTH'S ENVIRONMENT! NOW IN CHICAGO, U.S.A., SHE LIVES THE LIFE OF COLLEGE STUDENT LINDA DANVERS, BUT WHEN DANGER BECKONS, SHE FIGHTS INJUSTICE AS...
SUPERGIRL™
"HAIL, HAIL, THE GANG'S ALL HERE!"
HEADS UP, YOU TURKEYS! WE'RE BREAKING IN!
BWHAAASH
PAUL KUPPERBERG WRITER... CARMINE INFANTINO & BOB OKSNER ARTISTS... ANDY KUBERT LETTERS... TOM ZIUKO COLORIST... JULIUS SCHWARTZ EDITOR.
S-4066

MAY I HAVE YOUR *ATTENTION*, LADIES AND GENTLEMEN! I REALIZE YOU ALL HAVE BUSINESS TO CONDUCT HERE AT THE *AEROSPACE TECHNOLOGIES SHOW*, SO WE SHAN'T TAKE UP MUCH OF YOUR *VALUABLE* TIME.

ALL WE ASK IS THAT YOU REMAIN *CALM* WHERE YOU ARE AND NO ONE WILL BE *HURT*.

THAT'S *REAL* CONSIDERATE OF YOU, LADY... ONLY WE CAN'T *LET* YOU COME BUSTING IN HERE LIKE THAT!

YEAH--AND IN CASE YOU AIN'T *NOTICED*, WE'VE GOT THE GUNS!

¿OOOOH!¿ *I'M SCARED*--AREN'T *YOU*, KONG¿

GOSH-- I SURE AM, *MS. MESMER!* THINK WE OUGHTTA *HIDE*¿

TRUTHFULLY ...NO!

PEOPLE ATTENDING THE AEROSPACE TECHNOLOGIES SHOW AT *CHICAGO'S* McCORMICK PLACE EXHIBITION CENTER WILL LATER BE AT A BIT OF A *LOSS* TO EXPLAIN WHAT HAPPENED NEXT. THEY ALL SAW THE LIGHTS, HEARD THE YOUNG WOMAN MURMUR SOFTLY--

--BUT THE REST...WELL, IT *DOES* GET A BIT *CONFUSING* AFTER THAT...

WHAT'RE YOU *STOPPIN'* FOR, CHARLIE¿ WHAT'S A MATTER WITH YOU¿

THIS ONE *IS* AN ANNOYANCE, BIG GUY. DO YOU WANT I SHOULD HAVE MY CAPTIVE *SHOOT* HIM¿

NAW, BLUE EYES--

--DON'T BOTHER!

URK!

THIS JERK AIN'T GONNA BE *BOTHERIN'* NOBODY FOR A *LONG TIME!*

KRSSH!

2

I SUGGEST YOU CEASE THESE ANTICS, MY FRIENDS. ENJOYABLE THOUGH THEY MAY BE, WE DID NOT *ALLOW* FOR THEM ON OUR *TIMETABLE!*

BULLDOZER! *THIS* IS WHAT WE WERE INSTRUCTED TO OBTAIN--!

SURE THING, HONEY! YOU JUST STAND BACK NOW, *BRAINS*--

--'CAUSE BULLDOZER'S COMIN' THROUGH!

KHAWOOMP

ANY *OTHER* SMALL JOBS YOU NEED DONE, KIDDO?

YOU'VE DONE *YOUR* BIT, MAN. NOW STAND ASIDE WHILE *I* TAKE CARE'A THE *LIFTIN'!*

HA! I THOUGHT YOU SAID THIS THING WAS *HEAVY!* IT CAN'T WEIGH MORE 'N A COUPLA *TONS!*

WOULD I ACCEPT ANY MISSION THAT MIGHT *STRAIN* YOU, DEAR KONG? NOW COME ALONG, LEST WE *MISS* OUR APPOINTMENT WITH THE *MAN!*

FAREWELL THEN, FRIENDS. I APOLOGIZE FOR ANY INCONVENIENCE... BUT THEN, PERHAPS YOU'LL CONSIDER YOURSELVES *PRIVILEGED* TO HAVE *WITNESSED* THE PREMIERE OUTING OF *THE GANG!*

TILL WE MEET AGAIN... PARTING IS SUCH *SWEET* SORROW...!

THEN WHY NOT *STICK AROUND* AND SAVE YOURSELF THE *GRIEF*, LADY?

WHO--?!

WHAMM'N

3

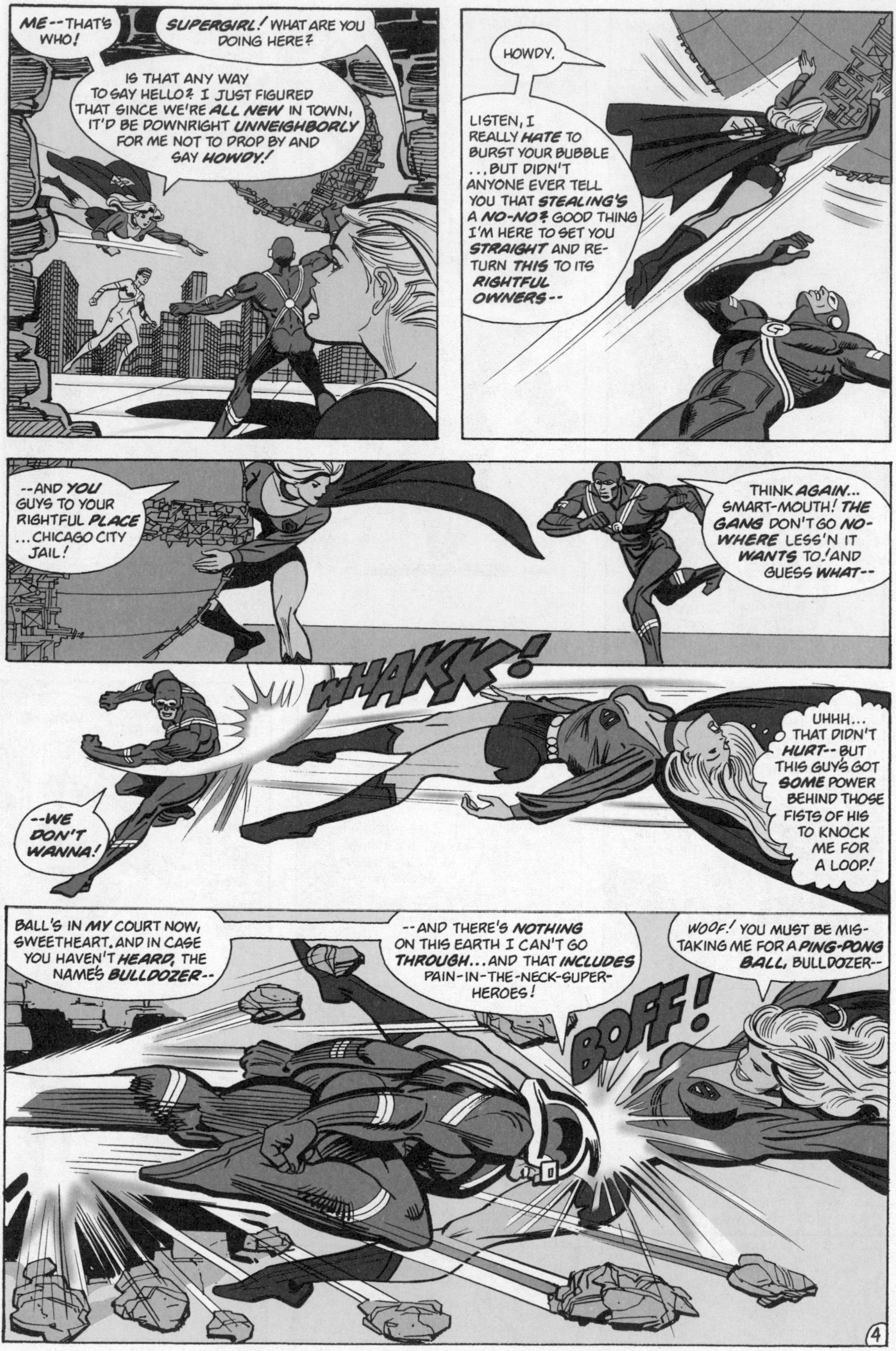
ME--THAT'S WHO!
SUPERGIRL! WHAT ARE YOU DOING HERE?
IS THAT ANY WAY TO SAY HELLO? I JUST FIGURED THAT SINCE WE'RE ALL NEW IN TOWN, IT'D BE DOWNRIGHT UNNEIGHBORLY FOR ME NOT TO DROP BY AND SAY HOWDY!
HOWDY.
LISTEN, I REALLY HATE TO BURST YOUR BUBBLE ...BUT DIDN'T ANYONE EVER TELL YOU THAT STEALING'S A NO-NO? GOOD THING I'M HERE TO SET YOU STRAIGHT AND RE-TURN THIS TO ITS RIGHTFUL OWNERS--
--AND YOU GUYS TO YOUR RIGHTFUL PLACE ...CHICAGO CITY JAIL!
THINK AGAIN... SMART-MOUTH! THE GANG DON'T GO NO-WHERE LESS'N IT WANTS TO! AND GUESS WHAT--
WHAKK!
--WE DON'T WANNA!
UHHH... THAT DIDN'T HURT--BUT THIS GUY'S GOT SOME POWER BEHIND THOSE FISTS OF HIS TO KNOCK ME FOR A LOOP!
BALL'S IN MY COURT NOW, SWEETHEART. AND IN CASE YOU HAVEN'T HEARD, THE NAME'S BULLDOZER--
--AND THERE'S NOTHING ON THIS EARTH I CAN'T GO THROUGH... AND THAT INCLUDES PAIN-IN-THE-NECK-SUPER-HEROES!
BOFF!
WOOF! YOU MUST BE MIS-TAKING ME FOR A PING-PONG BALL, BULLDOZER--
4

--AND IN CASE *YOU* HAVEN'T HEARD, THAT'S NOT MY SPEED AT ALL!

BUT I SEE NOW WHAT I DID WRONG. I FIGURED YOU FOR A BUNCH OF *PUNKS* IN FANCY COSTUMES, BUT I'VE GOTTEN A *HANDLE* ON YOU *NOW*--

--YOU'RE PUNKS WITH A *GIMMICK*!

THAT DOESN'T MAKE YOU *UNSTOPPABLE*... IT JUST MEANS I'VE GOT TO PUT A *TOUCH MORE EFFORT* INTO DOING IT!

OOOGG!

KNORF!

MAYBE THAT'D BE EASY IF WE WERE *ALONE*, SUPERGIRL--

--BUT THE GANG *STICKS TOGETHER*! TOUCH *ONE* OF US, AND YOU'VE GOT *THREE MORE* JUMPING DOWN YOUR THROAT ...*HUH*?!

JUMPING... NOW *THERE'S* AN IDEA! ALLEY-OOP!

RUNNING AND SMASHING SEEMS TO BE YOUR *THING*, BULLDOZER...ONLY YOU *CAN'T* RUN IF YOUR FEET *AREN'T* ON THE GROUND, CAN YOU?

NO--

--BUT *WHO SAID* I HAD TO RUN TO DO MY THING?

BLAM

GOT'CHA, LITTLE BUDDY!

5

WE DARE NOT DELAY ANY *LONGER,* GANG! MS. MESMER, I BELIEVE IT IS TIME FOR YOU TO SHOW SUPERGIRL WHAT *YOU* ARE CAPABLE OF!

MY THOUGHT EXACTLY, BRAINS--

--SO *READY* OR *NOT,* LADY....!

HHH--?!

THE SIMPLE DISC BEGINS ITS SLOW *SPIN,* BUILDING *GRADUALLY--*

--UNTIL *ALL* THE MAID OF MIGHT CAN SEE IS A BLINDING BARRAGE OF *COLORS* AND LIGHTS THAT WASH OVER HER--

--UNTIL, SUDDENLY...

THAT WAS A *PRETTY* LIGHT-SHOW, BUT YOU'LL HAVE TO DO A LOT *BETTER* THAN THAT TO...

...TO... *HUH?* THEY'RE... *GONE?!*

UH-HUH, AND THEY'VE *BEEN* GONE FOR ABOUT *FIVE MIN-UTES* WHILE *YOU* JUST HUNG IN THE AIR LIKE A CHRISTMAS TREE ORNAMENT! WHAT'S *WRONG* WITH YOU, SUPERGIRL?

BUT THAT'S *IMPOSSIBLE,* OFFICER! THEY WERE JUST HERE --NOT MORE THAN A *SECOND* AGO!

YOU BETTER GET YOUR *STOP-WATCH* FIXED THEN! ACCORDING TO EVERY WITNESS IN THE AREA, THEY TOOK OFF A *LONG* TIME AGO!

6

RAO--THAT *CAN'T* BE, I TELL YOU. I HAVE AN *INFALLIBLE* SENSE OF TIME. I *KNOW* THE DIFFERENCE BETWEEN FIVE MINUTES AND A SECOND!

YEAH, WELL, WELCOME TO THE WORLD OF *HUMAN FRAILTIES,* SUPERGIRL, 'CAUSE YOU'RE *WRONG!*

I'M *SORRY,* OFFICER...

SORRY DOESN'T GET BACK THAT STOLEN *SATELLITE*...AND IT'S *NOT* A WORD MY CHIEF LIKES TO SEE ON OUR *REPORTS!*

I CAN'T *BELIEVE* THIS! *HOW* COULD I CONFUSE A BLINK OF THE EYE WITH SO MUCH ELAPSED TIME...UNLESS--

--*UNLESS* THOSE LIGHTS THAT MS. MESMER CHARACTER HIT ME WITH GIVE HER SOME SORT OF *HYPNOTIC POWER* CAPABLE OF AFFECTING EVEN *ME!*

THAT *MUST* BE IT... AND THAT KIND OF ABILITY MAKES THE *GANG* AN AWFULLY *TOUGH* GROUP OF FOES TO ALLOW TO RUN FREE!

BUT I HAVEN'T THE *SLIGHTEST* IDEA WHERE TO START LOOKING FOR THEM...*OR* THE TIME RIGHT NOW, FOR THAT MATTER! *I WAS* IN THE MIDDLE OF SOMETHING WHEN MY SUPER-SENSES PICKED UP THE COMMOTION AT McCORMICK PLACE, AND I'D BETTER GET *BACK* TO THAT--

--OR RATHER, LAKE SHORE UNIVERSITY STUDENT *LINDA DANVERS* HAD BETTER--

--IF SHE EVER WANTS TO GET THAT RESEARCH PAPER FOR HER PSYCHOLOGY CLASS--

--*FINISHED* FOR TOMORROW!

BESIDES, THIS PAPER ISN'T THE *ONLY* THING I'VE GOT ON TAP FOR TODAY. I WOULDN'T WANT TO HAVE TO *CANCEL* MY APPOINTMENT FOR LATER.

EVEN *THEY* WOULD NEVER FORGIVE ME IF I DIDN'T SHOW UP!

7

AND SPEAKING OF APPOINTMENTS, WE HAVE A BRIEF ONE OF OUR *OWN* TO KEEP SEVERAL MILES DOWNTOWN, IN CHICAGO'S *LOOP*--

--AND THE OFFICE OF A CERTAIN *LESTER ADAMS*...

THE REPORT CAME IN OVER THE RADIO ALMOST AN *HOUR* AGO... *WHY* HAVEN'T THEY *CONTACTED* ME YET, BLAST THEM! IF THOSE FOOLS TAKE MUCH LONGER, THE WHOLE DEAL COULD BE IN *JEOPARDY!*

YOU *APPEAR* ANXIOUS, MR. ADAMS. *SURELY* YOU CAN RELAX NOW. THE *WORST* IS *OVER!*

HUH--?! WHO...?

SURELY YOU HAVE NOT *FORGOTTEN* ME SO *SOON*, SIR--I PRESUME IT *WAS* ME YOU WERE WAITING FOR.

BRAINS! GOOD LORD, WOMAN, HOW MANY TIMES HAVE I TOLD YOU NOT TO COME *HERE*... WE'VE *APPEARANCES* TO MAINTAIN!

I *ASSURE* YOU, SIR, I WAS *NOT* OBSERVED --NOR, WE DISCOVERED, DO WE LIKE TO *WAIT!*

IF YOU WILL, I'LL SAVE YOU THE *TROUBLE* OF HAVING OUR PAYMENT DELIVERED! THE SATELLITE HAS BEEN *DELIVERED* TO THE PREARRANGED SPOT!

I'M SURE IT *HAS* BEEN, BRAINS, BUT UNLIKE YOU, *I* GO BY THE *SYSTEM.* YOUR MONEY WAS SENT OVER VIA *MESSENGER* SOME TIME AGO...IN THE CARE OF SOME UN-SUSPECTING LACKEY *I* HIRED--

" --BY THE NAME OF *JOHN OSTRANDER*."

OH MANOMAN... I'M *NEVER* GONNA MAKE IT IN TIME! THESE LEGS JUST AIN'T *LONG* ENOUGH!

1537 WEST FARGO AVENUE IN CHICAGO'S ROGERS PARK SECTION IS *HOME* TO THIS YOUNG MAN... JUST AS IT IS TO *THIS* YOUNG WOMAN, LINDA DANVERS...

WELL *HELLO* DERE, LOVELY NEIGHBOR LADY! LONG TIME NO *SEE!*

*W*HICH, INCIDENTALLY, IS A GOOD PART OF THE *REASON* HE LIKES IT HERE SO MUCH...

HELLO, JOHN. NOPE--I'VE BEEN REAL BUSY GETTING SETTLED IN SCHOOL.

8

LISSEN, I'D *LOVE* TO RAP WITH YOU, GORGEOUS, BUT I'M IN A *RUSH.* I WAS HEADIN' DOWN TO THE *SOUTH SIDE* TO DELIVER THIS PACKAGE FOR MY BOSS--

--BUT I STOPPED OFF TO CHECK IN WITH MY *ANSWERING SERVICE,* AND THEY TOLD ME I HADDA GET DOWN TO DRURY LANE THEATRE FOR AN *AUDITION... PRONTO!*

AND I'M ONE LITTLE *ACTOR* WHAT CAN USE THIS GIG!

UHHH-- WHAT ABOUT YOUR *JOB,* FRIEND?

YOU CALL BEIN' A *MESSENGER* A *JOB...?* ANYWAY, IT'S ALL THE WAY DOWNTOWN... I'D *NEVER* MAKE IT THERE AND BACK HERE TO *CHANGE* BEFORE HITTIN' THE THEATRE. *WHOEVER'S* SUPPOSED TO GET THIS CAN *WAIT,* HONEY. CATCH YA LATER!

SHEESH! NO WONDER EVERYONE CALLS HIM THE BUILDING'S BIGGEST *CHARACTER...* ALTHOUGH CONSIDERING HOW *IRRESPONSIBLE* HE IS, I'M *SURPRISED* HE HASN'T BEEN *EVICTED* YET!

OH WELL. JOHNNY O'S NOT THE *ONLY* ONE IN A *HURRY.* I'VE GOT PEOPLE OF MY OWN TO MEET... AND... HUH?

THERE, YOU ARE, LINDA DARLING!

DON'T BE IN SUCH A *RUSH,* HONEY. I'VE BEEN WAITING FOR YOU TO GET HOME ALL AFTERNOON!

MRS. BERKOWITZ! I'D REALLY LOVE TO DISCUSS IT ...BUT CAN'T IT *WAIT?* I'M IN AN AWFUL *HURRY* AND...

SO? YOU THINK I DON'T *KNOW?* SO YOU'LL SLOW DOWN A BIT, IT WOULDN'T KILL YOU!

BUT... BUT PEOPLE ARE *EXPECTING* ME AND...

I KNOW DARLING. OY, YOU YOUNGSTERS NEED TO *LISTEN!*

9

SIGH!

OKAY, MRS. B--I SUPPOSE YOU'VE GOT SOMETHING TO *TELL* ME. BUT COULD WE *PLEASE* HURRY, BECAUSE THESE PEOPLE ARE EXPECTING ME AND...

TSK! "THESE *PEOPLE?*" THAT'S THE WAY YOU REFER, LINDA--

--TO YOUR LOVELY *MOTHER AND FATHER!?*

MOM...DAD...!

YOU SHOULDN'T BE SO *SURPRISED*, DEAR. PEOPLE SHOW UP AT THE DOOR OF ONE OF MY *FAVORITE TENANTS* WHEN NOBODY'S HOME, I'M GOING TO TURN *AWAY* WITHOUT A GLASS COFFEE?

IT'S SO *GREAT* TO SEE YOU BOTH AGAIN! HI! HELLO!

I'M *SURE* YOU THREE WANT TO TALK. GO--ENJOY!

I WANT TO *THANK* YOU FOR YOUR HOSPITALITY, MA'AM.

NONSENSE, MR. DANVERS. IT'S A *PLEASURE* IN THIS DAY AND AGE TO SEE A FAMILY SO *HAPPY* TOGETHER.

THANKS SO MUCH, MRS. B. YOU'RE A REAL SWEETHEART.

GO, MEIN KINDER--

--ENJOY...

10

IT'S GOOD TO SEE YOU AGAIN, HONEY. YOU DON'T KNOW HOW *HAPPY* I AM THAT WE HAD TO COME THROUGH CHICAGO ON *BUSINESS* FOR A FEW DAYS.

ME TOO, DAD. IT'S BEEN *TOO* LONG.

THIS IS SUCH A *LOVELY* CITY! HOW'RE YOU GET-TING ON HERE... *REALLY?*

DON'T I *LOOK* HAPPY? I *LOVE* CHICAGO AND SCHOOL, AND ALL THE FRIENDS I'VE MADE...IN FACT, I LOVE MY *WHOLE LIFE*, DAD. SO YOU CAN STOP *WORRYING!*

YOU LOOK *ECSTATIC*, LINDA. BUT WHAT ABOUT YOUR OTHER, ER... CAREER?

HA HA... YOU'RE AS *CAUTIOUS* AS EVER ABOUT MY SECRET IDENTITY, DAD.

BUT THAT'S GREAT TOO...I'VE *FINALLY* WORKED THAT OUT FOR MYSELF. YOU DON'T KNOW HOW *LONG* I LET SUPERGIRL GET OUT OF HAND UNTIL THE JOBS WERE ALMOST OVER-WHELMING ME... ER, LINDA, THAT IS.

IT TOOK A BIT OF *DOING*, BUT I *CONVINCED* MYSELF I DIDN'T HAVE TO BE SUPERGIRL 24 HOURS A DAY... THAT THERE ARE ACTUALLY THINGS I *DIDN'T* HAVE TO JUMP INTO MY LITTLE RED-HOT PANTS FOR.

BUT SURELY IF AN *EMERGENCY* POPS UP...?

THERE ARE EMERGENCIES AND *EMERGENCIES!* I SUPPOSE I'VE DEVELOPED SOME SORT OF *SIXTH SENSE* ABOUT THESE THINGS... WHAT I *NEED* TO HANDLE AND WHAT I CAN LEAVE UP TO *OTHERS.*

WELL, NOW I DON'T *KNOW* ABOUT THIS, LINDA. YOU MEAN YOU'LL JUST *IGNORE* TROUBLE IF YOU DON'T FEEL LIKE TACKLING IT--?

OF *COURSE* I DON'T *IGNORE* IT, DAD...BUT LET'S FACE IT. IF I WASN'T AT LEAST *SELECTIVE* ABOUT THE THINGS I HANDLE, I'D *NEVER* HAVE TIME TO BE ANYONE *BUT* SUPERGIRL--

--AND *LESS* THAN THAT HAS DRIVEN A LOT OF PEOPLE NUTS!

NOW, *FRED*... YOU KNOW OUR DAUGHTER *BETTER* THAN THAT! SHE'D *NEVER* LET ANYONE GET *HURT* BECAUSE OF HER *NEGLIGENCE!*

I *KNOW*, *EDNA*, BUT STILL, IT DOESN'T *SOUND*...

OH, *DAD*, LOOK-- I'M JUST MORE *SELECTIVE* THESE DAYS ...NOT *RECKLESS!*

ANYWAY, WE'RE... OH-OH!

OH-OH *INDEED!* I *REMEMBER* WHAT *THAT* LOOK MEANS.

YEAH, BUT I FEEL SO *SILLY* AFTER LECTURING YOU ABOUT HOW I DON'T GO CHARGING OFF AFTER *EVERY* CALL FOR *HELP!*

WE'RE YOUR *PARENTS*, DEAR--WE *UNDERSTAND!* YOU GO TAKE CARE OF WHATEVER IT IS YOU HAVE TO DO--AND *WE'LL* GET A *TABLE!* COME BACK AS SOON AS YOU CAN!

JUST TAKE *CARE* OF YOURSELF!

DON'T I *ALWAYS*?

ALL RIGHT--SO I *DIDN'T* TELL THEM THE *WHOLE* STORY! I MAY BE SUPERGIRL TO THE *WORLD*--

--BUT I'LL *ALWAYS* BE THE HELP-LESS LITTLE 16-YEAR-OLD ORPHAN THEY *ADOPTED* ALL THAT TIME AGO TO THEM!

*S*HE IS NO LONGER AN ORPHAN--

--AND BY NO *MEANS* IS THIS YOUNG WOMAN *HELPLESS*... ALTHOUGH AT THE *MOMENT*, SHE'S QUITE *CONCERNED*...

WEIRD! MY SUPER-HEARING PICKED UP STRANGE NOISES ...RIGHT *HERE*--IN MY *OWN APARTMENT BUILDING!*

12

IT COULD BE A COINCIDENCE...NO --IT'S GOT TO BE! I MEAN, EVEN THOUGH WE FOUGHT EARLIER TODAY, THERE'S NO WAY IN THE WORLD IT COULD BE KNOWN THAT SUPERGIRL LIVES HERE IN HER SECRET IDENTITY--

--EVEN BY THE GANG!

L-LISSEN...CAN'T WE...TALK THIS OVER...? I DON'T EVEN KNOW YOU...ER, PEOPLE!?

PERHAPS NOT, FOOL-- YET THAT DOES NOT MEAN YOU DO NOT HOLD SOMETHING OF OURS! YOU WOULD BE WISE TO TURN IT OVER TO US, LEST WE ...WHA...?

SUPERGIRL--?!

RIGHT THE FIRST TIME, BIG GUY! I THOUGHT YOU MIGHT PREFER PICKING ON ME FOR A WHILE INSTEAD OF HELPLESS CIVILIANS!

WHA4AMM

THAT OUGHT TO KEEP HIM BUSY FOR A BIT. I THINK YOU'D BETTER COME WITH ME, MISTER--IT'S A LOT SAFER!

WHAT IN THE NAME OF KRYPTON CAN LINDA'S ACTOR-NEIGHBOR HAVE TO DO WITH THESE CLOWNS?

WOOOF! THANKS A HEAP, SUPERGIRL!

13

WOULD YOU *MIND* TELLING ME WHAT THAT'S ALL ABOUT--OR IS *THAT* YOUR IDEA OF A *PARTY?*

YEAH... *SURE!* LOOK, DON'T ASK *ME.* I GOT HOME FROM MY AUDITION AND FOUND THOSE DUDES WAITING FOR ME--AND MAN, WERE THEY *TICKED!*

WHERE IS IT, PUNK? COUGH IT UP...OR NOT EVEN SUPERGIRL WILL *BE ABLE* TO PROTECT YOU!

HE SEEMS TO KNOW *YOU.*

DO I LOOK LIKE A SUPER-VILLAIN, LADY? I'M AN *ACTOR* FOR CRYIN' OUT LOUD!

KRSSH

WE'LL DISCUSS THIS *LATER,* MISTER.

AS FOR *YOU,* MAMMOTH--MY ADVICE IS TO *COOL* IT, BEFORE YOU GET *HURT!*

THIS IS *TWICE* YOU BUTTED INTO OUR BUSINESS, GIRLY--WHICH'S *TWO TIMES TOO MANY!* YOU'RE THE ONE WHAT BETTER *WATCH* YOURSELF--

--'CAUSE WE'RE DONE PLAYIN'!

BWASH

UNNNH!

AS I SUSPECTED, MS. MESMER--SHE HAS *RE*-TURNED TO PLAGUE US. WILL IT *WORK* AS PLANNED?

LIKE A *CHARM,* BRAINS. JUST YOU WAIT AN' *SEE!*

UGH! I NEED THIS ABUSE--?

14

THESE GUYS WORK TOGETHER LIKE THEY'VE BEEN DOING IT ALL THEIR LIVES! I CAN'T AFFORD TO LET MY GUARD DOWN FOR A *SECOND*--

--OR TURN MY *BACK* ON ANY *ONE* OF THEM!

I...*?GASP!?* OH MY GOD--

--NO!

HOW...?! I *KNOW* I CHANGED FROM *LINDA* TO *SUPERGIRL*...BUT *NOW*...WHAT IF *JOHN* SEES ME...?

LIKE I *SAID,* BRAINS--IT *WORKS!* THE POST-HYPNOTIC SUGGESTION I LEFT HER WITH THIS MORNING WAS A SURE BET TO TRIGGER *SOMETHING* IN HER *REFLECTION* THAT SHE'S *AFRAID* OF!

I DON'T KNOW *WHAT* THAT IS IN THAT CHICK, BUT JUDGING FROM THE WAY SHE *TOOK OFF* LIKE A BAT OUT OF HELL, I'D SAY IT WAS PRETTY *HEAVY,* HUH?

HEH-HEH... *QUITE!*

HEY! WHERE YOU *GOIN,* SUPERGIRL--?! AREN'T YOU GONNA--

--HELP..?

15

NEXT ISSUE: JOHNNY-O DOES SOME FAST TALKING... *SUPERGIRL* DOES SOME FAST THINKING... AND THERE'S PLENTY OF FAST ACTION... IN *"FEAR TIMES FOUR!"* ON SALE DEC. 23RD! IT'S A *DATE!*

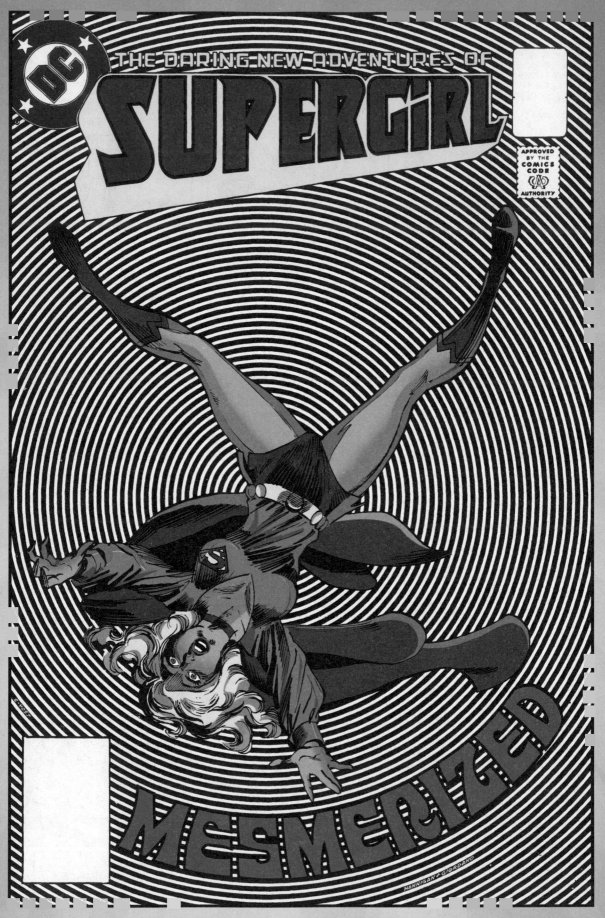

Cover by **Ed Hannigan & Dick Giordano**

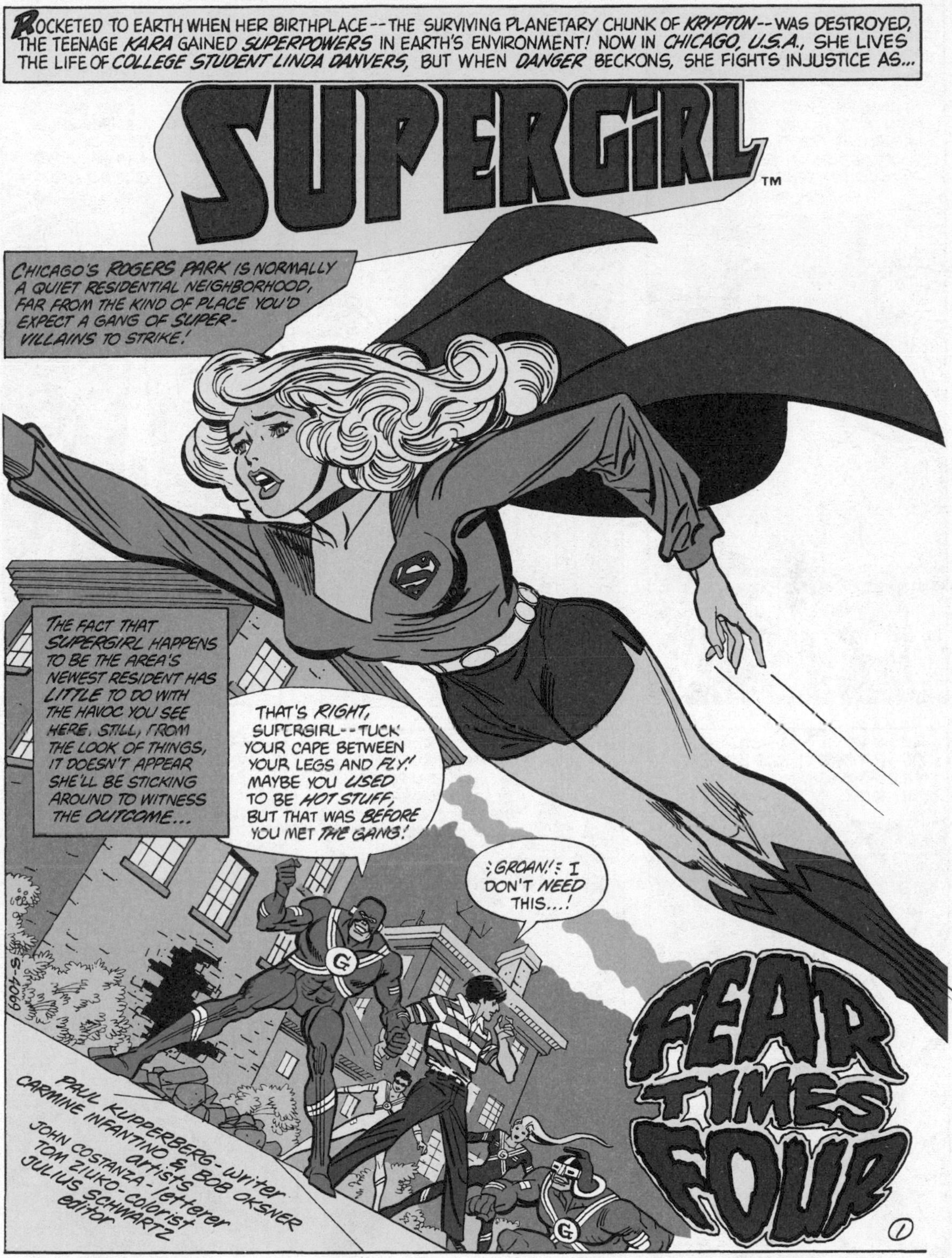
ROCKETED TO EARTH WHEN HER BIRTHPLACE -- THE SURVIVING PLANETARY CHUNK OF KRYPTON -- WAS DESTROYED, THE TEENAGE KARA GAINED SUPERPOWERS IN EARTH'S ENVIRONMENT! NOW IN CHICAGO, U.S.A., SHE LIVES THE LIFE OF COLLEGE STUDENT LINDA DANVERS, BUT WHEN DANGER BECKONS, SHE FIGHTS INJUSTICE AS...
SUPERGIRL™
CHICAGO'S ROGERS PARK IS NORMALLY A QUIET RESIDENTIAL NEIGHBORHOOD, FAR FROM THE KIND OF PLACE YOU'D EXPECT A GANG OF SUPER-VILLAINS TO STRIKE!
THE FACT THAT SUPERGIRL HAPPENS TO BE THE AREA'S NEWEST RESIDENT HAS LITTLE TO DO WITH THE HAVOC YOU SEE HERE. STILL, FROM THE LOOK OF THINGS, IT DOESN'T APPEAR SHE'LL BE STICKING AROUND TO WITNESS THE OUTCOME...
THAT'S RIGHT, SUPERGIRL--TUCK YOUR CAPE BETWEEN YOUR LEGS AND FLY! MAYBE YOU USED TO BE HOT STUFF, BUT THAT WAS BEFORE YOU MET THE GANG!
GROAN! I DON'T NEED THIS...!
FEAR TIMES FOUR
PAUL KUPPERBERG-writer
CARMINE INFANTINO & BOB OKSNER artists
JOHN COSTANZA-letterer
TOM ZIUKO-colorist
JULIUS SCHWARTZ editor
S-4069
1

MS. MESMER, YOUR *HYPNOTIC POWERS* IMPRESS ME MORE AND *MORE* AS WE GO ALONG!

FRANKLY, I WAS NOT *CERTAIN* EVEN *YOU* WOULD BE ABLE TO IMPLANT A *POST-HYPNOTIC SUGGESTION* IN SUPERGIRL THAT COULD SEND HER FLEEING THIS WAY!

THANKS, *BRAINS.* TO TELL THE TRUTH, I WASN'T SO SURE *MYSELF!*

BUT WHEN YOU GET RIGHT DOWN TO IT, EVEN A *SUPERGIRL'S* GOING TO HAVE *FEARS* SHE WON'T BE ABLE TO CONTROL... ESPECIALLY WHEN THEY'RE BROUGHT OUT BY *HYPNOSIS!*

IT WASN'T TOUGH TO IMPLANT THE SUGGESTION THAT WOULD MAKE HER *SEE* THOSE FEARS AFTER THE FIRST TIME WE MET AND...*

LISSEN, I HATE INTERRUPTING THIS MUTUAL ADMIRATION SOCIETY, BUT JUST BECAUSE SUPERGIRL'S *SPLIT* DON'T MEAN SHE *WON'T* BE COMING *BACK*--

*PREVIOUS ISSUE -- JULIE

--AND WE'VE *STILL* GOT THIS LITTLE *RAT* TO DEAL WITH!

A-ACTUALLY, I WAS *HOPING* YOU'D *FORGET...!*

N-NO... NO SUCH *LUCK...*

INDEED *NOT,* MR. OSTRANDER. NOW, I *BELIEVE* YOU POSSESS A CERTAIN PACKAGE THAT BELONGS TO *US* AND WE WILL HAVE IT FROM YOU--

-- REGARDLESS OF *WHAT* IT TAKES TO RETRIEVE IT!

MEANWHILE, THE SCENE IS QUITE A BIT MORE SERENE SEVERAL MILES TO THE SOUTH IN A POSH DOWNTOWN RESTAURANT...

RIGHT THIS WAY, MR. AND MRS. DANVERS. YOUR TABLE IS *READY.*

THANK YOU. OUR DAUGHTER SHOULD BE *JOINING* US IN JUST A FEW MINUTES.

2

OF COURSE, SIR. SHE WILL BE SHOWN TO YOUR TABLE AS SOON AS SHE ARRIVES. WHILE YOU'RE WAITING, MAY I GET YOU SOMETHING FROM THE BAR?

WE'D LIKE A GLASS OF MINERAL WATER WITH A TWIST OF LIME, PLEASE.

CERTAINLY, MR. DANVERS. YOUR WAITER FOR TONIGHT IS PIERRE AND HE WILL BE AT YOUR SERVICE. *PIERRE!*

IF THERE IS ANYTHING ELSE I MIGHT DO FOR YOU, PLEASE FEEL FREE TO CALL UPON ME AND... AND... *OHH!?!*

IS THIS THE TABLE THAT'S ORDERING THE DRINKS?

OF COURSE *NOT*, YOU DOLT! DO *YOU* SEE ANYONE SEATED HERE?

N-NO, SIR.... M-MY MISTAKE...

AND WHILE CONTROLLED CHAOS REIGNS WITHIN THE RESTAURANT, WE TURN OUR ATTENTION *ELSEWHERE* -- SOME SEVERAL HUNDRED FEET *ABOVE* THE STREETS OF CHICAGO, TO BE EXACT...

SORRY ABOUT THE SUPER-SPEED SNATCH, MOM AND DAD, BUT I *HAD* TO TALK WITH YOU --

-- AND I DIDN'T *DARE* SHOW UP IN THE RESTAURANT LIKE *THIS!*

OF COURSE, LINDA. WHAT WOULD PEOPLE *SAY* IF THEY SAW SUPERGIRL WALKING UP TO US IN PUBLIC?

WHAT'RE YOU *TALKING* ABOUT, DAD? SOME VILLAINS MANAGED TO SWITCH ME INTO MY LINDA DANVERS IDENTITY *WITHOUT* MY KNOWING IT... IN *PUBLIC!*

THANK GOODNESS YOU WERE ABLE TO GET BACK INTO YOUR SUPER-GIRL OUTFIT WITHOUT ANYONE *SEEING* YOU, HONEY.

3

SOMEBODY'S AWFULLY CONFUSED HERE... I'M JUST NOT SURE *WHO!*

LOOK AT ME, MOM-- AM I *CRAZY,* OR ISN'T *THIS* ONE OF *LINDA'S* GET-UPS?

NOT UNLESS YOU'VE STARTED HAVING DINNER IN A *RED-AND-BLUE* COSTUME!

THIS IS VERY *WRONG.* LINDA, TELL ME *EXACTLY* WHAT YOU *SEE* YOU'RE *WEARING!*

THIS, DAD... MY *STREET-CLOTHES!* I *COULDN'T* MAKE A MISTAKE ABOUT *THAT...* COULD I?

I'M AFRAID SO! REACH INSIDE THE POUCH IN YOUR CAPE WHERE YOU KEEP YOUR *CIVVIES.*

...OR *THINK* YOU'RE WEARING? SOMEBODY'S PLAYING *TRICKS* ON YOUR MIND! BELIEVE ME, LINDA-- YOU *ARE* DRESSED AS SUPERGIRL!

I DON'T KNOW WHAT GOOD *THAT'LL* DO SINCE I'M ALREADY WEARING ...*HUH?!* IT'S A *DUPLICATE* OF THE OUTFIT I'M WEARING!

GREAT! THEN *WHY* CAN'T I SHAKE THE *FEAR* THAT I'M *NOT*-- THAT THE WHOLE *WORLD* CAN SEE RIGHT THROUGH MY SECRET IDENTITY AT THE MOMENT?

THIS IS *TERRIBLE!* I'M AFRAID TO *ACT...* AND ONE OF MY NEIGHBORS IS GOING TO *SUFFER* FOR THAT AT THE HANDS OF *THE GANG!*

SPEAKING OF WHOM...

THIS IS THE *SOUTH SIDE OF CHICAGO,* THE "*BADDEST PART OF TOWN*" IMMORTALIZED IN SONG--

OF COURSE, THE SONGWRITER HAD NO WAY OF KNOWING THAT IT WAS *ALSO* THE PLACE THE GANG CALLED *HOME...*

IN *HERE,* CREEP!

CAN'T WE TALK THIS *OVER,* GUYS? *TELL* ME WHAT IT IS YOU *WANT* FROM ME, FER CRYIN' OUT LOUD!

4

REALLY, MR. OSTRANDER, THESE DELAYING TACTICS OF YOURS ARE QUITE *USELESS*. THOUGH WE WERE FORCED TO FLEE TO AVOID THE POLICE, WE ARE WELL AWARE OF THE FACT THAT *YOU* HOLD SOMETHING OF OURS.

WHERE IS IT?

WHAT IT? I DON'T KNOW FROM ANY "*IT*"!

BRAINS *TOLD* YOU TO *CAN IT*, PUNK! YOU TRYIN' TO TELL US YOU *WASN'T* GIVEN A PACKAGE TO DELIVER BY MR. ADAMS?

ADAMS--?! SURE... I WORK FOR HIM. BUT WHAT'S THAT GOT TO DO WITH *YOU?*

YOU *ARE* DENSE, AIN'T YOU? THAT WAS *OUR* BREAD YOU WAS HOLDIN'!

YOUR--?! LOOK, MAN, I JUST DO THIS DELIVERY STUFF TO PAY THE RENT, Y'KNOW? SURE, ADAMS GAVE ME A PACKAGE TO DELIVER, BUT I HAD TO MAKE AN *AUDITION*... I'M AN *ACTOR*, REALLY!

HONEST, I WAS GOING TO DELIVER IT--*LATER!* I DON'T EVEN CARE *WHY* ADAMS WOULD HAVE DEALINGS WITH YOU GUYS...

MY COMPANIONS AND I ARE SOMETIME *EMPLOYEES* OF MR. ADAMS AND HIS ORGANIZATION--OR DIDN'T YOU KNOW THAT? TELL ME--WHAT MANNER OF OUTFIT DID YOU THINK HE IS RUNNING?

HEY--I DON'T ASK *QUESTIONS*, Y'KNOW. LIKE I SAID, IT WAS JUST A JOB--TO MAKE SOME QUICK MONEY!

BUT IF YOU SAY THE PACKAGE IS *YOURS*, IT'S *YOURS*, LADY! ME--I AIN'T THE TYPE TO ASK FOR HASSLES FROM ANYBODY WHO CAN MAKE SUPERGIRL RUN OFF SCREAMING!

YOU *WANT* IT, YOU *GOT* IT! NO QUESTIONS AND... ;*GULP!*... N NO ENVELOPE--!

OH-OH... I MUST'VE *LEFT* IT BACK AT THE AUDITION! BUT I CAN *GET* IT FOR ;*OOOFF!*

HE'S *LYIN'*, BRAINS! THE PUNK *KNEW* IT WAS MONEY AND RIPPED US OFF! LEMME DO THE SAME FOR *HIM*... WITH HIS *HEAD!*

NO, BULLDOZER. THAT WILL NOT *DO*. PLEASE RELEASE HIM.

HUH?! WE OUGHTTA...

REMEMBER OUR AGREEMENT, OLD FRIEND. THERE WILL BE *NO* KILLING--

5

"--NOTHING THAT WILL *LOWER* US TO THAT DESPICABLE LEVEL OF BARBARISM WE SOUGHT SO HARD TO AVOID WHILE GROWING UP IN THESE MEAN STREETS OF THE SOUTH SIDE!

"HAVE YOU ALREADY *FORGOTTEN* THE POVERTY WE WERE MADE TO SUFFER THROUGH GROWING UP HERE? THE FILTH, THE GARBAGE... AND THE *IGNORANCE?*

"AHHH, BUT *WE* WERE DIFFERENT, MY FRIENDS. EVEN AT AN *EARLY* AGE, WE SAW THAT COMMON STREET *HOOLIGANISM* WAS NOT THE WAY TO RAISE OURSELVES FROM DESTRUCTION. NO, WE WOULD FIND OUR WAY FROM THE STREETS *ELSEWISE*--

"--SO THAT WE WOULD NOT END UP IMPRISONED OR ADDICTED TO THE VILE NAR-COTICS THAT FLOODED OUR NEIGHBORHOOD BY THE TIME WE WERE IN HIGH SCHOOL.

"--AND *DEVELOP* THEM INTO OUR SO-CALLED '*TICKETS*' OUT OF POVERTY! WE FORMED *THE GANG* AND KEPT TO OURSELVES IN THIS VERY BASEMENT *CLUB-HOUSE*--

"*EACH* OF US HAD CERTAIN *TALENTS* WITH WHICH TO WORK, SO DID WE TAKE THE *NICKNAMES* OUR CON-TEMPORARIES SOUGHT TO *MOCK* US WITH--

"--MAKING OURSELVES INTO YOUNG MEN AND WOMEN WITH *ABILITIES* SUFFICIENT TO MAKE A *MARK* ON THIS CITY, AVOIDING CRIME AND POLICE RECORDS UNTIL WE WERE ABLE--WITH *ASSISTANCE* FROM *MR. ADAMS* AND HIS ORGANIZATION--

"--TO MAKE OUR DEBUT AS... *THE GANG!*"

6

BUT DO NOT LET THIS DESIRE TO *AVOID* SUCH PRATFALLS *DECEIVE* YOU, MR. OSTRANDER. FOR WE *DID* ORGANIZE TO MAKE OUR-SELVES *RICH*--

--AND WE *SHAN'T* ALLOW THAT DESIRE TO BE FOILED BY SOME *THIEVING* LACKEY. WE *WILL* HAVE OUR *MONEY,* SIR-- OR ITS FULL VALUE IN *BLOOD!*

ULP

MEANWHILE...

RAO, BUT THIS IS *SPOOKY!* NO MATTER *WHAT* MY FOLKS TELL ME, I *CAN'T* SHAKE THE FEELING I'M ACTUALLY FLYING AROUND AS *LINDA DANVERS* INSTEAD OF SUPERGIRL!

FIVE WILL GET YOU *TEN* THAT GIRL WITH THE *BIG EYES* IS BEHIND THIS! SHE HYPNOTIZED ME *ONCE*-- AND *THIS* HAS THE MARKINGS OF FULL-FLEDGED *MESMERISM!*

FAT LOT OF GOOD KNOWING THAT DOES ME, THOUGH. I *TRIED* BREAKING THE HYPNOTIC HOLD... AND *NOTHING!* EVEN KNOWING I'M UNDER HYPNOSIS ISN'T HELPING.

I *STILL BELIEVE* THE WHOLE WORLD CAN SEE RIGHT THROUGH MY *SECRET IDENTITY!*

WAITAMINNIT! MAYBE... *MAYBE* THE HYPNOTIC COMPULSION'S ONLY IN FORCE WHEN I'M IN MY *SUPERGIRL* GARB--! SO... IF I *AM* DRESSED AS LINDA--

--THEN I WON'T BE SUPERGIRL JUST *THINKING* I'M DRESSED AS LINDA... I *WILL* BE!

SEVERAL SECONDS LATER, AFTER A SUPER-SPEED SWITCH OF CLOTHING...

BETTER... NOT BY A *LOT,* BUT BETTER! I *STILL* HAVE THE UN-EASY FEELING MY *CAPE* IS SHOWING, BUT I THINK I CAN GET A GRIP ON MYSELF NOW!

UH-OH, THE GANG AND JOHN ARE GONE... BUT MRS. BERKOWITZ'S TROUBLES ARE *STARTING.* THANK GOODNESS SHE'S GOT SUCH WONDERFUL TENANTS TO *HELP* HER--!

IT WAS LIKE A *TORNADO* HIT, OFFICER! *OY!*... AND *POOR* JOHNNY! THAT'S *HIS* APARTMENT.

7

MRS. BERKOWITZ! ARE YOU ALL RIGHT? I JUST GOT HOME AND *SAW...*

SHE'S *FINE*, LIN...BUT I DON'T THINK THIS *BUILDING'S* EVER GONNA BE THE *SAME*!

SOME *WEIRD* KIND OF DUDES CAME BY AND *SNATCHED* POOR JOHNNY-O! I MEAN, I *KNOW* ACTORS HAVE *STRANGE* FRIENDS, BUT *THESE* WERE *UNREAL*!

WHAT AM I GOING TO DO, LINDA? MY POOR BUILDING...AND WHAT ABOUT *JOHNNY?* SUPPOSE HE'S BEEN *HURT...?*

CALM DOWN, MRS. B. EVERYTHING'LL BE *FINE*. I'M *SURE* JOHNNY'S *OKAY*--

--AND ALL *YOU* NEED IS A NICE GLASS OF TEA... ER, AND SOME ADVICE FROM YOUR *INSURANCE* AGENT, OKAY, MRS. B?

..., THIS IS ROLAND WILSON ON THE SCENE *LIVE* FOR THE NEWS AT SIX! EYEWITNESSES HERE AT THE ROGERS PARK LOCATION OF THIS AFTERNOON'S DISTURBANCE--

--CONFIRM POLICE SUSPICIONS THAT THE ATTACKERS OF THIS BUILDING'S *RESIDENT*, ACTOR JOHN OSTRANDER, ARE THE *SAME* SUPER-POWERED VILLAINS WHO *EARLIER* STAGED THE *DARING* ROBBERY AT THE *MCCORMICK PLACE* EXHIBITION CENTER. AN ALL-POINTS...

FOOLS!

THOSE BLASTED *FOOLS!* DON'T THEY REALIZE THEIR *STUPIDITY* THREATENS *EVERYTHING* WE'VE BEEN WORKING SO *HARD* FOR? AND FOR *WHAT*--? FOR A PITIFUL SUM OF *CASH* I WOULD'VE *EASILY REPLACED*!

IT'S TOO LATE TO DO ANYTHING ABOUT THEM *NOW*. ALL WE *CAN* DO IS TRY AND SALVAGE OUR *OWN* POSITIONS--!

DENNIS! SEND OUT *WORD*...I'M CALLING A MEETING OF THE COUNCIL IMMEDIATELY!

AT *ONCE*, SIR!

I HOPE THEY HAVEN'T RUINED IT ALL--AND THAT MY FELLOW *COUNCIL MEMBERS* WILL *HEED* MY ADVICE ON THE GANG'S RATHER *LIMITED* FUTURE--!

8

THE GOODMAN THEATER NEAR LAKE MICHIGAN...

MR. OSTRANDER, YOU ARE *CERTAIN* THIS IS WHERE YOU LAST RECALL HAVING POSSESSION OF OUR MONEY?

YEAH-- OF *COURSE* I REMEMBER! I WAS AUDITION-ING FOR THE PART OF "BYSTANDER" FOR THE "CHRISTMAS CAROL" AND...

WE DON'T *CARE*, PUNK--

--SO *SHUT* YOUR YAP!

OH! CONSIDER IT SHUT!

RRRIPPP

LEAD THE WAY! THE TIME SPENT WAITING FOR THE THEATER TO *CLOSE* HAS MADE ME *MOST* IMPATIENT. I WISH TO *HAVE* WHAT IS OURS AND BE *DONE* WITH THIS!

YOU AND ME *BOTH!* LEMME SEE... YEAH!

I WAS FIDDLING WITH IT WHILE WAITING FOR THE DIRECTOR TO GIVE ME A CALL. I WAS STANDIN' RIGHT *HERE*--IN THE WINGS. IF IT'S *ANYWHERE*, IT'S GONNA BE *HERE!*

I *HOPE* SO, CREEP-- FOR *YOUR* SAKE!

LADY--YOU *WANT* INTIMIDATED, YOU *GOT* INTIMIDATED! YOU DON'T *NEED* MORE THREATS. *ONE* IS *PLENTY* FOR M... HUH?

JUST *HOLD STILL* NOW, YOUNGSTERS, AND YOU *WON'T* GET HURT--

--'CAUSE THE *COPS'LL* BE HERE ANY MINUTE TO TAKE YOU TO A NICE, SAFE *JAIL* FOR BREAK-ING AND ENTERING!

9

SORRY, OLD MAN. THAT'S NOT *PART* OF TONIGHT'S PLANS.

BUT DON'T FEEL BAD. MATTER OF FACT, JUST KEEP LOOKING *MY* WAY, AND I CAN ARRANGE IT SO YOU DON'T EVEN *REMEMBER* SEEING US--

--AT ALL!

I...I....DIDN'T... SEE...NOTH...

NO! YOU AIN'T PLAYIN' NO *TRICKS* ON ME, GIRL! I WAS A COP IN THIS TOWN *TWENTY* YEARS BEFORE THIS!

UGH!

BLAMM

HERE'S *ONE* LITTLE ACTOR WHAT KNOWS HIS *CUE* WHEN HE SEES IT-- AND *THIS* IS MY CUE TO EXIT... *STAGE RIGHT...LEFT...UP AND DOWN!* ANY OLD WAY--LONG AS I *EXIT*--

--AND MAKE MYSELF *MONDO SCARCE!*

SHE'S *HIT*, KONG! THAT CREEP *SHOT* MS. MESMER!

COME *BACK!* MESMER WILL BE *FINE*...IF WE GET HER OUT OF HERE *BEFORE* THE POLICE ARRIVE! LET THE OLD MAN *GO!*

10

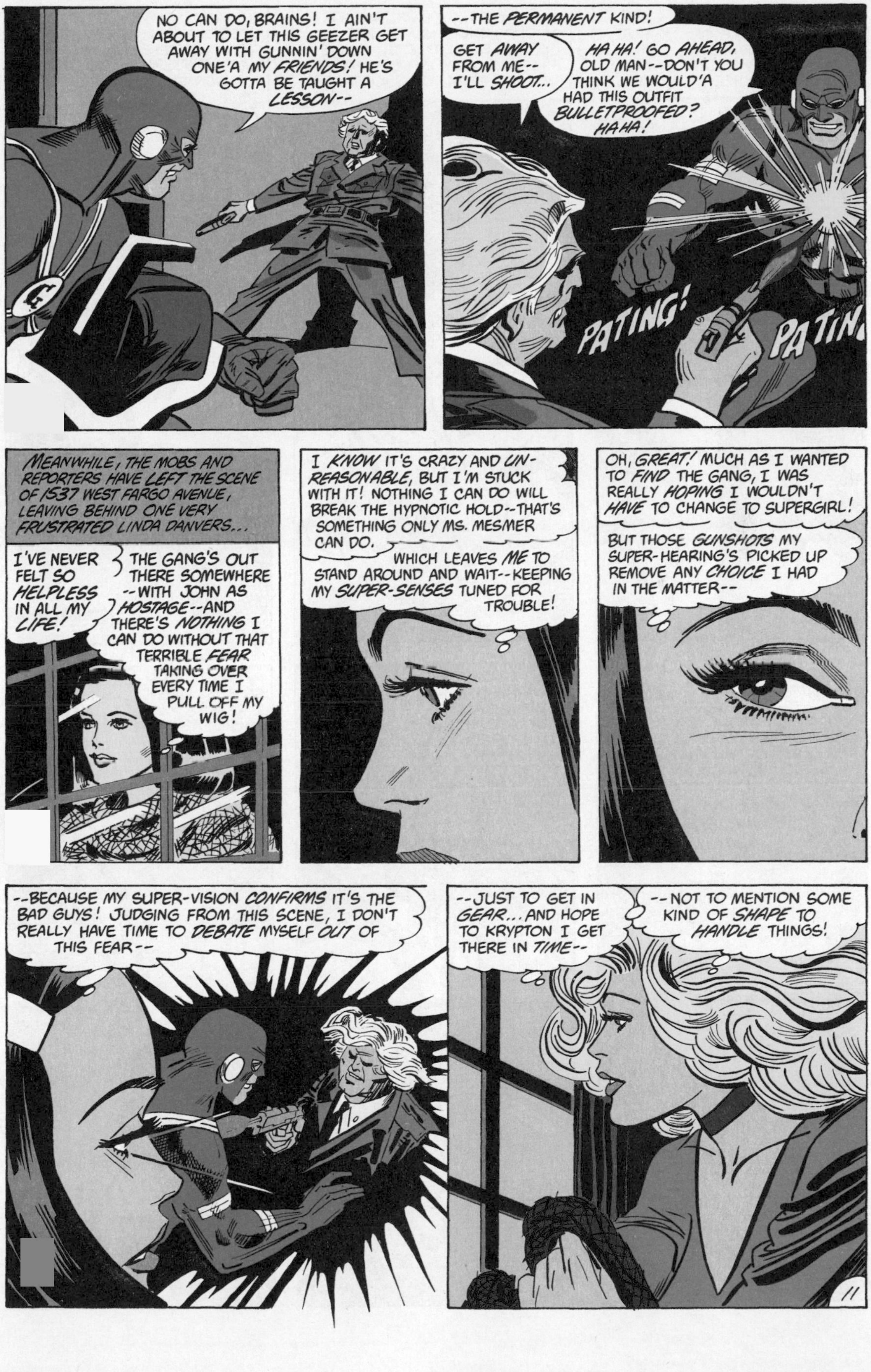

NO CAN DO, BRAINS! I AIN'T ABOUT TO LET THIS GEEZER GET AWAY WITH GUNNIN' DOWN ONE'A MY FRIENDS! HE'S GOTTA BE TAUGHT A LESSON--
--THE PERMANENT KIND!
GET AWAY FROM ME-- I'LL SHOOT...
HA HA! GO AHEAD, OLD MAN--DON'T YOU THINK WE WOULD'A HAD THIS OUTFIT BULLETPROOFED? HA HA!
PATING!
PATIN
MEANWHILE, THE MOBS AND REPORTERS HAVE LEFT THE SCENE OF 1537 WEST FARGO AVENUE, LEAVING BEHIND ONE VERY FRUSTRATED LINDA DANVERS...
I'VE NEVER FELT SO HELPLESS IN ALL MY LIFE!
THE GANG'S OUT THERE SOMEWHERE --WITH JOHN AS HOSTAGE--AND THERE'S NOTHING I CAN DO WITHOUT THAT TERRIBLE FEAR TAKING OVER EVERY TIME I PULL OFF MY WIG!
I KNOW IT'S CRAZY AND UNREASONABLE, BUT I'M STUCK WITH IT! NOTHING I CAN DO WILL BREAK THE HYPNOTIC HOLD--THAT'S SOMETHING ONLY MS. MESMER CAN DO.
WHICH LEAVES ME TO STAND AROUND AND WAIT--KEEPING MY SUPER-SENSES TUNED FOR TROUBLE!
OH, GREAT! MUCH AS I WANTED TO FIND THE GANG, I WAS REALLY HOPING I WOULDN'T HAVE TO CHANGE TO SUPERGIRL!
BUT THOSE GUNSHOTS MY SUPER-HEARING'S PICKED UP REMOVE ANY CHOICE I HAD IN THE MATTER--
--BECAUSE MY SUPER-VISION CONFIRMS IT'S THE BAD GUYS! JUDGING FROM THIS SCENE, I DON'T REALLY HAVE TIME TO DEBATE MYSELF OUT OF THIS FEAR--
--JUST TO GET IN GEAR...AND HOPE TO KRYPTON I GET THERE IN TIME--
--NOT TO MENTION SOME KIND OF SHAPE TO HANDLE THINGS!

SWELL! I GO THROUGH ALL THE TROUBLE OF CHANGING CLOTHES-- AT LEAST I *THINK* I CHANGED CLOTHES-- AND WHAT DO I SEE IN THE MIRROR--?

ME... BUT THE *WRONG* ONE!

C'MON, KARA... YOU *KNOW* IT'S ALL IN YOUR *MIND!* YOU'RE *NOT* GONNA LET A LITTLE THING LIKE A HYPNOTICALLY-INDUCED *PHOBIA* STOP YOU FROM DOING YOUR JOB!

ALL RIGHT, YOU'RE *SCARED* SILLY TO BE SEEN OUT THERE LIKE THIS-- *BIG DEAL!* YOU GONNA LET SOMETHING LIKE *THAT* KEEP YOU FROM DOING YOUR *STUFF?*

HECK-- STOP TALKING AND GET *FLYING!*

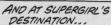
AND AT SUPERGIRL'S *DESTINATION...*

YOU MADE A WHOLE *BUNCH* OF *BAD* MISTAKES TODAY, OLD MAN-- THE *LEAST* OF WHICH WAS COMING TO WORK! YOU SHOULDN'T'A OUGHTTA SHOT MS. MESMER LIKE THAT, 'CAUSE THAT MAKES ME *MAD*--

--AN' I DON'T EVEN WANNA *SAY* WHAT I DO WHEN I'M MAD... BUT YOU'RE GONNA FIND OUT *ANYWAY...* HEY!!?

STOP IT, KONG... *NOW!*

RESTRAIN YOURSELF, MY FRIEND. I REALIZE YOU ARE *ANGRY,* AS ARE WE *ALL*-- BUT SLAYING THE OLD MAN WILL ACCOMPLISH *NOTHING,* DO YOU NOT AGREE?

I...YEAH, I SUPPOSE SO, BRAINS. WHAT-EVER YOU SAY.

12

MOMENTS LATER... SIRENS! I DISLIKE OUR TACKLING THE POLICE AT *LESS* THAN FULL CAPACITY. I SUGGEST WE TAKE *REFUGE* WHILE MS. MESMER RECEIVES *PROPER* MEDICAL ATTENTION!

BREEEEEEEEEE

HOPE YOU'VE GOT *TWO* DOCTORS WAITING, BRAINS... OTHERWISE BULLDOZER HERE'S GOING TO BE *AWFULLY* SORE!

BWHAAAM

S-SUPERGIRL!? I THOUGHT YOU SAID SHE WASN'T GONNA *BOTHER* US ANY MORE, BRAINS! I GOTTA--

NO, KONG! *YOUR* JOB IS TO GET MS. MESMER HELP. BULLDOZER AND I SHALL HANDLE THIS PEST!

PEST? AND HERE I THOUGHT WE WERE GETTING TO BE *BUDDIES!*

MAN, BUT I'VE *NEVER* HEARD *HOLLOWER*-SOUNDING BANTER--! *FACE* IT, GIRL--YOU'RE *SCARED* BEING HERE. DESPITE WHAT *REASON* TELLS YOU, YOU *KNOW* THEY'RE ALL LOOKING *STRAIGHT THROUGH* YOU TO YOUR SECRET IDENTITY, DON'T YOU?

IT'S LIKE I'M WEARING A SIGN THAT SAYS, "LINDA DANVERS IS SUPERGIRL!"

CUT IT OUT, KIDDO! IT'S IN YOU *HEAD*--ALL OF IT! THERE'S *NO DANGER*... NOBODY BUT *YOU* SEES ANYTHING OUT OF THE ORDINARY!

RIIIGHT! JUST KEEP TELLING YOURSELF THAT, HERO!

OH--*SORRY*, FRIEND. WERE YOU TRYING TO ATTRACT MY ATTENTION?

SPEAK UP! NO NEED TO BE *SHY* WITH *ME.* I *LOVE* TALKING WITH *STRANGERS*, AND BELIEVE ME WHEN I TELL YOU--

--THEY *DON'T COME* MUCH STRANGER THAN *YOU!*

YEEEE-OWWW!

13

NOOOOOOOO!

BHAWHOOOMP!

WH-WHY, YOU... LOUSY...!

WHAT, BULLDOZER--?

I...I'M GONNA... PUNCH OUT YOUR...LIGHTS...

OOOH, STOP IT, BIG MAN--

--YOU'RE SCARIN' ME TOO MUCH!

BLAMM!

THAT'S THE TICKET-- KEEP A GRIP ON YOURSELF! THAT'S ONE DOWN--

14

--AND FROM THE LOOKS OF 'EM, TWO AND THREE SHOULDN'T BE ALL THAT *TOUGH* TO HANDLE *EITHER!*

BESIDES, IF I LET MESMER GET AWAY, I'LL *NEVER* STOP SHAKING IN MY LITTLE RED *BOOTIES.* IT'S HARD ENOUGH STICKING AROUND *NOW--*

--SO *NO WAY* IS IT A CONDITION I INTEND TO LET STICK!

NOT SO *FAST*, BOY AND GIRL! AUNTIE SUPERGIRL'S GOT SOMETHING SHE WANTS TAKEN CARE OF *BEFORE* YOU SAY YOUR BYEBYES... LIKE HAVING HER *RIGHT MIND* RESTORED!

GIVE HER A *BREAK,* SUPERGIRL-- SHE'S... *HURT!*

I GOTTA GET HER *HELP--* HONEST! I-I DON'T WANNA *FIGHT* YOU!

GLAD TO HEAR IT, BIG GUY-- BUT THAT *STILL* DOESN'T HELP ME GET OUT FROM UNDER THE HYPNOTIC COMPULSION SHE'S PUT ME UNDER.

GROAN. IT *HURTS,* SUPERGIRL ...A....A LOT. JUST GET ME... TO A DOCTOR AND... AND I'LL *RELEASE* YOU...I... SWEAR...

MESMER--

--YOU JUST BOUGHT YOURSELF ONE *SUPER-SPEED* AMBULANCE RIDE TO COOK COUNTY HOSPITAL!

THEY ARE... *GONE...!*

IT WOULD SEEM I AM THE ONLY ONE *LEFT--* FOR *NOW!*

BUT THAT *WILL* CHANGE. I *SWEAR* IT--MY FRIENDS WILL BE FREED! I-- AND THE *COUNCIL--* SHALL SEE TO THAT!

NEXT: WHAT LANDS AT CHICAGO'S AIRPORT IS NOT A BIRD *OR* A PLANE--IT'S *TROUBLE!* **"BATTLEGROUND O'HARE!"** ON SALE JAN. 20! IT'S A *DATE!* 15

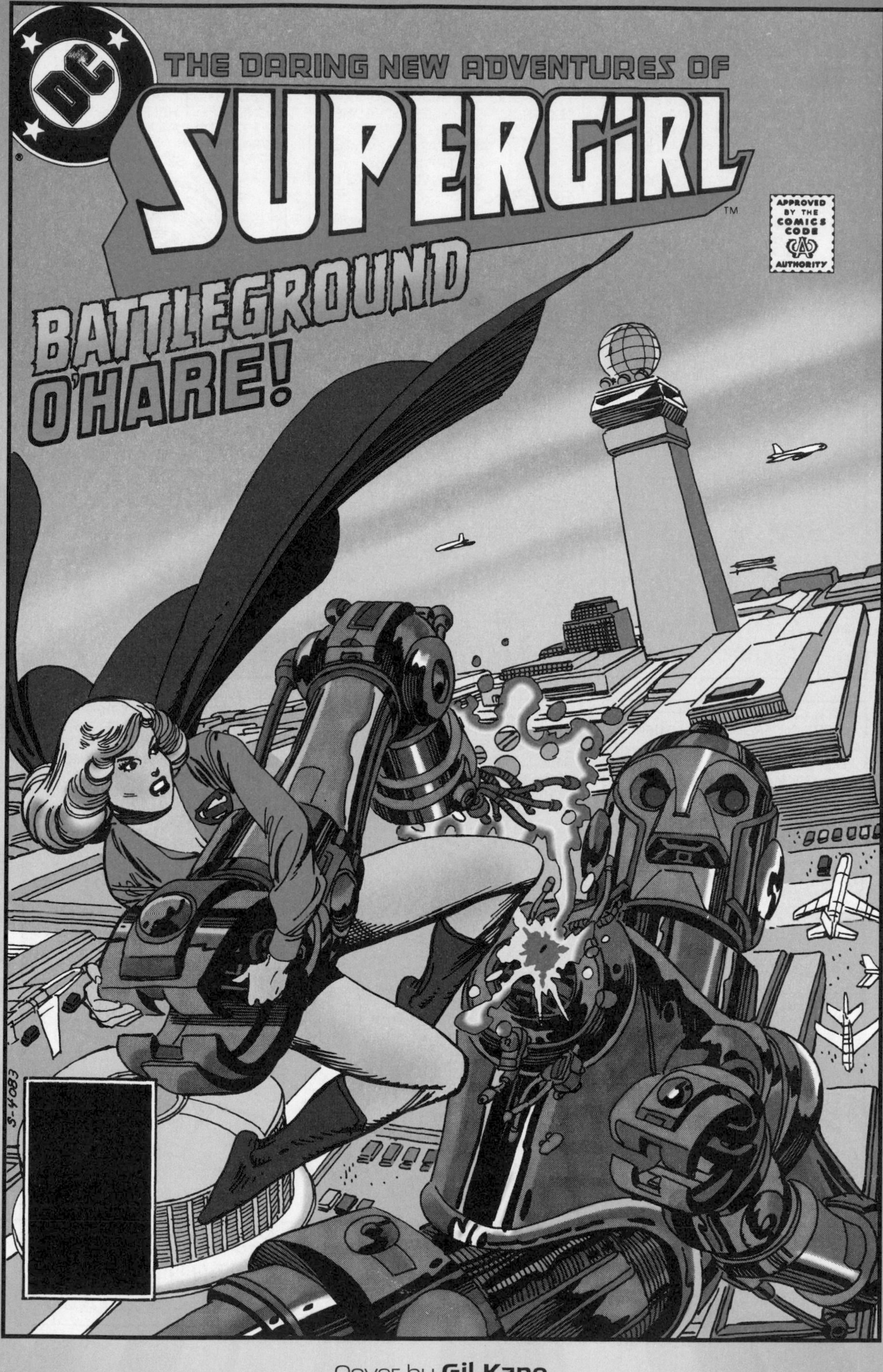
DC
THE DARING NEW ADVENTURES OF
SUPERGIRL
TM
APPROVED BY THE COMICS CODE AUTHORITY
BATTLEGROUND O'HARE!
S-4083

Cover by **Gil Kane**

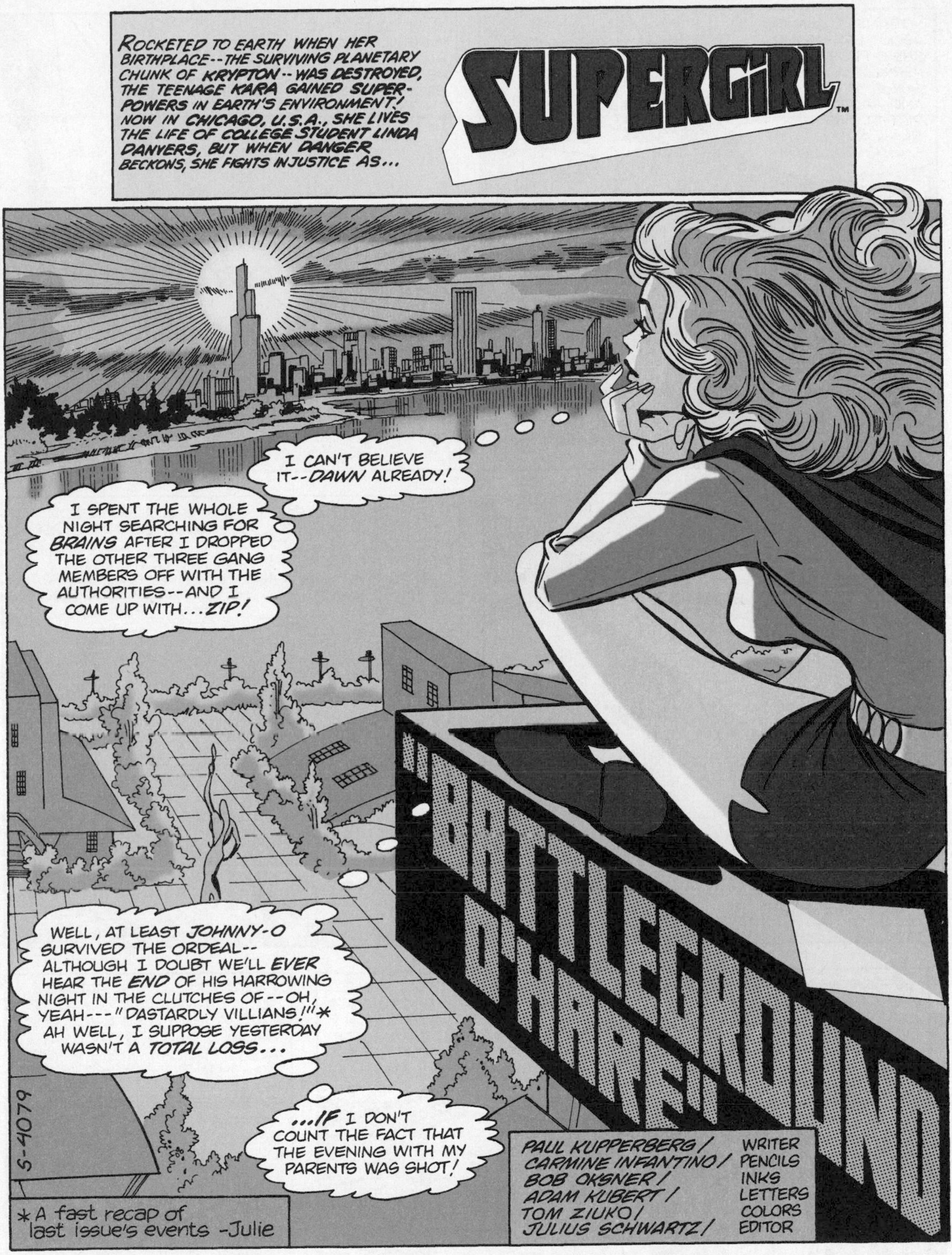

ROCKETED TO EARTH WHEN HER BIRTHPLACE--THE SURVIVING PLANETARY CHUNK OF KRYPTON--WAS DESTROYED, THE TEENAGE KARA GAINED SUPER-POWERS IN EARTH'S ENVIRONMENT! NOW IN CHICAGO, U.S.A., SHE LIVES THE LIFE OF COLLEGE STUDENT LINDA DANVERS, BUT WHEN DANGER BECKONS, SHE FIGHTS INJUSTICE AS...
SUPERGIRL™
I CAN'T BELIEVE IT--DAWN ALREADY!
I SPENT THE WHOLE NIGHT SEARCHING FOR BRAINS AFTER I DROPPED THE OTHER THREE GANG MEMBERS OFF WITH THE AUTHORITIES--AND I COME UP WITH...ZIP!
"BATTLEGROUND O'HARE!!"
WELL, AT LEAST JOHNNY-O SURVIVED THE ORDEAL--ALTHOUGH I DOUBT WE'LL EVER HEAR THE END OF HIS HARROWING NIGHT IN THE CLUTCHES OF--OH, YEAH---"DASTARDLY VILLIANS!"* AH WELL, I SUPPOSE YESTERDAY WASN'T A TOTAL LOSS...
...IF I DON'T COUNT THE FACT THAT THE EVENING WITH MY PARENTS WAS SHOT!
PAUL KUPPERBERG/ WRITER
CARMINE INFANTINO/ PENCILS
BOB OKSNER/ INKS
ADAM KUBERT/ LETTERS
TOM ZIUKO/ COLORS
JULIUS SCHWARTZ/ EDITOR
S-4079
*A fast recap of last issue's events -Julie

NOTHING I CAN DO ABOUT BRAINS *NOW*. SHE'S PROBABLY DUG HERSELF A *DEEP HOLE* TO HIDE IN... AND HAS PULLED THE DIRT IN OVER HER-- RIGHT ALONG WITH *"MR. ADAMS"*--

--THE GUY WHO GAVE JOHNNY-O THE PACKAGE THE GANG WAS AFTER! BY THE TIME THE COPS GOT THERE, HIS OFFICE WAS *DESERTED*.

THEY CAN'T FIND HIDE NOR HAIR OF HIM... OR THAT HE EVER REALLY *EXISTED*! STILL, FINDING HIM IS THE LAW'S JOB--

--WHILE I SEEM TO REMEMBER SOME CHORES OF MY *OWN* I'VE BEEN NEGLECTING DURING ALL THIS--

--NAMELY THE *LIFE* OF *LINDA DANVERS*... HER *COLLEGE*... AND ASSISTANT/SECRETARY JOB TO *PROF. METZNER* IN THE PSYCH DEPARTMENT.

IT'S TOO EARLY FOR CLASS...BUT CONSIDERING THE PERPETUAL STATE OF *DISORDER* IN HIS OFFICE, IT'S *NEVER* TOO EARLY TO REPORT FOR WORK.

A FEW MINUTES LATER, IN THE EMPTY CORRIDORS OF LAKE SHORE UNIVERSITY'S COUGHLIN HALL...

HELL-*O!* LOOKS LIKE A CERTAIN PSYCHOLOGY PROFESSOR'S *FOR-GOTTEN* TO LOCK HIS DOOR FOR THE NIGHT--*AGAIN!*

FORTUNATELY, BURGLERS WOULD NEVER BE ABLE TO *FIND* ANYTHING UNDER ALL THIS *RUBBLE* EVEN IF THEY *DID* BREAK IN! I...*HUH?!*

OH, HI, PRO-FESSOR. SURE, THANKS.

WELL, WELL... GOOD *MORN-ING*, LINDA! CARE FOR A CUP? JUST MADE IT FRESH.

THERE YOU GO. IT'S AWFULLY *EARLY*, ISN'T IT? FRANKLY, THAT'S *MORE* DEDICA-TION THAN I WOULD'VE *EXPECTED* FOR THE SALARY.

ACTUALLY, I WAS UP EARLY, SO I THOUGHT I'D GET A *HEAD START* ON THINGS.

2

I COULD *USE* THE HELP. I CAN'T FIGURE *WHY* THIS PLACE CAN NEVER STAY *NEAT!* AHHHH... I *KNEW* I HAD ANOTHER ONE SOMEWHERE--!

A *FILING SYSTEM* WOULDN'T *HURT*, PROF.

I SUPPOSE *NOT*... ALTHOUGH IT'S A BLAMED *NUISANCE*, HAVING TO DIG THROUGH ALL THOSE *DRAWERS.*

≤PUFF!≥

HMMMM. I SEE YOUR *POINT. STILL*, IF I *DID* SOMEHOW MANAGE TO TURN THIS MESS INTO A COHERENT, ALPHA-BETICAL SYSTEM, WHAT D'YOU THINK ITS CHANCES OF *STAYING* THAT WAY ARE?

NOT, ER... VERY GOOD, I'M AFRAID.

I DIDN'T *THINK* SO...!

MEANWHILE, SEVERAL MILES UPTOWN, AT 1537 WEST FARGO AVENUE...

NOW, JOHNNY! DON'T YOU WANT TO DO WHAT'S *GOOD* FOR YOU? BE A GOOD BOY--

--AND LAY DOWN AND DRINK YOUR CHICKEN SOUP!

UH, *SURE* THING, MRS. BERKOWITZ. I'M *REALLY* OKAY! *HONEST!* THOSE WEIRDOS NEVER LAID A GLOVE ON ME.

SO? YOU DON'T THINK BEING *KIDNAPPED* DOESN'T MAKE A PERSON A NERVOUS WRECK *ANY-WAY!?* NOT TO MENTION SPENDING HALF THE MORNING ANSWERING ALL THOSE *QUESTIONS* FROM THOSE POLICEMEN! ≤TSK≥

WELL, I GOTTA *ADMIT*, I COULD'VE LIVED WITHOUT THE *WHOLE THING*. AND, ER... LOOK, MRS. B.-- I'M *REALLY* SORRY ABOUT YOUR WALL, I'LL PAY YOU BACK *WHAT-EVER* IT'LL COST TO FIX IT!

DON'T BE *SILLY!* I SHOULD SAY IT'S *YOUR* FAULT AND MAKE ONE OF MY TENANTS PAY? THE *INSURANCE* WILL COVER IT. I'M JUST HAPPY *YOU'RE* ALL RIGHT.

COULDN'T BE *BETTER*...CONSIDERING I WAS KIDNAPPED, SCHLEPPED AROUND CHICAGO ALL NIGHT BY A GANG OF *SUPER-VILLAINS, AND* LOST MY JOB... ALL IN ONE NIGHT! *SHEESH*. MUST BE *SOME KINDA RECORD!*

GOOD CHICKEN SOUP, THOUGH!

3

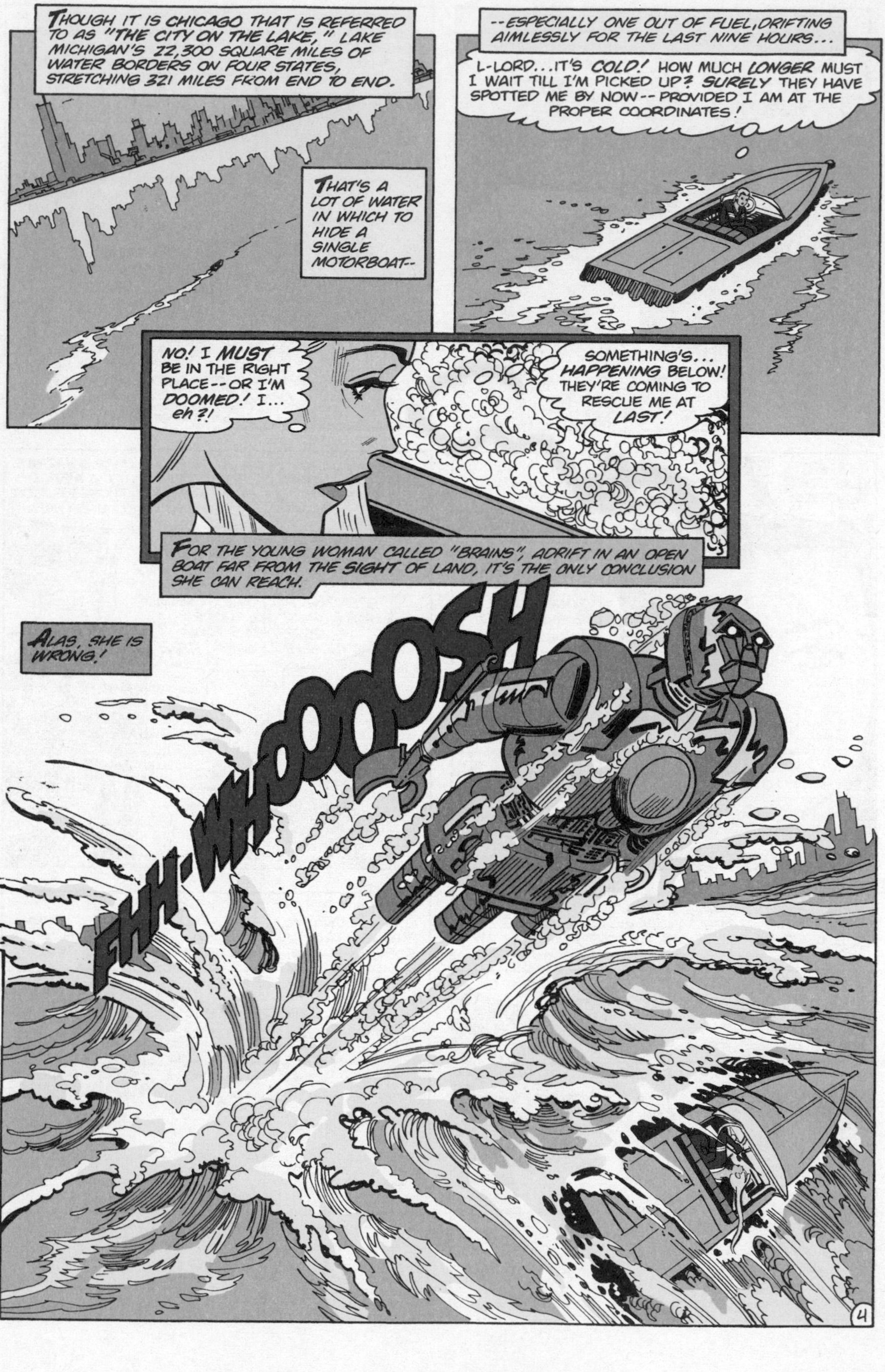
THOUGH IT IS CHICAGO THAT IS REFERRED TO AS "THE CITY ON THE LAKE," LAKE MICHIGAN'S 22,300 SQUARE MILES OF WATER BORDERS ON FOUR STATES, STRETCHING 321 MILES FROM END TO END.
THAT'S A LOT OF WATER IN WHICH TO HIDE A SINGLE MOTORBOAT--
--ESPECIALLY ONE OUT OF FUEL, DRIFTING AIMLESSLY FOR THE LAST NINE HOURS...
L-LORD...IT'S COLD! HOW MUCH LONGER MUST I WAIT TILL I'M PICKED UP? SURELY THEY HAVE SPOTTED ME BY NOW -- PROVIDED I AM AT THE PROPER COORDINATES!
NO! I MUST BE IN THE RIGHT PLACE--OR I'M DOOMED! I... eh?!
SOMETHING'S... HAPPENING BELOW! THEY'RE COMING TO RESCUE ME AT LAST!
FOR THE YOUNG WOMAN CALLED "BRAINS", ADRIFT IN AN OPEN BOAT FAR FROM THE SIGHT OF LAND, IT'S THE ONLY CONCLUSION SHE CAN REACH.
ALAS, SHE IS WRONG!
FHH-WHOOOOOSH
4

I--I don't UNDERSTAND--! WHO WOULD LAUNCH SUCH AN...OBJECT FROM THE MIDDLE OF THE LAKE...STRAIGHT AT CHICAGO!?

COULD THEY HAVE BEGUN A NEW OPERATION OF WHICH I AM UNAWARE--?

STAY JUST THE WAY YOU ARE, SWEETHEART! WHAT YOU'VE SEEN WAS SUPPOSED TO BE TOP SECRET--

--WHICH MEANS THERE'RE SOME PEOPLE BELOW WHO ARE GONNA WANT TO TALK TO YOU!

OHH--

BRAINS RAISES HER HANDS SLOWLY INTO THE AIR. SHE HAD WANTED TO BE RESCUED, AFTER ALL--EVEN IF SHE DID HAVE SOMETHING A BIT DIFFERENT IN MIND.

SEVERAL HOURS LATER, ON A NORTHBOUND EL TRAIN...

≷GROAN≷ YOU'VE READ THE CONSTITUTION, HAVEN'T YOU--?

DOESN'T THIS COME UNDER THE CATEGORY OF "CRUEL AND UNUSUAL PUNISHMENT"?

I DON'T THINK THE EL TRAIN'S EXACTLY WHAT THEY HAD IN MIND WHEN THEY WROTE THE THING, JOAN--BUT, YEAH! RUSH-HOUR GETS ME A LOT CLOSER TO PEOPLE I'D JUST AS SOON NOT BE CLOSE TO!

OOOOF!

REMINDS ME OF SOME OLD PSYCH EXPERIMENT I READ ABOUT, LIN--THE ONE WHERE THEY CROWDED RATS TOGETHER IN A SMALL ENCLOSED SPACE TO SIMULATE THE TRAINS ...AND THEY WOUND UP KILLING EACH OTHER!

GEE--I WONDER WHY!

5

SARCASM WILL GET YOU NOWHERE... ESPECIALLY SINCE YOU'RE THE ONE MAJORING IN ALL THAT PSYCHOLOGICAL GOBBLEDYGOOK!

PRAISE ALLAH-- A SEAT! WHAT MADE YOU PICK PSYCH ANYWAY?

OH, I SUPPOSE I'VE ALWAYS BEEN INTERESTED IN HOW THE HUMAN MIND FUNCTIONS. FIGURED I MIGHT AS WELL CHANNEL THAT INTEREST INTO SOMETHING CONSTRUCTIVE.

HO-KAY! IT'S YOUR SANITY. ME--I'M GONNA STICK WITH SOMETHING SIMPLE...LIKE THEATER! I...HEY! MY SEAT--!

'SCUSE ME.

NOW I KNOW WHAT MADE THOSE RATS KILL...OTHER RATS! AWW, WHAT THE HECK! WE'VE ONLY GOT TEN MORE STOPS TO GO ANYWAY!

AND SO, TEN STOPS LATER...

SEE YOU TOMORROW, LIN. I'VE GOT A BIG DATE TO GET READY FOR TONIGHT.

YOU USUALLY DO, FROM WHAT I'VE NOTICED. WHEN DO YOU EVER FIND TIME TO STUDY?

WHAT'S "STUDY"?

NEVER MIND.

WELL, NOW,... WHAT'VE WE GOT HERE? HIYA, LITTLE KITTYCAT! YOU LIVE AROUND HERE?

I'VE SEEN HER SCROUNGING AROUND THE BLOCK FOR DAYS NOW. I FIGURE SHE'S A STRAY.

NOT ANY MORE, FRIEND--'CAUSE THIS LITTLE DARLING'S JUST BEEN ADOPTED! ISN'T THAT RIGHT, LITTLE STREAKY?

YOU SURE DON'T WASTE TIME THINKING UP NAMES! HOW'CUM STREAKY?

OH...LET'S JUST SAY SHE REMINDS ME OF A CAT I USED TO OWN!

6

HERE WE ARE, STREAKY... YOUR NEW HOME, SWEET HOME. GO AHEAD, SNIFF AROUND.

OH, YOU'RE *HUNGRY*, AREN'T YOU? LOOK, I'M *SORRY* THAT I DON'T HAVE MUCH IN THE WAY OF CAT FOOD ON HAND...

...I WASN'T *EXPECTING* VISITORS--

MEEOWLL!L

--BUT I THINK MAYBE I CAN DIG UP *SOME-THING* TO PLEASE YOUR PALATE UNTIL I GET TO THE STORE. LET'S SEE NOW...

...AND AT THE TOP OF THE HOUR, HERE'S THE NEWS ON WXTR RADIO.

KL!K!

PURRRRRRRR

HOW DOES A BOWL OF GRADE-A MILK SOUND TO YOU, STREAKY? YEAH, I KIND OF *FIGURED* THAT'D TICKLE YOUR LITTLE FURRY FANCY.

THE MAYOR'S OFFICE ANNOUNCED AN INVEST-IGATION OF CITY HALL WORKERS USING THEIR POSITIONS TO SELL PATRONAGE JOBS TO THE HIGHEST BIDDERS--

MILK

--A SITUATION THE MAYOR DENOUNCED AS "DEPLORABLE!" SHE ALSO SAID...HOLD ON! I'VE JUST BEEN HANDED A BULLETIN FROM O'HARE AIRPORT--

--WHERE A... *GIANT ROBOT* IS REPORTEDLY RUNNING AMOK! THAT'S WHAT IT SAYS HERE, PEOPLE --A GIANT ROBOT--

--WHICH HAS, APPARENTLY, TAKEN OVER THE FIELD AND IS LEADING POLICE ON A WILD CHASE! NO ONE'S DETER-MINED YET IF IT'S DANGEROUS--

--BUT ALL TAKE-OFFS AND LANDINGS HAVE BEEN *SUSPENDED* TILL THE THING CAN BE *CAUGHT!* WE'LL HAVE MORE ON THAT STORY AS IT COMES IN...

LINDA DANVERS HAS HEARD ALL SHE NEEDS TO HEAR.

O'HARE FIELD:

CHICAGO'S MUNICIPAL AIRPORT'S REPUTATION AS THE BUSIEST AIRFIELD IN THE COUNTRY IS WELL DESERVED, FOR MORE PEOPLE AND PLANES PASS THROUGH ITS CONTROL EVERY DAY THAN MANY AIRPORTS EXPERIENCE IN A MONTH.

7

THAT IT RUNS AS WELL AS IT DOES IS A TRIBUTE TO MODERN TECHNOLOGY AND SHREWD MANAGEMENT. STILL, IT DOESN'T TAKE MUCH TO DISRUPT SUCH A DELICATELY BALANCED ORDER--

EMPLOYEES ONLY

EMPLOYEES ONLY

--AND FRANKLY, A DISRUPTION LIKE THIS IS EASILY MORE THAN ENOUGH!

HEY, SARGE... HOW'RE WE SUPPOSED TO GET THAT THING OFF'A THE FIELD?!

ONE THING'S FOR SURE-- BULLETS AIN'T THE WAY!

AFFIRM- ATIVE, HUMANS. YOUR WEAPONS ARE USELESS--

--AGAINST MATRIX- PRIME!

THE NAME MEANS NOTHING TO THE OFFICERS OF THE LAW--

--BUT THAT SITUATION IS QUICKLY AND EFFICI- ENTLY REMEDIED WHEN, WITH A SMOOTH, BARELY AUDIBLE ELECTRONIC HUM, THE ROBOT'S CHEST OPENS--

--DISGORGING A HOST OF ARMOR- PLATED TERRORS--

--EVIDENTLY CREATED TO DEAL WITH JUST THIS CONTINGENCY!

HOL-EE--! SCATTER, MEN-- THESE BUGGERS ARE OUT FOR BLOOD!

BWEEET!

BWL!P!

BWEEET!

FZZZZT! BWEET!

THE DRONES WILL OCCUPY THE HUMANS WHILE MATRIX- PRIME UNDERTAKES THE PRIMARY MISSION.

SENSORS INDICATE THIS CRAFT CONTAINS OBJECTIVE.

HANGAR 12

8

MATRIX *CONFIRMED.* PROCESSING WORKER-DRONES.

DRONES ON *AUTOMATIC RETRIEVAL* PROGRAM.

ALERT! DEFENSE-SENSORS REGISTERING *AIRBORNE* INTRUDER.

WHAT *ELSE* DO YOU EXPECT AT AN *AIRPORT,* TINMAN-- *MOLES?*

INTRUDER *IDENTIFIED.* NAME: *SUPERGIRL.* CLASSIFICATION : *ALIEN HUMANOID.* ANALYSIS: *DEFENSIVE* MODE REQUIRED.

IF WHAT YOU MEAN IS I'M *NOT* HERE TO PLAY *PATTY-CAKE* WITH YOU--

--YOU'VE HIT IT ON THE *HEAD!*

WHAT...?! STILL *STANDING*--?! THAT SHOT *SHOULD'VE* TURNED YOU INTO *SCRAP!*

YOUR ASSUMPTION IS BASED ON INSUFFICIENT DATA. MATRIX-PRIME IS CONSTRUCTED OF *TYLENMINIUM ALLOY*--

--RESISTANT UP TO 12 MILLION POUNDS PER SQUARE-INCH PRESSURE.

DO TELL? LET'S SEE WHAT I CAN DO ABOUT DELIVERING 12 MILLION AND *ONE* POUNDS!

KLANG

OPPONENT ANALYZED. MATRIX CONFIRMED. COMMENCING DEFENSIVE PROGRAM. ⸮KLIK!⸮

WHY DON'T I THINK I'M GOING TO *LIKE* THIS IN THE *LEAST*--?

IS *THIS* WHAT YOU'RE PLANNING TO STOP ME WITH, MATRIX? TO TELL YOU THE TRUTH, WITH AN ACT AS *FEEBLE* AS YOURS, YOU'RE NOT GOING TO LAST VERY LONG IN THE BAD-GUY BIZ!

KRUNCH!

SNKK!

SNKK!

IF THIS MATRIX WASN'T SO TOUGH, SO *WELL-BUILT,* I COULD TAKE THE WHOLE SITUATION AS A *JOKE!* BUT IT'S AFTER *SOMETHING*--

--AND UNLESS I CAN SHAKE THESE BUZZING BEASTIES OFF, THE MECHANICAL BOZO *MIGHT* GET AWAY WITH IT!

THWAK

KRUNCH!

10

SUDDENLY...

≡UNGGH!≡ TH-THAT *HURTS*--!? BUT HOW...?!

DEFENSIVE DRONES EQUIPPED WITH LIFE-FUNCTION SENSORS, HUMANOID.

MATRIX-PRIME HAS SYNTHE-SIZED DRONES WITH CIRCUITS CAPABLE OF SEEKING WEAK-NESSES AND ATTACKING.

FIGHTER DRONES HAVE COMPLETED ASSIGNED PROGRAMMING.

DE-SYNTHE-ZISING PROCESS RUNNING.

DRONES RETURNING TO BASIC RAW MATERIALS FOR *REUSE*.

OH, *GREAT!* THIS HEAP'S A WALKING, TALKING *ROBOT-FACTORY*--

--CAPABLE, NO LESS, OF COMING UP WITH LITTLE METAL CRITTERS THAT CAN EMIT POWERFUL *ELECTRO-MAGNETIC* WAVES TO KNOCK ME SILLY!

I *COULD* STAND THIS ASSAULT FOR A BIT LONGER--

--BUT WHY *BOTHER* WHEN I CAN *AVOID* IT? FORTUNATELY, THESE THINGS ZIP AROUND ON *JET-ENGINES*...ENGINES THAT NEED *AIR* IN THEIR FUEL MIXTURE!

LET'S HEAR IT FOR *SUPER-LUNGS*--

WHOOOOOOSSSHH-

--AND THE INCREDIBLE AMOUNT OF AIR THEY CAN HOLD! ENOUGH, AT LEAST, TO CREATE A TEMPORARY *VACUUM* IN THE IMMEDIATE AREA OF THE DRONES... RESULTING IN A WHOLE LOT OF *USELESS* ROCKETS!

CLATTER

CRUNCH

11

'COURSE, IT GOES AGAINST MY *COMMUNITY SPIRIT* TO LEAVE THIS LITTER LYING AROUND, SO GUESS I OUGHTTA *CLEAN UP.*

ALERT! HUMANOID HAS DEACTIVATED DRONES. MATRIX-PRIME PROGRAMMED TO INITIATE OWN DEFENSIVE MODE.

WHOOSH

HUMANOID MUST BE DELAYED UNTIL WORKER DRONES RETURN TO PRIME COORDINATES.

WHO PROGRAMMED YOU, ANYWAY? --WILLIAM BUCKLEY?

LISTEN, I *HATE* TO PUT A DAMPER ON YOUR TRANSISTORS, MATRIX--BUT THIS IS *ONE* SUPER-HERO TYPE WHO DOESN'T CARE MUCH TO BE *MANHANDLED*--

WAAK

--OR *ROBOT*-HANDLED EITHER, FOR THAT MATTER--

--UNLESS YOU HAPPEN TO HAVE A *LIKING* FOR HAVING YOUR HANDLER *HANDED* TO YOU!

¿*BWEEP! BWEEP!*? *DAMAGE TO MASTER-UNIT. APPENDAGE COUPLINGS TO BE REINFORCED AT EARLIEST OPPORTUNITY.*

SKRYAK!
WAK!

GEE, I FEEL KINDA BAD HAVING TO TELL YOU THIS, TINMAN--

--BUT GUESS *WHICH* ROBOT DOESN'T *HAVE* ANY FUTURE...*HUH?!*

INOPERATIVE STATEMENT!

12

OOOFF! THIS ISN'T *EXACTLY* WHAT I HAD IN MIND...!

THAM!

THAT'S *IT*, MATRIX! THAT HIDE OF YOURS *MAY* BE TOUGH, BUT YOU WOULDN'T *BELIEVE* SOME OF THE THINGS I'VE MANAGED TO PUNCH MY WAY THROUGH!

THAT STATEMENT IS NON-FUNCTIONAL. WORKER DRONES HAVE REACHED PRIME-COORDINATES--

--AS MATRIX-PRIME MUST NOW DO.

NOT SO *FAST!* *YOU* MIGHT BE VIEWING THIS ON A COLD, MECHANICAL BASIS--

--BUT *ME*, I TAKE IT *PERSONALLY!*

THE HUMANOID PURSUES MATRIX-PRIME. PRIME-COORDINATES MUST REMAIN SECRETED FROM INTRUDERS.

FWHOOOSSHHH!

DRONE MISSLES SYNTHESIZED. LAUNCH SEQUENCE COMPLETED.

SIGH! I *HATE* SURPRISES.

STILL, I DON'T SUPPOSE THERE CAN BE ANYTHING IN THE MISSLES THAT CAN HURT *ME*--!

TRUE, SUPERGIRL--

13

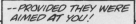

--PROVIDED THEY WERE AIMED *AT YOU!*

RAO...NO! MATRIX MUST KNOW ABOUT MY *INVULNERABILITY!* THE MISSILES ARE HEADED FOR THE CITY!

FWIIISSSH!

FWIIISSSHHH!

BLAST HIM! MATRIX WILL HAVE TO *WAIT*--!

BUT MATRIX-PRIME DOESN'T *WAIT!* FASTER THAN THE SPEED OF SOUND *STREAKS* THE ROBOT TOWARDS THE *LAKE FRONT*--

--AND IS QUICKLY LOST TO SIGHT BENEATH BLUE WATERS.

SPLAAASSH

MEANWHILE...

UH-UH... IT WOULDN'T DO TO TRASH THE *SEARS TOWER!* THESE THINGS CAN'T BE BOUGHT OUT OF A *CATALOG*, Y'KNOW!

ALLEZ-OOP!

14

ONE *DOWN*-- OR SHOULD I SAY *UP*... AND ONE TO GO! AHH, THERE IT GOES NOW... RIGHT FOR A BRIDGE OVER THE CHICAGO RIVER!

GOOD THING THESE MISSILES ARE JUST *SLOGGIN'* ALONG AT *MACH FIVE*--

--A NICE, *LEISURELY* PACE COMPARED TO WH*T* I CAN POUR ON!

GOTCHA!

TSK, TSK! THAT'S QUITE A *VIOLENT* TEMPER YOU'VE GOT THERE!

BWOOOOOOOM

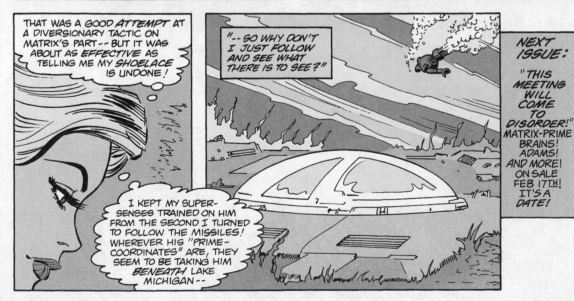

THAT WAS A GOOD *ATTEMPT* AT A DIVERSIONARY TACTIC ON MATRIX'S PART-- BUT IT WAS ABOUT AS *EFFECTIVE* AS TELLING ME MY *SHOELACE* IS UNDONE!

"-- SO WHY DON'T I JUST FOLLOW AND SEE WHAT THERE IS TO SEE?"

I KEPT MY SUPER-SENSES TRAINED ON HIM FROM THE SECOND I TURNED TO FOLLOW THE MISSILES! WHEREVER HIS "PRIME-COORDINATES" ARE, THEY SEEM TO BE TAKING HIM *BENEATH* LAKE MICHIGAN--

NEXT ISSUE:

"THIS MEETING WILL COME TO *DISORDER!*" MATRIX-PRIME BRAINS! ADAMS! AND MORE! ON SALE FEB 17TH! IT'S A DATE!

Cover by **Paris Cullins** & **Dick Giordano**

LAKE MICHIGAN, SOME 50 MILES DUE NORTHEAST OF CHICAGO...

THIS IS PRETTY MUCH WHAT YOU'D EXPECT TO SEE OUT HERE ON A TYPICAL DAY-- A LOT OF NOTHING MUCH SAVE WATER.

OF COURSE, THE IMPLICATION IN THE USE OF A WORD LIKE TYPICAL IS THAT THERE ARE INSTANCES WHEN THE REPRESENTATIVE TYPE EXPECTED IS NOT ALWAYS MET.

WELCOME TO SUCH A DAY!

NATURALLY, SINCE THE SITUATION HAS BEGUN TO TURN TOWARDS THE SLIGHTLY BIZARRE ALREADY, IT'S NOT FOR US TO BE TERRIBLY SURPRISED WHEN THE TREND CONTINUES--

--AND FOR THE SECOND TIME IN A MOMENT, THE NORMALLY PLACID SURFACE OF THE NATION'S THIRD LARGEST GREAT LAKE IS RUDELY DISTURBED BY INTRUDERS FROM THE SKY--

--BEFORE RETURNING TO ITS NATURAL STATE, WITH BUT THE GENTLY SPREADING RIPPLES THE ONLY REMINDER OF THEIR EVER HAVING BEEN THERE.

A NOT SO TYPICAL DAY FOR LAKE MICHIGAN--

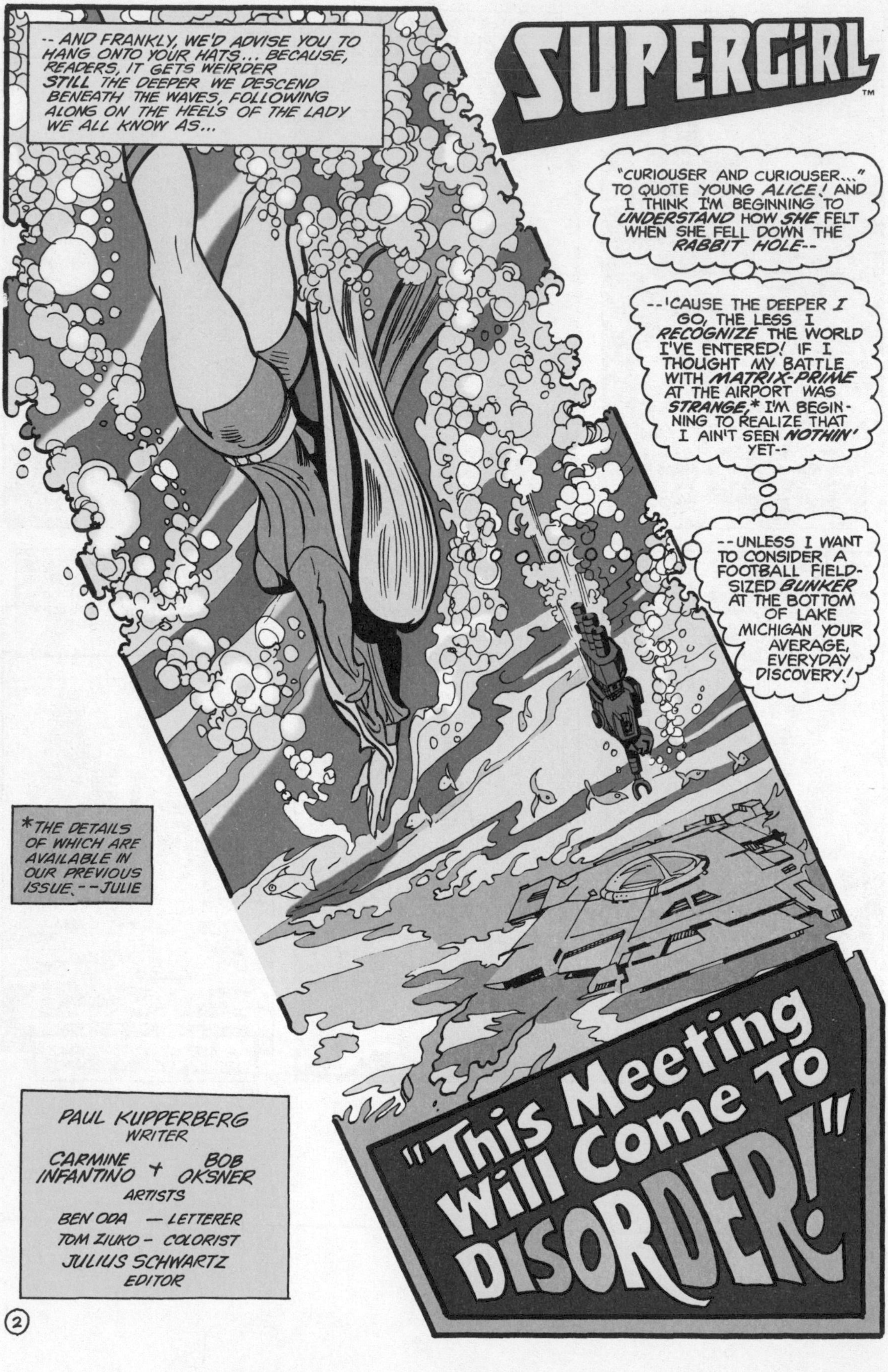
-- AND FRANKLY, WE'D ADVISE YOU TO HANG ONTO YOUR HATS... BECAUSE, READERS, IT GETS WEIRDER STILL THE DEEPER WE DESCEND BENEATH THE WAVES, FOLLOWING ALONG ON THE HEELS OF THE LADY WE ALL KNOW AS...
SUPERGIRL™
"CURIOUSER AND CURIOUSER..." TO QUOTE YOUNG ALICE! AND I THINK I'M BEGINNING TO UNDERSTAND HOW SHE FELT WHEN SHE FELL DOWN THE RABBIT HOLE--
--'CAUSE THE DEEPER I GO, THE LESS I RECOGNIZE THE WORLD I'VE ENTERED! IF I THOUGHT MY BATTLE WITH MATRIX-PRIME AT THE AIRPORT WAS STRANGE,* I'M BEGINNING TO REALIZE THAT I AIN'T SEEN NOTHIN' YET--
--UNLESS I WANT TO CONSIDER A FOOTBALL FIELD-SIZED BUNKER AT THE BOTTOM OF LAKE MICHIGAN YOUR AVERAGE, EVERYDAY DISCOVERY!
*THE DETAILS OF WHICH ARE AVAILABLE IN OUR PREVIOUS ISSUE. --JULIE
PAUL KUPPERBERG WRITER
CARMINE INFANTINO + BOB OKSNER ARTISTS
BEN ODA — LETTERER
TOM ZIUKO - COLORIST
JULIUS SCHWARTZ EDITOR
"This Meeting Will Come To DISORDER!"
2

STILL, I SHOULDN'T BE *TOO* BLOWN AWAY BY THIS, I SUPPOSE. *WHOEVER* BUILT MATRIX *MUST* HAVE A LOT OF *KNOW-HOW* AT HIS DISPOSAL--

--ENOUGH, I GUESS, TO MAKE THE CONSTRUCTION OF SOMETHING LIKE *THIS* A *SNAP!* AND *SPEAKING* OF *SNAPS*--

-- I BETTER SNAP *OUT* OF TRYING FOR *DEEP THOUGHTS* AT THE MOMENT... 'CAUSE THAT WALKING, TALKING MECHANICAL *ROBOT-FACTORY* IS AT IT *AGAIN*--

--AND *WHY* SHOULD I BOTHER PLAYING WITH HIS *TOYS* WHEN I'D MUCH *RATHER* ENGAGE IN A GAME OF *"KICK-THE-CAN"* WITH MATRIX *ITSELF!*

WELL, AT LEAST I KNOW MATRIX'S *DRONES* CAN'T REALLY *HURT* ME ...EVEN IF THEY *ARE* ANNOYING LITTLE DISTRACTIONS--

--OR THEY *WOULD* BE, IF I *LET* 'EM GET TO ME!

A LITTLE CLEVERLY APPLIED *HEAT VISION* AND THESE THINGS'LL BE *SLAG* BEFORE THEY CAN GET WITHIN STRIKING RANGE!

YIKES!

THINK *AGAIN*, KARA! THE DRONES ARE *ABSORBING* THE HEAT *BEFORE* IT CAN AFFECT THEM! SCORE *ONE* FOR THE ROBOT-- HIS COMPUTER-MIND *ANALYZED* MY ABILITIES ...PICKED ON HEAT VISION AS MY BEST *DEFENSE*--

--AND CONCOCTED THESE BUGGERS WITH THE ABILITY TO *ABSORB* THE HEAT... AND TURN IT *BACK* ON ME!

SUPER I *MAY* BE, BUT NOT NECESSARILY AGAINST MY *OWN* POWERS! IF THOSE BEAMS TOUCH ME, I COULD WIND UP ONE *PARBOILED* LITTLE LADY!

3

OF COURSE, JUST BECAUSE HE'S *SMART* DOESN'T MEAN HE KNOWS *EVERYTHING*... INCLUDING ABOUT MY *SUPER-BREATH!*

THAT OUGHT TO PUT THE LITTLE *DOOHICKIES* ON *HOLD.* MAYBE THEY *CAN* BURN FREE OF IT *IF* THE ICE HASN'T ALREADY *DEACTIVATED* THEM--

--BUT BY THE TIME *THAT* HAPPENS, I'LL BE LONG *GONE.*

...JUST LIKE *MATRIX-PRIME!* SHERLOCK HOLMES I'M *NOT*... BUT WHO WANTS TO BET HE'S *INSIDE* HERE?

HO-KAY...SO THE WALLS ARE *LEAD-LINED,* BLOCKING MY X-RAY VISION FROM SEEING IF THAT'S THE *CASE--!* WHO CARES--

--ESPECIALLY WHEN THERE'S MORE THAN *ONE* WAY TO SEE WHAT'S GOING ON IN HERE--

--VIA THE *DIRECT ROUTE!*

KREE-KRAAAK!

4

AHHH, THERE'S NOTHING LIKE SUPER-STRENGTH TO TAKE THE *DRUDGERY* OUT OF EVERYDAY HOUSEHOLD CHORES--!

OH, NOW ISN'T THAT *SWEET!* YOU GUYS WENT THROUGH ALL THE *TROUBLE* OF ARRANGING A WELCOMING COMMITTEE FOR ME! SORRY ABOUT PUTTING A *DAMPER* ON THE PARTY--

FWHOOOOOSHH!

--BUT YOU BETTER HAUL YOURSELVES *OUT* OF HERE... OR YOU'RE GONNA GET YOUR SHOES AWFULLY *WET!*

TSK! DON'T YOU PEOPLE *EVER* LEARN THAT YOU'RE JUST *WASTING* PERFECTLY GOOD AMMUNITION ON ME--?

POW! POW!

P-TING!

BLAM!

NOW *THAT'S* MORE LIKE IT! THERE'S NO DISGRACE IN RUNNING AWAY... ESPECIALLY WHEN THE *ALTERNATIVE* IS TO STAY AND GET THOSE GUNS WRAPPED AROUND YOUR HEADS!

AS MUCH FUN AS THAT'D BE, I'M AFRAID IT'S GOING TO HAVE TO *WAIT,* THOUGH--

WHFUMPF!

--UNTIL I TAKE CARE OF THIS BIT OF BUSINESS!

THE RATE THE WATER'S POUR-ING IN, THIS PLACE'LL BE ONE BIG *CONDOMINIUM* FOR THE FISHES IN JUST A COUPLE OF MINUTES--

--UNLESS I PUT A *CORK* IN IT!

THWAMM!

THAT SHOULD HOLD FOR NOW-- AND WHATEVER WATER DID GET IN IS BEING REMOVED BY AUTOMATIC *PUMPS--*

--WHICH MAKES IT TIME TO TAKE A *LOOK-SEE* AROUND THIS JOINT!

5

MEANWHILE, ELSEWHERE IN THE UNDERWATER COMPLEX...

LADIES AND GENTLEMEN OF THE *COUNCIL*, A DIRE SITUATION HAS DEVELOPED WITHIN OUR CHICAGO OPERATION THAT REQUIRES OUR IMMEDIATE ATTENTION CONCERNING THE ACTIONS OF *LESTER ADAMS!*

YOU ARE *CHARGED*, MR. ADAMS, WITH GROSS *INCOMPETENCE* AND SEVERELY COMPROMISING THE WORKINGS AND PLANS OF THIS *COUNCIL!*

YOU KNOW WELL THE *PENALTY* FOR THESE ACTIONS. HOW DO YOU *PLEAD?*

P-PLEASE... I--I KNOW MY ACTIONS WERE *WRONG*, BUT I ONLY DID WHAT I THOUGHT *NECESSARY* TO INSURE THE...

SILENCE, ADAMS! THE *CHAIRMAN* HAS AGREED TO PERSONALLY HEAR YOUR CASE... HE HAS NO TIME TO *WASTE* ON YOUR FEEBLE EXCUSES!

THE MASSIVE CHAMBER FALLS SILENT AS THE LARGE VIEW-SCREEN LIGHTS UP--AND EVERY MAN AND WOMAN PRESENT SHUDDERS GRATEFULLY. *THEY* ARE NOT TO BE *JUDGED* BY THE DARK VISAGE IT SHOWS.

YOU WERE *TRUSTED* WITH A MOST *SENSITIVE* MISSION, LESTER ADAMS-- ONE THAT CARRIED GREAT *RESPONSIBILITY* IN THE EXECUTION OF THIS COUNCIL'S GOALS --

--*CONTROL OF THE WORLD'S EXCHANGE OF INFORMATION!*

TOWARDS THAT END HAVE SCIENTISTS DEVISED THIS SATELLITE TO BE LAUNCHED INTO EARTH ORBIT-- WITH THE *BULK* OF THE *COMPONENTS* NEEDED TO BE OBTAINED FROM VARIOUS CORPORATIONS AND GOVERNMENT INSTALLATIONS.

THAT WAS *YOUR* JOB, ADAMS...VIA YOUR CHICAGO OFFICE, YET RATHER THAN DO SO *QUIETLY*, YOU CHOSE TO EMPLOY VARIOUS... *COLORFUL* BEINGS--

--WHICH SERVED ONLY TO *ATTRACT* ATTENTION TO YOUR MISSION... AND IN-VOLVE *SUPERGIRL* IN WHAT WAS TO BE A *SECRET* OPERATION. *THAT*, SIR, IS *INTOLERABLE!*

6

OUR WORK IS NOW IN JEOPARDY, ADAMS. WE HAVE *YOU* TO THANK FOR THIS.

B-BUT YOU'VE GOT TO *UNDERSTAND*... HOW WAS I SUP-POSED TO KNOW THE *GANG* WOULD GO AFTER THAT DUPE I'D HIRED AS COURIER AND...

FAILURE, MR. ADAMS, REGARDLESS OF CAUSE, IS *UNACCEPTABLE!*

P-PLEASE... *WAIT--!* I... I...

...NO...

NO!

NOOOOOOO!

FHA-BLAM!

BLAM!

HUH--?!

BWEEET!

BWEEET!

BWEEEET!

7

THE GUARDS' SURPRISE IS QUITE UNDERSTANDABLE, ACTUALLY... THEY NEVER EXPECTED TO BE CALLED TO DEFEND THIS FORTRESS FROM *OUTSIDE* ATTACKERS. AFTER ALL, WHO POSSESSES THE ABILITY TO LAUNCH AN ATTACK HERE, ALMOST 900 FEET UNDER WATER?

ONE GUESS!

P-TINK!

PON

BLAMM!

HEY, NOW--NO NEED TO GET *NASTY*, BUSTER! I WANT THE GUYS WHO PUT TOGETHER MATRIX-PRIME... YOU'RE JUST THE *HIRED HELP!*

MAYBE, BIG MOUTH... BUT I BEEN HIRED TO *PROTECT* THOSE PEOPLE!

IN THAT CASE, WHATEVER THEY'RE *PAYING* YOU TO DO THAT--

HEY--!

--THEY'RE *NOT* GETTING THEIR MONEY'S WORTH!

THERE SHE IS... GET HER!

DON'T BE *SILLY!* THE LIKES OF YOU COULDN'T "GET" ME UNLESS I *WANTED* TO BE GOT--

--AND IN CASE YOU HAVEN'T *NOTICED*, GETTING GOT'S THE *LAST* THING I HAD IN MIND!

SWOOOOOOOSSSH!

I SEEM TO BE MAKING QUITE A *HIT* HERE... OR DON'T THEY *WANT* TO HIT ME? DOESN'T MATTER--SO FAR, THEY HAVEN'T TROTTED OUT ANYTHING THAT CAN STOP ME!

NO, THEY HAVEN'T, SUPERGIRL--

8

--AT LEAST, NOT UNTIL *NOW!*

KHWAAM!

UHHH! WHAT HAPPENED...?!

DIDN'T EVEN SEE WHAT *HIT* ME...NOT THAT I REALLY *CARE*, 'CAUSE UNLESS IT'S ANOTHER *KRYPTONIAN*--

--IT'S GONNA BE MIGHTY *SORRY* IT GOT INVOLVED IN THIS FRACAS! I'M GOING TO...*OH!*

BRAINS...OF THE GANG--AND *MATRIX-PRIME!*

CORRECT THE FIRST TIME, *SUPERGIRL* --ONLY NOW, THANKS TO THIS WONDROUS DEVICE, THE ROBOT IS UNDER *MY* DIRECT *TELEPATHIC CONTROL*, SUPPLANTING ITS INDEPENDENT "THOUGHT"--

--THE PROGRAMMING OF WHICH, ALAS, WAS THOROUGHLY *INADEQUATE* TO THE TASK AT HAND...NAMELY, *DESTROYING YOU!*

THOUGH YOU PROVED CAPABLE OF *CAPTURING* MY FELLOW *GANG* MEMBERS, OUR ENCOUNTER SHOWED ME ONE THING ABOUT YOU--

BHWOMPF!

--THE *BEST* MEANS OF DEFEATING YOU IS THROUGH *DIRECT ATTACK!*

SURE, SURE, I'VE HEARD THAT ONE BEFORE, LADY...ONLY YOU'RE *FORGETTING* THAT I HAPPEN TO BE *INVULNERABLE*--

THWAMM!

KROOOM!

--AND NO MATTER *WHO* CONTROLS THIS PILE OF BOLTS, HE'S JUST ANOTHER *POTENTIAL SCRAP HEAP* TO ME!

YOUR TAUNTS FAIL TO MOVE ME TO FOOLISH ACTIONS, GIRL! I KNOW *WELL* THE FULL POTENTIAL OF THIS ROBOT...AND INVULNERABLE THOUGH YOU MAY BE--

9

OOOFF!

--EVEN *YOU* MUST HAVE A *WEAKNESS!*

WHERE ARE YOUR BOASTS *NOW,* SUPERGIRL? WHY DO YOU NOT *GLOAT* AS YOU DID WHEN YOU IMPRISONED MY FRIENDS AND ALLIES?

HA HA HA! CAN IT *BE* THE PAIN OF THIS BEATING HAS RENDERED YOU *SENSELESS!*

BWARM!

BOFF!

IT.... *UGH!*.... *COULD* BE, BRAINS--

--BUT IT *AIN'T!*

I DIDN'T MEAN TO GET YOUR *HOPES* UP, LADY, BUT ALL YOUR WALKING *ERECTOR-SET* DID WAS CATCH ME *OFF-GUARD* FOR A COUPLE OF SECONDS--

--BUT I THINK I'VE GOT THINGS IN HAND *NOW--*

--SO IT'S *BYE-BYE,* ROBBIE THE ROBOT!

NO.... NO.... NO*OOOOO!* AI*IIIEEEEE!*

WHAM!

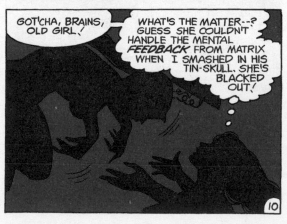

GOT'CHA, BRAINS, OLD GIRL!

WHAT'S THE MATTER--? GUESS SHE COULDN'T HANDLE THE MENTAL *FEEDBACK* WHEN I SMASHED IN HIS TIN-SKULL. SHE'S *BLACKED OUT!*

10

ELSEWHERE:

HURRY IT UP, DAVEY, THE ORDERS TO LOAD THIS CONTRAPTION ONTO THE *SUB* CAME FROM THE *CHAIRMAN* HIMSELF!

DON'T WORRY, MAN-- I'M *HUSTLIN'!* THAT'S ONE DUDE I DON'T WANNA GET *ANGRY* AT ME!

WHAT D'YOU THINK'S GOIN' ON, ANYWAY? EVERY ALARM IN THE JOINT'S RINGIN' LIKE *CRAZY!*

I DON'T THINK I *WANNA* KNOW! BUT IF THE CHAIRMAN'S PLANNIN' TO *SPLIT* AND HE'S TAKIN' *PROJECT SKYEYE* WITH HIM, YOU *KNOW* IT'S *BAD NEWS!* ONLY THING WORRYIN' ME NOW--

--IS HOW DO *WE* GET OUTTA HERE?!

THE CRAFT SEPARATES SMOOTHLY FROM THE AIRLOCK AND SLICES SWIFTLY TOWARD THE SURFACE. WITHIN MINUTES, IT WILL BE GONE--

--LEAVING A CERTAIN MAID OF MIGHT WITHOUT A *CLUE* TO WHAT SHE'S JUST FOUND.

THAT TAKES CARE OF JUST ABOUT *EVERYTHING* I CAN DO. I'LL GET THE *COAST GUARD* IN ON THE ARRESTS ONCE I CHECK OUT THIS ONE LAST CHAMBER AND...

OH!

JUDGING FROM THE DESCRIPTION *JOHNNY OSTRANDER* GAVE OF THE MAN HE WAS WORKING FOR WHEN THE *GANG* KIDNAPPED HIM, I'D SAY *THIS* IS....OR *WAS*... THE ELUSIVE MR. *ADAMS!*

TALK ABOUT REACHING A *DEAD END!*

HERE I AM IN THE MIDDLE OF SOMETHING REALLY *HOT*... AND THERE'S NO WAY FOR ME TO FIND OUT JUST WHAT I'M DEALING WITH!

11

THE FOLLOWING DAY, IN THE QUIET ROGERS PARK SECTION OF CHICAGO'S NORTH SHORE...

HOME, SWEET HOME... AT *LAST!*

THERE'S NOTHING LIKE SPENDING THE NIGHT SHUTTLING *PRISONERS* FROM THE BOTTOM OF LAKE MICHIGAN TO COAST GUARD SHIPS TO MAKE ME APPRECIATE MY APARTMENT. ALL I WANT TO DO IS *RELAX* AND...

KNOCK! KNOCK! KNOCK!

AWWW, NO! WHAT *NOW*--?!

WHOEVER IT IS, MAYBE I CAN GET RID OF 'EM AND TAKE IT *EASY!*

'BOUT *TIME* YOU ANSWERED YOUR DOOR, NEIGHBOR. YOU MUST SLEEP LIKE A *LOG!*

CHERYL DELARYE AND *DARYLL SIMMONS!* WELL, WHAT BRINGS YOU FOLKS AROUND ON A SATURDAY AFTERNOON?

LISTEN, WHEN I GET A DAY TO REST, I USE IT TO *REST!* COME ON IN! I WAS JUST GOING TO PUT UP SOME COFFEE.

NONE FOR US, LINDA. WE WERE ON OUR WAY OVER TO *GRANT PARK* TO PARTAKE OF A FREE *JAZZ CONCERT* AND THOUGHT YOU MIGHT WANT TO TAG ALONG.

12A

NOW THAT'S *MY* KIND OF MUSIC, MR. SIMMONS! AFTER THE WORK I'VE PUT IN THIS WEEK, I THINK I *DESERVE* THE TREAT, TOO. YOU'RE *ON!*

THEN WHAT'RE YOU JUST *STANDING* THERE FOR, GIRL? GET SOME CLOTHES ON... WE'RE GONNA MISS *DIZZY GILLESPIE* IF YOU DON'T HUSTLE!

JUST GIVE ME A *MINUTE*, FOLKS. DON'T EVEN *BOTHER* SITTING DOWN... I'M A *FAST* DRESSER!

12

LET'S BOOGIE, BOYS AND GIRLS. I'VE BEEN MEANING TO GET DOWN TO THE LAKEFRONT SINCE I GOT INTO TOWN, BUT THIS IS THE FIRST....!

AH-*HA!* I SEE THE GIRL'S SPOTTED OUR NEWEST NEIGHBOR, DARYLL.

HIS NAME'S *JAKE HELLER,* LINDA...AND THAT *IS* THE INFORMATION YOU WERE AFTER, JUDGIN' FROM THE *SPARK* IN YOUR EYES!

OH, WELL, I'M JUST A NATURAL-BORN *SNOOP,* CHERYL...

...BUT LET'S *FACE* IT, KIDDO-- THIS MR. HELLER'S ONE *CUTIE,* ALL RIGHT.

MORE ON JAKE HELLER IN THE *FUTURE.* FOR NOW, WE SPEED AHEAD ONE HALF HOUR TO *GRANT PARK,* ALONG CHICAGO'S DOWNTOWN DISTRICT AND THE FESTIVITIES IN *PROGRESS*--

--FESTIVITIES WHICH INCLUDE LINDA AND COMPANY...

YUMMIE! THERE'S NOTHING LIKE A BAD, OVERLY *GARLICKED* HOT DOG IN THE PARK ON SATURDAY AFTERNOON!

ALL DEPENDS ON WHETHER OR NOT YOU'RE A BIG FAN OF *HEARTBURN.*

I'D RISK *ANYTHING* FOR ONE OF THESE ...EVEN HEARTBURN. IF THE MUSIC'S *HALF* AS ENJOYABLE, TODAY'S GONNA BE *GREAT!*

YOU KIDDING? WHAT COULD BE *BETTER* THAN GILLESPIE AND BRUBECK, LADY?

THE MAN'S GOT A POINT. MAYBE TODAY DIDN'T START OUT AS ONE OF THE ALL-TIME WINNERS-- BUT *THAT* WAS FOR SUPERGIRL! NOW LINDA DANVERS ...SHE'S GONNA HAVE A *SWELL* OLD TIME!

WHAT COULD *POSSIBLY* RUIN A SUNNY DAY IN THE PARK?

13

DO YOU REALLY WANT TO KNOW, LINDA?

IF SO, TAKE A LOOK AROUND AT THOSE WHO HAVE COME TO GRANT PARK FOR THE SUN AND MUSIC. AT LEAST ONE OF THEM IS *NOT* AS SHE SEEMS TO BE.

IT'S NOT JUST THE HEAVY *OVERCOAT*, SO OUT OF PLACE IN THE SUMMER-LIKE HEAT OF THIS SEPTEMBER THAT SIGNALS THIS WOMAN'S DIFFERENCE TO THE CROWD.

NO, THERE'S SOMETHING ELSE--

--REALLY NOTHING MORE THAN A FEELING... A FLASH OF INTUITIVE CERTAINTY THAT SHE IS NOT TRULY ONE OF THE ASSEMBLAGE--

--THAT HER PURPOSE FOR BEING HERE HAS NOTHING TO DO WITH A DESIRE TO TAKE ADVANTAGE OF THE SUN, TO ENJOY THE SPIRIT OF THE MUSIC.

AND, OF COURSE, THERE ARE HER EYES!

SHE HAS COME SEEKING SOMETHING THAT THE PEOPLE IN THIS PARK WOULD FIND TOTALLY ALIEN... IF THEY COULD EVEN *UNDERSTAND*.

BUT MOST OF THEM CANNOT, SO THEY MERELY DRAW BACK FROM HER IN FEAR.

ONE OF THEIR NUMBER, HOWEVER, IS ALL TOO *FAMILIAR* WITH THIS WOMAN AND HER PURPOSE. SHE JUST DOESN'T YET RECOGNIZE IT...

THAT WOMAN -- I'M GETTING INCREDIBLY BAD VIBES FROM HER--! MAYBE I OUGHT TO SLIP AWAY AND...

WHOA THERE, LINDA--GET A GRIP ON YOURSELF! THERE'S GOTTA BE A COUPLE OF *THOUSAND WEIRDOS* LOOSE ON THE STREETS IN THIS CITY! THAT DON'T MAKE 'EM ALL A JOB FOR *SUPERGIRL!*

14

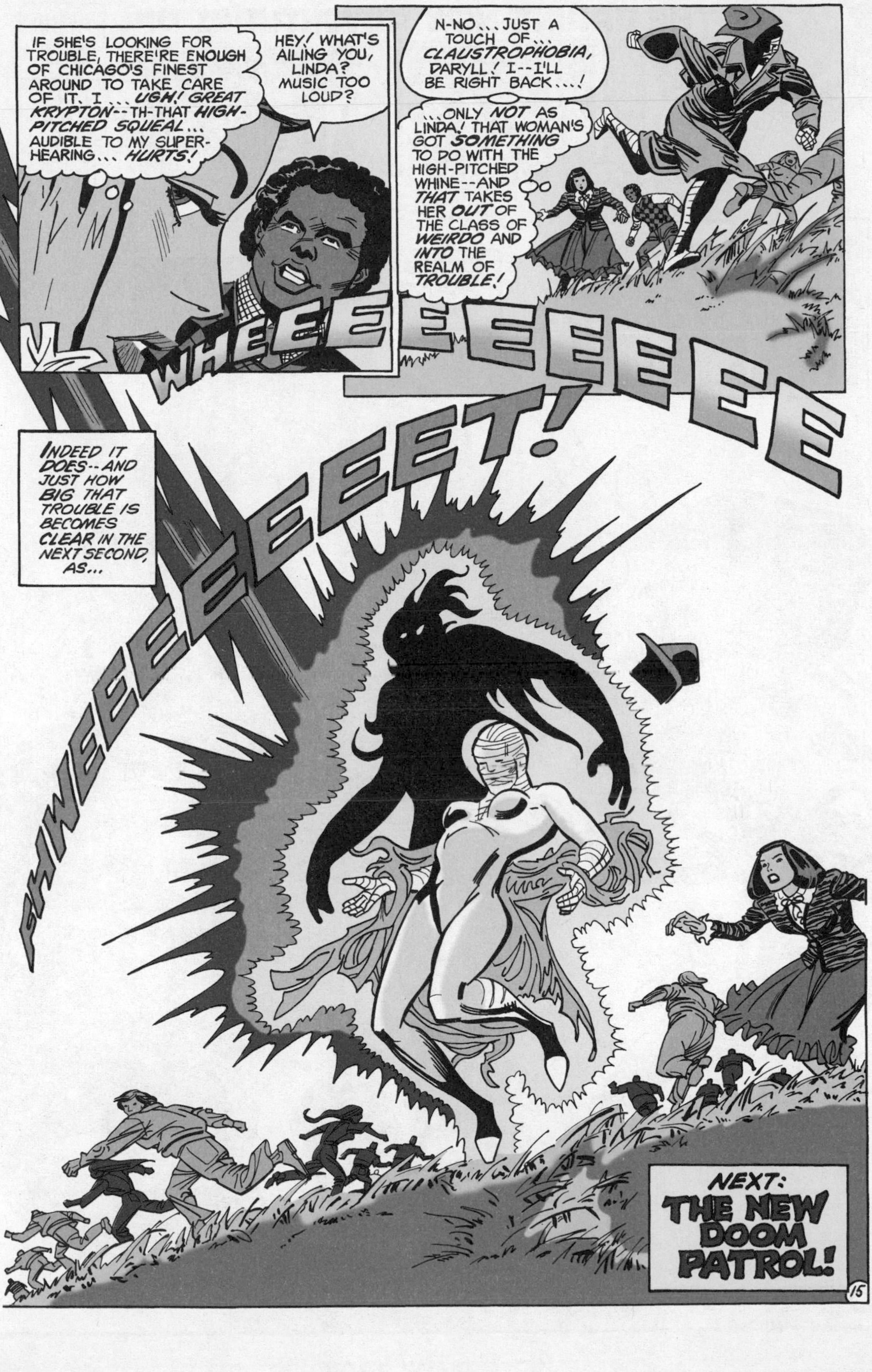

IF SHE'S LOOKING FOR TROUBLE, THERE'RE ENOUGH OF CHICAGO'S FINEST AROUND TO TAKE CARE OF IT. I... UGH! GREAT KRYPTON--TH-THAT HIGH-PITCHED SQUEAL... AUDIBLE TO MY SUPER-HEARING... HURTS!
HEY! WHAT'S AILING YOU, LINDA? MUSIC TOO LOUD?
N-NO... JUST A TOUCH OF... CLAUSTROPHOBIA, DARYLL! I--I'LL BE RIGHT BACK...!
...ONLY NOT AS LINDA! THAT WOMAN'S GOT SOMETHING TO DO WITH THE HIGH-PITCHED WHINE--AND THAT TAKES HER OUT OF THE CLASS OF WEIRDO AND INTO THE REALM OF TROUBLE!
WHEEEEEEEEE
SHWEEEEEEEET!
INDEED IT DOES--AND JUST HOW BIG THAT TROUBLE IS BECOMES CLEAR IN THE NEXT SECOND, AS...
NEXT: THE NEW DOOM PATROL!

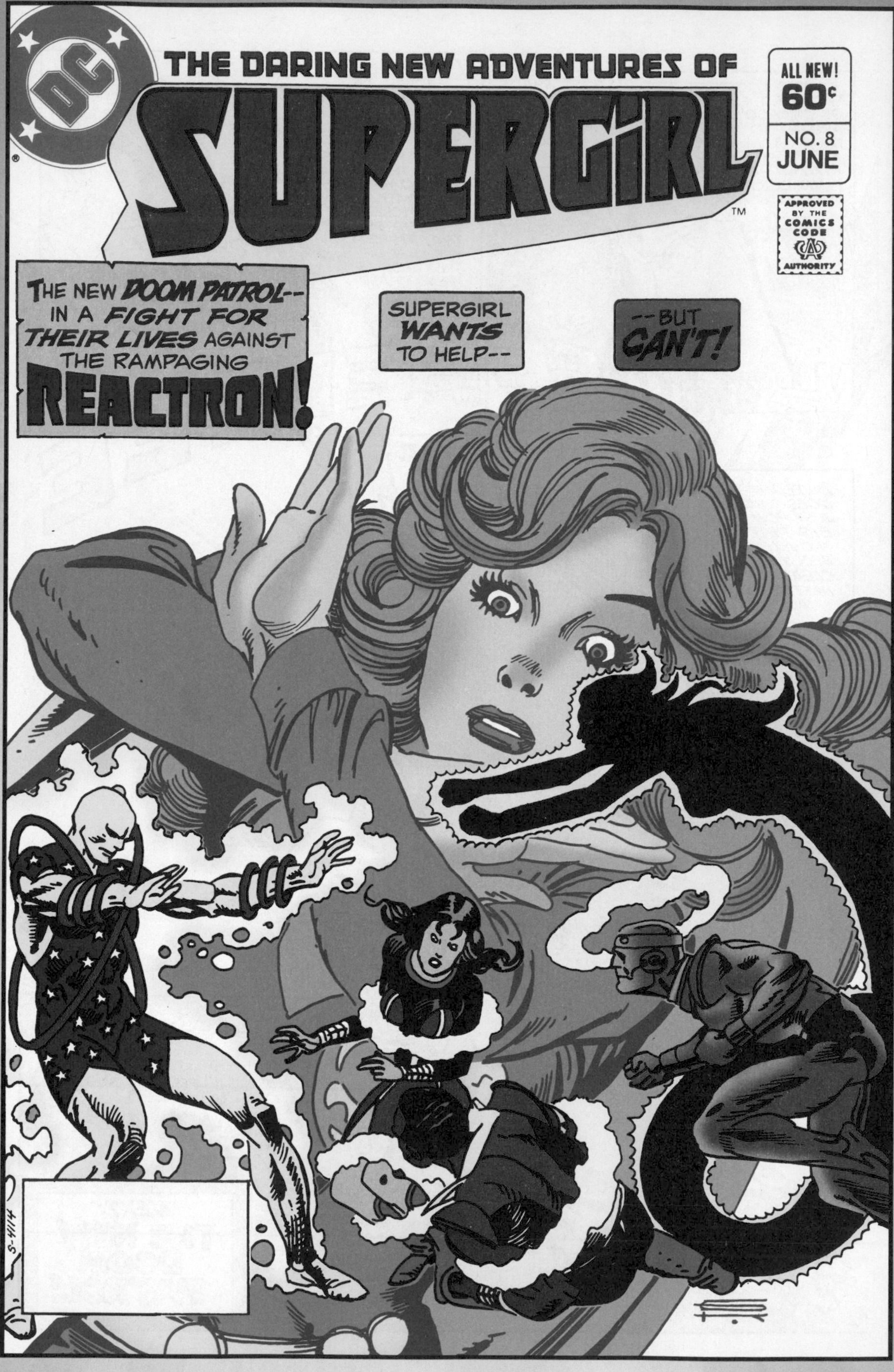

DC
THE DARING NEW ADVENTURES OF
SUPERGIRL
TM
ALL NEW!
60¢
NO. 8
JUNE
APPROVED BY THE COMICS CODE AUTHORITY
THE NEW DOOM PATROL-- IN A FIGHT FOR THEIR LIVES AGAINST THE RAMPAGING REACTRON!
SUPERGIRL WANTS TO HELP--
--BUT CAN'T!
S-4114

Cover by **Gil Kane**

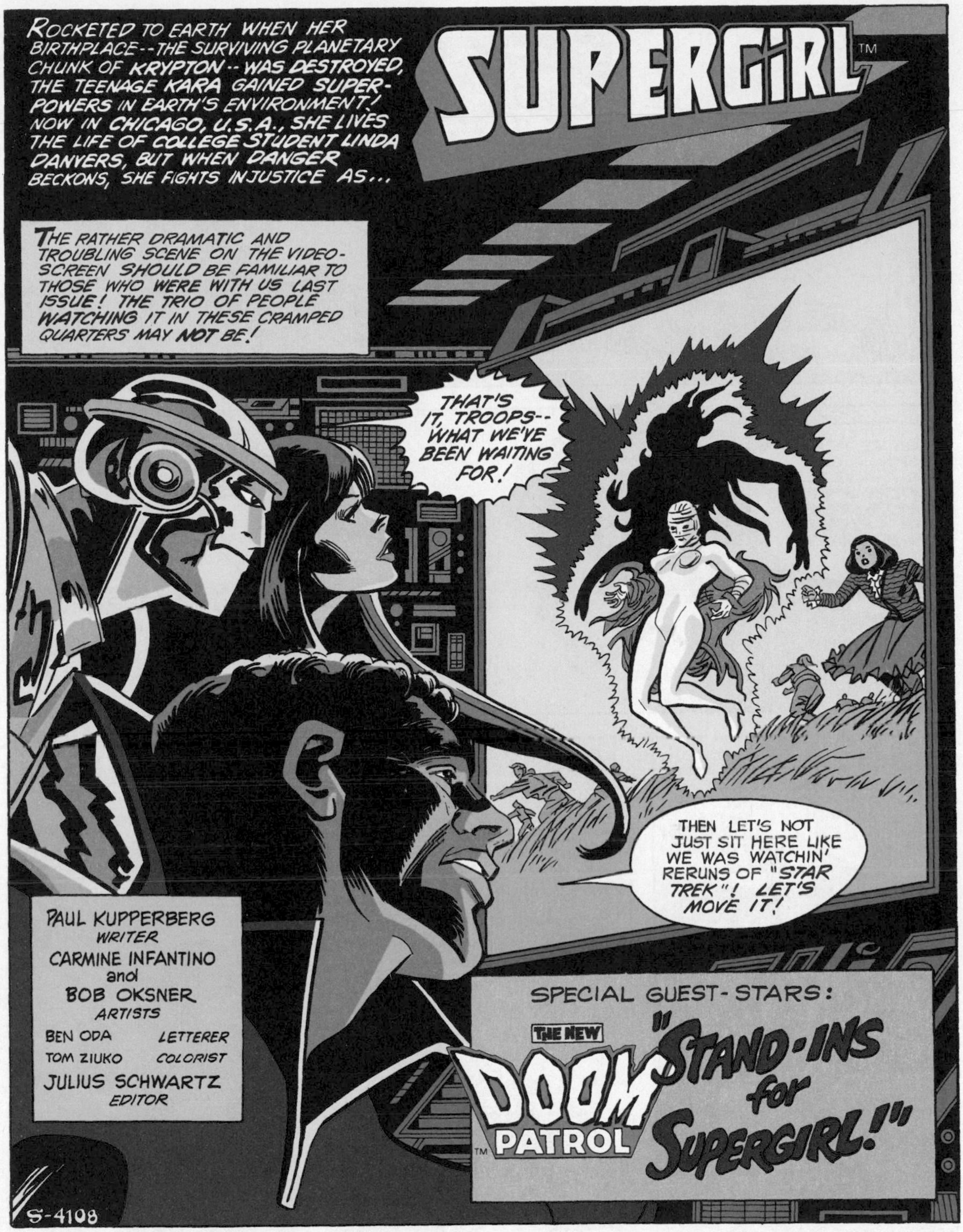
SUPERGIRL™
ROCKETED TO EARTH WHEN HER BIRTHPLACE--THE SURVIVING PLANETARY CHUNK OF KRYPTON--WAS DESTROYED, THE TEENAGE KARA GAINED SUPER-POWERS IN EARTH'S ENVIRONMENT! NOW IN CHICAGO, U.S.A., SHE LIVES THE LIFE OF COLLEGE STUDENT LINDA DANVERS, BUT WHEN DANGER BECKONS, SHE FIGHTS INJUSTICE AS...
THE RATHER DRAMATIC AND TROUBLING SCENE ON THE VIDEO-SCREEN SHOULD BE FAMILIAR TO THOSE WHO WERE WITH US LAST ISSUE! THE TRIO OF PEOPLE WATCHING IT IN THESE CRAMPED QUARTERS MAY NOT BE!
THAT'S IT, TROOPS--WHAT WE'VE BEEN WAITING FOR!
THEN LET'S NOT JUST SIT HERE LIKE WE WAS WATCHIN' RERUNS OF "STAR TREK"! LET'S MOVE IT!
PAUL KUPPERBERG WRITER
CARMINE INFANTINO and BOB OKSNER ARTISTS
BEN ODA LETTERER
TOM ZIUKO COLORIST
JULIUS SCHWARTZ EDITOR
SPECIAL GUEST-STARS:
THE NEW DOOM PATROL™
"STAND-INS for SUPERGIRL!"
S-4108

DON'T HAVE TO TELL ME *TWICE*, JOSH! WE BEEN TRAILING THIS BOZO ACROSS COUNTRY FOR *WEEKS*... I AIN'T *ABOUT* TO LOSE HIM *NOW*!

YEAH, BUT I *STILL* AIN'T THRILLED ABOUT SENDIN' *VAL* IN AS A *DECOY* TO FLUSH 'EM OUT FOR US!

WHAT'RE YOU GRIPIN' ABOUT, MAN? WE'VE BEEN *WATCHING* HER LIKE A *MOTHER-HEN* WITH A *REMOTE SPY-EYE*, HAVEN'T WE?

WE ARE *AWARE* OF YOUR FEELINGS FOR *NEGATIVE WOMAN*, TEMPEST--BUT SHE *IS*, AFTER ALL, A MEMBER OF THE TEAM, SUBJECT TO THE SAME *RISKS* AS THE REST OF US!

YEAH, YEAH... I *KNOW*! AND HER *RADIOACTIVE NEGATIVE FORM* IS ALL WE HAD TO BAIT THE TRAP WITH.

SO HOW'CUM THAT *DON'T* MAKE ME FEEL ANY BETTER 'BOUT SENDIN' HER OUT THERE *ALONE*--?

THE LADY UNDER DISCUSSION IS ONE *VALENTINA VOSTOK*, LATE OF THE *U.S.S.R.*, CURRENTLY A MEMBER IN GOOD STANDING OF --

--THE NEW DOOM PATROL--?!

I DON'T RECOGNIZE THE *BANDAGES*, BUT THE *NEGATIVE FORM* WAS FAMILIAR!* AND CONSIDERING THE *BLAST* THAT JUST SENT HER REELING, I DON'T HAVE TO ASK *WHY* THEY'RE IN *CHICAGO*!

SUPERGIRL MET THE *NEW DOOM PATROL* IN *SUPERMAN FAMILY #191-193 -- Julie*

WHOOPS! GOT SO CAUGHT UP MAKING SURE NEGATIVE WOMAN'S ALL RIGHT THAT I ALMOST *FORGOT* WHAT MADE HER *NOT* ALL RIGHT!

BWAMM

BWEEP!

FWOOM!

2

JUST WHAT'N BLAZES DO YOU THINK YOU'RE *DOIN'*? CAN'T YOU TELL THIS PLACE'S GONNA MAKE *D-DAY* LOOK LIKE KINDER-GARTEN *RECESS* IN A COUPLE'A SECONDS...?

BUT SHE'S BEEN *HURT*...

WHY DON'T YOU JUST ACT LIKE A GOOD LITTLE *CITIZEN* AND RUN AWAY IN *PANIC*, HUH? SHE AIN'T *HURT*...HER BODY ALWAYS COLLAPSES LIKE THAT WHEN HER *NEGATIVE FORM* IS WORKIN'.!

LISTEN, MISTER, I...

JEEZ! YOU WANNA *ARGUE*, SWEETIE--OR DO YOU GET SOME KINDA *KINKY CHARGE* OUTTA RISKIN' YOUR NECK? THIS AIN'T NO MORE *DAY IN THE PARK*--SEE!

...OH....!

YOU FREAKS *NEVER* GIVE UP, DO YA? IF THAT'S THE WAY IT'S GOTTA BE, THEN I'M *GAME*--BUT *BEFORE* I BLAST YA TO SCATTERED NEUTRINOS, YER GONNA *KNOW* YA WAS SMASHED BY--

--REACTRON, THE LIVING REACTOR!

3

SO IT'S YOUR CHOICE, HONEY-- RUN AWAY AN' LIVE TO RUN ANOTHER DAY... OR STAY AND GET *BARBECUED!*

I'M *GOING,* FRIEND-- --BUT I'LL BE *BACK...* AS *SUPERGIRL!*

REACTRON'S NO RUN-OF-THE-MILL *BADDIE!* ACCORDING TO WHAT MY *SUPER-SENSES* CAN DETERMINE, HIS BODY ACTS LIKE A LIVING, BREATHING *NUCLEAR REACTOR*--

--PRODUCING *RADIATION* THAT HE CAN DIRECT BY MEANS OF *CONTROL RODS* ON HIS WRISTS AND CHEST! UH-UH-- *NOT A GOOD PERSON* TO HAVE ON THE LOOSE--

--WHICH IS WHY *SUPERGIRL'S* GOING TO LEND THE *DP* A HAND IN ROUNDING HIM UP AND... *HUH?!*

DARYLL!

THANK GOD I *FOUND* YOU, *LINDA!* WHEN WE GOT *SEPARATED,* I THOUGHT YOU WERE A *GONER!* COME ON... THIS'S *NO PLACE* FOR *ANYBODY* TO BE!

CHERYL'S WAITING FOR US IN MY *CAR!*

. . . . . *HOOO-BOY!*

DARRY'LL MEANS WELL, BUT HE DOESN'T KNOW I'D BE BETTER OFF STAYING BEHIND AND *HELPING--!*

PERHAPS *LINDA DANVERS* HAS REASON TO WORRY..

--BUT THEN, THE *DOOM PATROL* SEEMS TO BE HOLDING ITS OWN *WITHOUT* HER ASSISTANCE!

I KNEW YOU WOULDN'T BE FAR BEHIND IF THE *NEGATIVE BROAD* WAS AROUND, *JOSHUA CLAY!* DON'T THINK IT AIN'T GONNA BE A *PLEASURE* TO SKAG *YER HIDE!*

GO *AHEAD,* *SARGE...* YOU CAN *TRY,* BUT YOU AIN'T GONNA HAVE MUCH LUCK IF MY *FORCE-BLASTS* HAVE ANYTHING TO SAY ABOUT IT!

4

YEAH, BUT THEY *DON'T*, CLAY... THEY *DON'T*... UGH!

THE NEGATIVE BEING THAT IS PART OF VALENTINA VOSTOK *PHASES* THROUGH THE GLOWING FORM OF REACTRON, WITH *DEVASTATING* RESULTS TO THE VILLAIN...

THAT *HURT*, YA LOUSY DAME... BUT PROBABLY NOT *HALF* AS MUCH AS IT DID *YOU*--

--OR ONE-*TENTH* AS MUCH AS THE PAIN YER GONNA FEEL WHEN I *SPEED UP* THE *DECAY* OF YER RADIOACTIVE BODY ELEMENTS!

THE NEGATIVE BEING DOES THE *ONLY* THING IT *CAN* DO-- *RETREATS* TO THE SAFETY OF ITS *HUMAN* FORM, AND...

VAL, HONEY! WHAT'D THAT CRUMB *DO* TO YOU, BABE?

HE *HURT* YOU, VALENTINA-- AND FOR *THAT*--

NOTHING I WILL NOT *SURVIVE*, COMRADE! DO NOT *CONCERN* YOURSELF, PLEASE!

--REACTRON *WILL PAY!* TEMPEST... *STAND BACK!*

HER NAME IS *ARANI*, BUT THANKS TO HER *MUTANT-BORN* POWERS, GIVING HER TOTAL CONTROL OF HEAT AND COLD, SHE IS LIKEWISE KNOWN AS *CELSIUS*...

...QUITE APTLY, WOULDN'T YOU SAY?

ATTACKIN' ON *TWO* FRONTS, HUH, LADY? NOT *BAD*-- YER *HEAT'S* BLOCKIN' MY RADIATION-BLASTS AND THE WEIGHT OF THE *ICE* IS DRAGGIN' ME *DOWN*--!

YOU CATCH ON *QUICK*, BUSTER! GETTING YOU DOWN TO *MY* LEVEL'S THE WHOLE *IDEA*, SO'S I CAN DO--

5

--THIS!

THWAAAM!

KRAAK!

YOU AN' YER BUDDIES ARE *WORSE'N* THE *CONG*, CLAY. ONLY THING IS, *THEY* WERE *LUCKY* THAT I WAS JUST A *REGULAR DOGFACE* WHEN I WAS IN 'NAM--

--BUT *NOW* I'M *REACTRON...* **EEEUGH!**

YOU'RE *DOGMEAT*, PAL! AND YOU CAN *FORGET* USING ANY OF YOUR *RADIATION* ON *ME!* THIS ROBOT BODY OF MINE WAS BUILT TO STAND UP TO *ANYTHING* YOU CAN TOSS MY WAY!

MAYBE IT *WAS*, TIN-MAN ...BUT ME, I'M THE KINDA GUY WHAT LIKES TO SEE THINGS FER *HIMSELF!*

SO LET'S SEE HOW THAT *HUMAN BRAIN* OF YERS STANDS UP TO A *DIRECT ASSAULT* FROM *HIGH-INTENSITY PROTON BOMBARDMENT!*

THE ANSWER, AS THE *DOOM PATROLLER* IS ABOUT TO FIND OUT--

HA HA HA HA!

--IS NOT VERY WELL AT ALL!

M-MY BRAIN... ON *FIRE*--!

6

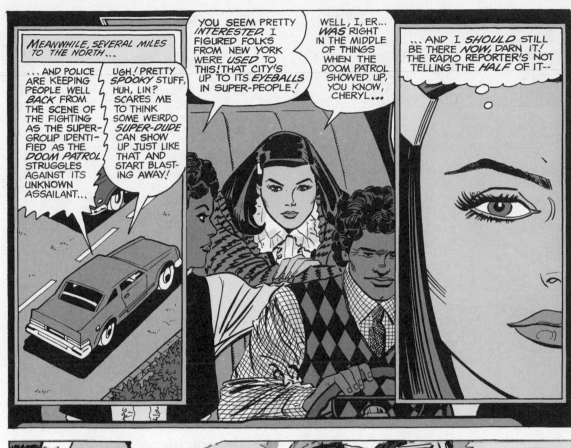

MEANWHILE, SEVERAL MILES TO THE NORTH...

...AND POLICE ARE KEEPING PEOPLE WELL *BACK* FROM THE SCENE OF THE FIGHTING AS THE SUPER-GROUP IDENTIFIED AS THE *DOOM PATROL* STRUGGLES AGAINST ITS UNKNOWN ASSAILANT...

UGH! PRETTY *SPOOKY* STUFF, HUH, LIN? SCARES ME TO THINK SOME WEIRDO *SUPER-DUDE* CAN SHOW UP JUST LIKE THAT AND START BLASTING AWAY!

YOU SEEM PRETTY *INTERESTED.* I FIGURED FOLKS FROM NEW YORK WERE *USED* TO THIS! THAT CITY'S UP TO ITS *EYEBALLS* IN SUPER-PEOPLE!

WELL, I, ER... *WAS* RIGHT IN THE MIDDLE OF THINGS WHEN THE DOOM PATROL SHOWED UP, YOU KNOW, CHERYL...

...AND I *SHOULD* STILL BE THERE *NOW,* DARN IT! THE RADIO REPORTER'S NOT TELLING THE *HALF* OF IT--

--WHILE I'VE GOT A *RINGSIDE SEAT,* THANKS TO MY *TELESCOPIC VISION* AND *SUPER-HEARING!* THE DP'S NOT DOING SO *HOT* AGAINST REACTRON--

ARRRGHH!

HA HA! KEEP SCREAMIN', PAL -- IT'S *MUSIC* TO MY *EARS!*

UHHH-- WHA--?!

BWATTZZZ

÷WHEW!÷ TH-THANKS A *HEAP,* VAL... A COUPLA SECONDS *MORE* OF THAT AND THE INSIDE OF MY SKULL WOULD'VE BEEN HOLDIN' *SCRAMBLED EGGS* INSTEAD'A MY *BRAINS!*

YOU CREEPS'VE BEEN *PRACTICIN'* SINCE THE LAST TIME IN ARIZONA, AIN'T YA? I STILL AIN'T *IMPRESSED*--

7

--BUT I *DO* KNOW I AIN'T *GAININ'* NOTHIN' BY TRADIN' PUNCHES WITH YOU CLOWNS!

CRIPES! WHAT'S HE DOING *NOW*--?

DON'T ASK *ME*, MAN...ASK *HIM*!

DON'T YAH *REMEMBER* YER *TRAININ'* LIEUTENANT CLAY, SIR"?! IT'S CALLED--

-- A *STRATEGIC* *WITHDRAWAL*, HA HA!

REACTRON USED A *CONCENTRATED* *STREAM* OF PARTICLES TO OPEN UP SOME SORT OF *WARP* TO *ESCAPE* THROUGH!

BAMPFF!

THAT'S NOT A TRICK HE CAN DO A WHOLE *LOT*, I'LL BET--IT'S *GOT* TO TAKE AN *INCREDIBLE* AMOUNT OF ENERGY!

BUT WITH HIM GONE, THAT LEAVES ME IN THE *DARK*. I STILL DON'T KNOW *WHO* HE IS, OR WHAT GOT THE *DP* ON HIS TAIL!

BUT *NEXT* TIME HE POPS UP, I'LL MAKE IT MY *BUSINESS* TO BE ON HAND!

WE JUMP AHEAD NOW, APPROXIMATELY 24 UNEVENTFUL HOURS TO THE CAMPUS OF CHICAGO'S LAKE SHORE UNIVERSITY...

I'M REALLY *EXCITED* ABOUT TODAY... BUT THEN, AS ONE OF ONLY 15 PSYCHOLOGY MAJORS TO MAKE IT INTO A *SPECIAL SEMINAR COURSE* ON *CRIMINAL PSYCH*, I GUESS I OUGHT TO BE!

OF COURSE, I *STILL* HAVEN'T FORGOTTEN ABOUT YESTERDAY'S *MELÉE* IN THE PARK! BUT I HAVEN'T SEEN HIDE NOR HAIR OF EITHER THE DP *OR* REACTRON *SINCE--*

--MEANING THE BATTLE'S EITHER *MOVED* ON, OR THEY'RE ALL *LYING* *LOW* FOR NOW.

MYSTERY SURROUNDING GRANT PARK BATTLE

ALL I CAN DO IS KEEP A SUPER-EAR PEELED FOR THEM. I'M NOT ABOUT TO LET IT *RUIN* MY DAY!

AND *SPEAKING* OF MYSTERIES --WONDER WHAT'S GOING ON OVER AT COUGHLIN HALL?

8

WELL, I CAN *SEE* WHY EVERYBODY'D BE SO *EXCITED*. IF I'M NOT MISTAKEN-- AND WE LASSES WITH *TOTAL RECALL* SELDOM ARE--THAT'S *PHILIP DECKER*, THE COMPOSER AND CONDUCTOR!

I REMEMBER READING HE'D BE TEACHING A FEW COURSES HERE IN CONJUNCTION WITH HIS DUTIES AS THE NEW *MUSICAL DIRECTOR* FOR THE *CHICAGO SYMPHONY.*

JAZZ AND *ROCK* MAY BE MY CUR-RENT FAVORITES, BUT EVEN *I'VE* GOT A FEW OF *HIS* ALBUMS AT HOME!

WHOOPS! CAN'T AFFORD THE TIME TO BE IMPRESSED NOW...NOT IF I DON'T WANT TO BE *LATE* FOR THE FIRST LECTURE--!

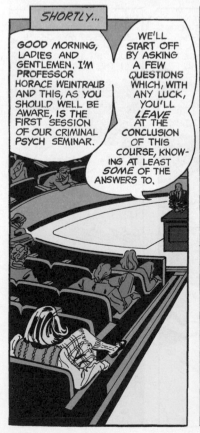

SHORTLY...

GOOD MORNING, LADIES AND GENTLEMEN. I'M PROFESSOR HORACE WEINTRAUB AND THIS, AS YOU SHOULD WELL BE AWARE, IS THE FIRST SESSION OF OUR CRIMINAL PSYCH SEMINAR.

WE'LL START OFF BY ASKING A FEW QUESTIONS WHICH, WITH ANY LUCK, YOU'LL *LEAVE* AT THE CONCLUSION OF THIS COURSE, KNOW-ING AT LEAST *SOME* OF THE ANSWERS TO.

WHAT *ELEMENTS* GO INTO CREATING THE SO-CALLED CRIMINAL MENTALITY? WHAT DRIVES PREVIOUSLY HONEST, SUPPOSEDLY *RATIONAL* PEOPLE TO CRIME?

NOW *THIS* IS WHAT I CAME TO SCHOOL *FOR!* I DEAL WITH CRIMINALS PRACTICALLY EVERY DAY OF MY LIFE, BUT I NEVER STOPPED TO CON-SIDER WHAT MAKES THEM *TICK.*

AND THAT'S A SUBJECT EVEN A *SUPERGIRL*--WHO COULD MEMORIZE EVERY BOOK EVER WRIT-TEN ON A SUBJECT IN A FEW HOURS-- NEEDS TO *STUDY!*

...THUS, OUR COURSE OF INVESTIGATION WILL TRACE CASE-HISTO-RIES OF CRIMINALS AND *ATTEMPT* TO PIECE TOGETHER A *PICTURE* OF...

9

MEANWHILE, ACROSS CAMPUS...

THAT'S A *WRAP*, PEOPLE! WE CAN *SHUT DOWN* THE SYSTEMS NOW. THE TEST WENT OFF *TEXTBOOK PERFECT!*

FLETCHER HALL

I CAN'T BELIEVE WE'RE ACTUALLY *ON SCHEDULE* WITH THIS THING, DR. TUCKER. WE CAN ACTIVATE THE *REACTOR* TOMORROW, AS PLANNED!

HMMM....YES...

Y'KNOW, IT'S ALMOST A *SHAME* THAT NO-BODY'LL EVER REALLY KNOW WHAT WE'VE MANAGED TO ACCOMPLISH DOWN HERE ON A *SHOESTRING BUDGET!*

I KNOW WHAT YOU MEAN, DR. *KENSINGTON*. BUT IF PEOPLE FOUND OUT WE'D PUT TOGETHER AN *EXPERIMENTAL NUCLEAR REACTOR* ON A COLLEGE CAMPUS...

...IN THE MIDDLE OF ONE OF THE *DENSEST* POPULATION CENTERS IN THE COUNTRY, THERE'D BE HELL TO PAY!

-*SIGH!*- TOO BAD. IT'S *UNREASONABLE* FEARS LIKE THAT WHICH COULD KEEP BACK THE *ADVANCE* OF TECHNOLOGY.

WELL NOW, THIS *IS* AN EXPERIMENTAL PROCESS, DOCTOR. MAYBE THEY'RE NOT *ENTIRELY* UNREASONABLE...

WATCH IT, JACK! YOU'RE STARTING TO SOUND LIKE ONE OF THOSE *NO-NUKES REACTIONARIES!* YOU'RE A *SCIENTIST.* YOU KNOW THERE ARE NO ADVANCES WITHOUT SOME *SMALL* RISK.

BUT OUR EQUATIONS AND PLANS HAVE BEEN CHECKED AND *RECHECKED* SO MANY TIMES, THE INK'S JUST ABOUT RUBBED OFF THE PAPERS!

SO *RELAX!* THIS IS NO TIME TO GET *JITTERY!*

NO, NO TIME AT *ALL*... NOT SO CLOSE TO *SUCCESS!* MY BOSSES IN THE *COUNCIL* WOULDN'T LIKE THAT IN THE *LEAST!*

10

THE MUNICIPAL GARAGE, BENEATH MICHIGAN AVENUE...

ANYTHING, JOSH?

ZILCH, MAN. WHATEVER ROCK REACTRON FOUND TO HIDE UNDER, HE'S KEEPIN' HIMSELF *BURIED DEEP!*

THIS WHOLE CAPER'S GETTIN' ON MY *NERVES!* AND CAN'T WE FIND SOMEPLACE *BETTER'N* THIS TRUCK TO WORK OUT OF? I'M GETTIN' *CLAUSTROPHOBIC* IN HERE!

SURE! CAN YOU SEE THE FOUR OF *US* WALTZING INTO A HOTEL LOBBY AND CHECKIN' INTO A ROOM WITH A *TON* OF ELECTRONICS GEAR?

MUST YOU TWO *ALWAYS* BE BICKERING? NONE OF US LIKES BEING HERE, JOSHUA -- BUT WE ARE A LONG WAY FROM OUR *MIDWAY CITY* HEADQUARTERS, SO WE MUST MAKE THE *BEST* OF IT.

NOW *PLEASE* TRY TO *THINK*, MY FRIEND. YOU KNOW REACTRON *BEST*. *WHERE* MIGHT HE BE HIDING?

IF HE WERE NORMAL, HE'D BE HOLED UP SOMEWHERE WITH A BOTTLE AND A WOMAN--BUT HE *AIN'T* NORMAL...HE'S *NOTHIN'* LIKE THE GUY I KNEW IN 'NAM-- 'CEPT FOR STILL BEING ONE *MEAN MOTHER!*

SHOOT! WHERE WOULD *YOU* BE IF YOU WAS A *RADIOACTIVE FREAK*...

THAT'S *RIGHT*, CLAY-- STICK YOUR FOOT DOWN YOUR *THROAT*, WHY DON'T YOU--! I-I'M *SORRY* ABOUT THAT, VAL HONEY! I...I...

PLEASE, DEAR JOSHUA, I TOOK NO *OFFENSE*. I AM...ADJUSTING TO MY CONDITION*...

*The details of which were recounted in *DC COMICS PRESENTS #52* -- Julie

CAN WE GET *TOGETHER* ON THIS, YOU GUYS?

WE GOT OURSELVES A BAD-GUY TO FIND... ONE, I GOTTA *REMIND* YOU--

--WITH ENOUGH *RAW POWER* AT HIS COMMAND TO MAKE THE HUMAN RACE AWFUL SORRY IT EVER CLIMBED OUTTA THE SLIME!

11

LAKE SHORE UNIVERSITY, LATE AFTERNOON...

÷WHEW!÷ AM I EVER *GLAD* THAT'S OVER WITH, LIN! TOO MUCH ENGLISH LIT AND I START TO GO *CROSS-EYED--!*

BUT, JOAN--I THOUGHT YOU WERE AN ENGLISH *MAJOR--?*

NEVER MIND! I DON'T THINK I WANT TO KNOW!

WHAT SAY WE BOOGEY BACK UP NORTH TO THE APARTMENT AND SPLIT A *PIZZA* FOR DINNER, MS. RAYMOND?

NAW... THAT WAS *LAST* WEEK!

MUCH *APPRECIATED,* MS. DANVERS, 'CEPT I *CAN'T.* GOT A *DATE* TONIGHT.

ANOTHER DATE WITH DANNY?! YOU WERE OUT WITH HIM *LAST* NIGHT! SERIOUS, HUH?

TONIGHT'S *MIKE'S* TURN! DANNY'S *OLD* NEWS!

I *AM* IMPRESSED! YOU MUST GO OUT *FOUR* OR *FIVE* TIMES A WEEK! WHEN DO YOU FIND TIME TO *STUDY?*

AU CONTRAIRE, LIN... AT *LEAST* FIVE OR *SIX* TIMES! AND I, UH...FIND *TIME* TO CATCH A GLANCE AT MY BOOKS HERE AND THERE!

BUT ENOUGH ABOUT *ME...* HOW'CUM *YOU* HAVEN'T MET ANYBODY SINCE YOU BLEW INTO TOWN?

WHO'S TO MEET? *YOU'RE* DATING EVERY SINGLE GUY IN TOWN!

HARDE*HAR* HAR! I...AY-YI-*YI!* *PINCH* ME, DANVERS-- *QUICK!* EITHER I'M *DREAMING,* OR THAT *IS* WHO I *THINK* IT IS COMIN' STRAIGHT INTO MY LONELY LITTLE LIFE!

UH...*DON'T* YOU *EVER* GIVE UP?

YOU'RE ONLY YOUNG *ONCE,* KIDDO. NOW, WATCH THE OL' JOANIE RAYMOND TECHNIQUE IN *ACTION!*

OOOPS! OH, I'M *TERRIBLY* SORRY, ÷TSK÷... I'M SUCH A *KLUTZ--!*

NONSENSE, MISS, IT WAS ENTIRELY *MY* FAULT FOR NOT WATCHING WHERE I WAS -- WELL... HELL-*O* THERE!

I, ER... AREN'T *YOU* PHIL DECKER, THE...THE...

HELLO *YOURSELF.*

OH, *BRO-THER!*

⑫

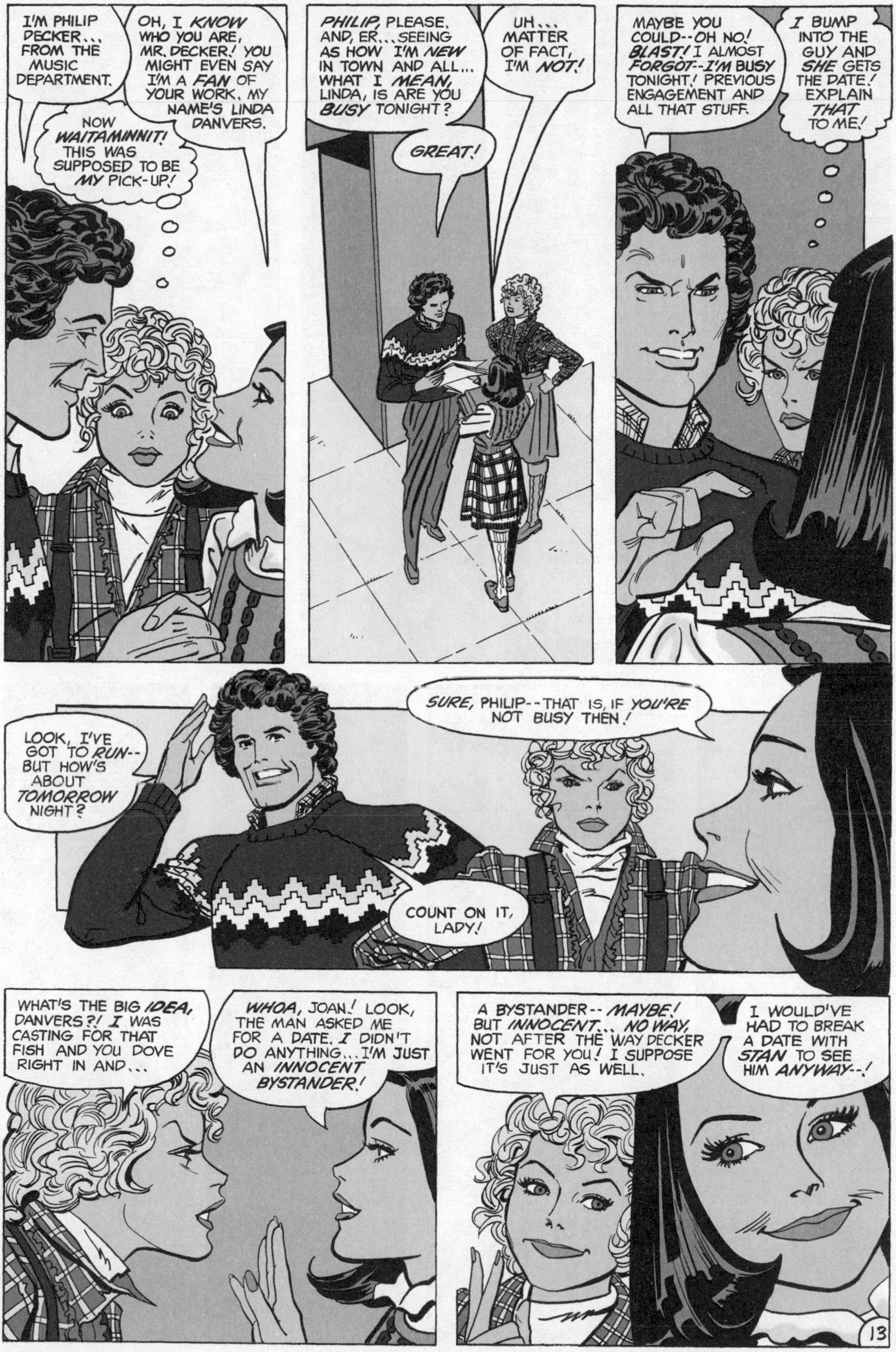
I'M PHILIP DECKER... FROM THE MUSIC DEPARTMENT.
OH, I KNOW WHO YOU ARE, MR. DECKER! YOU MIGHT EVEN SAY I'M A FAN OF YOUR WORK. MY NAME'S LINDA DANVERS.
NOW WAITAMINNIT! THIS WAS SUPPOSED TO BE MY PICK-UP!
PHILIP, PLEASE. AND, ER...SEEING AS HOW I'M NEW IN TOWN AND ALL... WHAT I MEAN, LINDA, IS ARE YOU BUSY TONIGHT?
UH... MATTER OF FACT, I'M NOT!
GREAT!
MAYBE YOU COULD--OH NO! BLAST! I ALMOST FORGOT--I'M BUSY TONIGHT! PREVIOUS ENGAGEMENT AND ALL THAT STUFF.
I BUMP INTO THE GUY AND SHE GETS THE DATE! EXPLAIN THAT TO ME!
LOOK, I'VE GOT TO RUN-- BUT HOW'S ABOUT TOMORROW NIGHT?
SURE, PHILIP--THAT IS, IF YOU'RE NOT BUSY THEN!
COUNT ON IT, LADY!
WHAT'S THE BIG IDEA, DANVERS?! I WAS CASTING FOR THAT FISH AND YOU DOVE RIGHT IN AND...
WHOA, JOAN! LOOK, THE MAN ASKED ME FOR A DATE. I DIDN'T DO ANYTHING...I'M JUST AN INNOCENT BYSTANDER!
A BYSTANDER--MAYBE! BUT INNOCENT... NO WAY, NOT AFTER THE WAY DECKER WENT FOR YOU! I SUPPOSE IT'S JUST AS WELL.
I WOULD'VE HAD TO BREAK A DATE WITH STAN TO SEE HIM ANYWAY--!
13

EVENING, IN THE SECRET LABORATORY BENEATH LSU'S FLETCHER HALL...

MMM. THOUGHT EVERYBODY'D GONE *HOME* BY NOW. THERE SHOULDN'T BE A LIGHT ON IN HERE.

AWW, PROBABLY ONE OF THEM ABSENT-MINDED PROFESSOR TYPES *FORGOT* TO TURN IT OFF WHEN HE... HUH?!

HEY! WHAT'RE *YOU*--?

WHAT'S IT TO *YOU*, CREEP? AIN'T GONNA *MATTER* MUCH ONE WAY OR THE OTHER IN A *SECOND*, ANYWAY--

--'CAUSE YOU'RE ABOUT TO BE MADE *DEAD!* HA HA HA!

S-STAY BACK...

BLAM! POW POW

THEM'S PRETTY *ROTTEN LAST* WORDS, GUY!

ARRRGHH!

14

THAT'S WHAT YA GET FER STICKIN' YER NOSE IN WHERE IT DON'T *BELONG!* 'LEAST I *LEFT* ENOUGH OF YA FER YER FAMILY TO *BURY!* HA!

WHERE WAS I *NOW...?* COUPLE'A MORE MINUTES WITH THIS COMPUTER, AN' I CAN GET THE HELL OUTTA HERE WITH WHAT I *CAME* FOR!

YOU'RE OUT OF LUCK ON *THAT* SCORE, FRIEND!

AWWW, WHO *NOW--?*

THE NAME'S *SUPERGIRL,* GOLDEN BOY--YOU KNOW, AS IN THE ONE WITH *SUPER-HEARING* THAT CAN PICK UP GUNSHOTS AND *SCREAMS* EVEN IN THE *SUB-BASEMENT* HERE!

I GOT *NEWS* FOR YOU, BABYDOLL--

-- YER ABOUT TO BE MADE AWFUL SORRY YOU GOT THEM POWERS!

GO AHEAD AND *SCARE* ME SOME *MORE--!*

AND ON THAT NOTE, WE TAKE OUR LEAVE OF THE MAID OF MIGHT, BUT BE BACK WITH US NEXT ISSUE FOR..."RE-ENTER--REACTRON!"

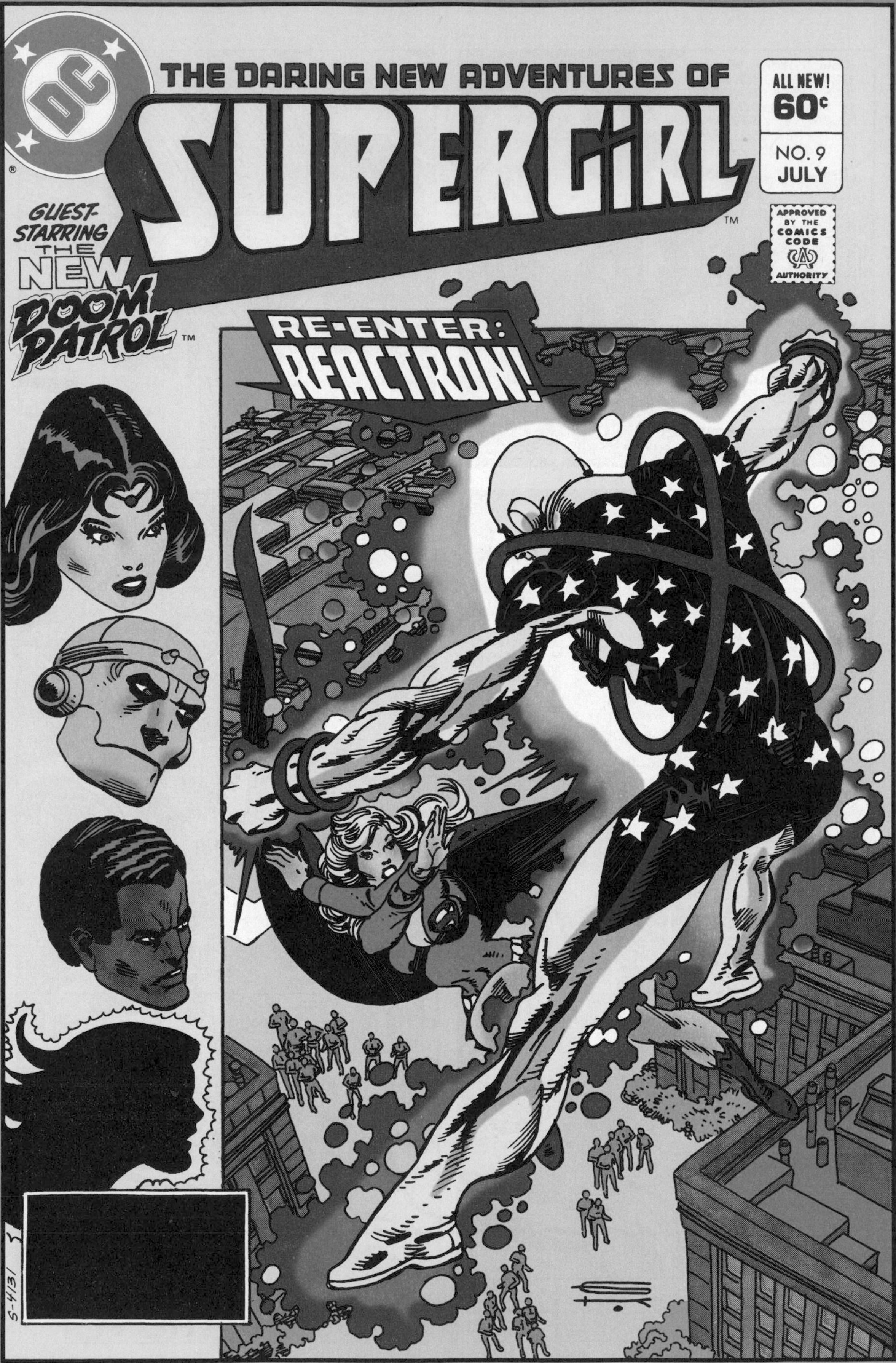
THE DARING NEW ADVENTURES OF
SUPERGIRL
ALL NEW!
60¢
NO. 9
JULY
APPROVED BY THE COMICS CODE AUTHORITY
GUEST-STARRING THE NEW DOOM PATROL
RE-ENTER: REACTRON!

Cover by **Gil Kane**

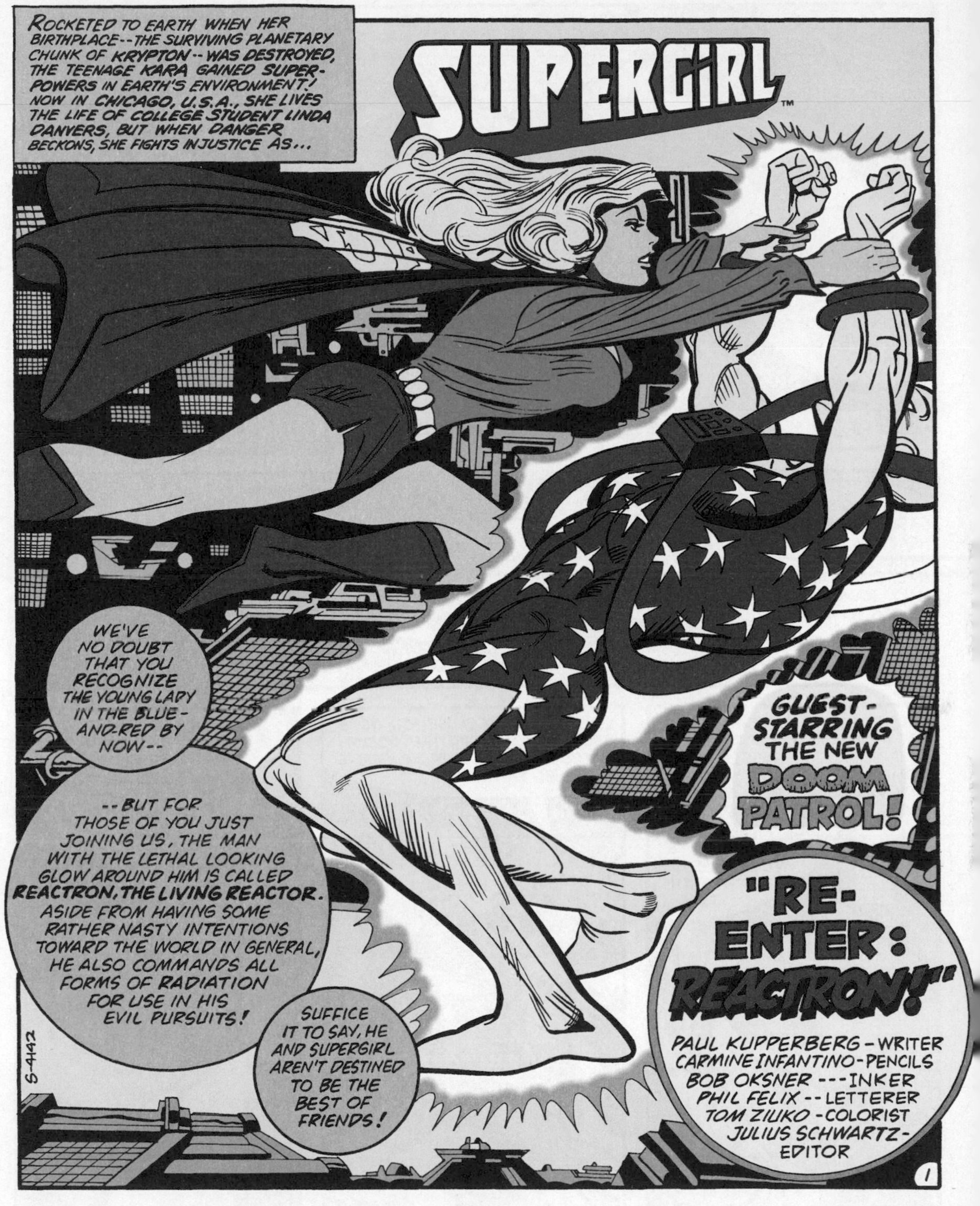
ROCKETED TO EARTH WHEN HER BIRTHPLACE--THE SURVIVING PLANETARY CHUNK OF KRYPTON--WAS DESTROYED, THE TEENAGE KARA GAINED SUPER-POWERS IN EARTH'S ENVIRONMENT! NOW IN CHICAGO, U.S.A., SHE LIVES THE LIFE OF COLLEGE STUDENT LINDA DANVERS, BUT WHEN DANGER BECKONS, SHE FIGHTS INJUSTICE AS...
SUPERGIRL™
WE'VE NO DOUBT THAT YOU RECOGNIZE THE YOUNG LADY IN THE BLUE-AND-RED BY NOW--
--BUT FOR THOSE OF YOU JUST JOINING US, THE MAN WITH THE LETHAL LOOKING GLOW AROUND HIM IS CALLED REACTRON, THE LIVING REACTOR. ASIDE FROM HAVING SOME RATHER NASTY INTENTIONS TOWARD THE WORLD IN GENERAL, HE ALSO COMMANDS ALL FORMS OF RADIATION FOR USE IN HIS EVIL PURSUITS!
SUFFICE IT TO SAY, HE AND SUPERGIRL AREN'T DESTINED TO BE THE BEST OF FRIENDS!
GUEST-STARRING THE NEW DOOM PATROL!
"RE-ENTER: REACTRON!"
PAUL KUPPERBERG - WRITER
CARMINE INFANTINO - PENCILS
BOB OKSNER --- INKER
PHIL FELIX -- LETTERER
TOM ZIUKO - COLORIST
JULIUS SCHWARTZ - EDITOR
S-4142
1

PAIN IN THE NECK, INTERFERIN' BROAD--LEMME *ALONE!* I WASN'T BOTHERIN' YOU ...I CAME HERE TO TAKE CARE'A SOME *BIZNESS!*

--LIKE THAT SECURITY GUARD YOU *KILLED* BECAUSE HE STUMBLED ON YOU TAKING CARE OF BUSINESS, HUH? *

✷ Last issue -- Julie

QUIT BEIN' SO *RIGHTEOUS,* SUPER-GIRL! IT AIN'T THE WAY TO SPEND THE LAST COUPLE'A MINUTES YOU GOT TO *LIVE!*

YOU'RE REALLY SCARING ME, REACTRON --

--BECAUSE IN CASE YOU HAVEN'T HEARD, YOU MIGHT AS WELL THROW *SPIT-BALLS* FOR ALL THE HARM RADIATION DOES TO ME!

CATCHING ON YET--OR DO I HAVE TO DO SOME MORE CONVINCING?

YOU AIN'T NO *ORDINARY* HASSLE, I'LL GIVE YA *THAT!* BUT YOU'RE GONNA BE SORRY YOU EVER EVEN HEARD'A MY *NAME* WHEN I GET DONE WITH YA!

LOOK, JUST BECAUSE YOU WERE ABLE TO HOLD OFF THE *DOOM PATROL,* DON'T THINK *I'M* GOING TO BE THAT EASY!

OH, I AIN'T NEVER THOUGHT YOU WAS *EASY,* SUPERGIRL ...

②

OOOOOFF!

--BUT THEN AGAIN, I NEVER *WAS* THE KIND'A GUY TO RUN AWAY FROM A *TOUGH FIGHT!*

THROWING ME AROUND LIKE A *BEANBAG!* LOOKS LIKE I UNDERESTIMATED HIS *RAW POWER!*

BUT POWER ALONE DOESN'T WIN BATTLES! DESPITE HIS RADIATION CONTROL, *REACTRON* DOESN'T RATE THAT HIGH IN THE *SMARTS DEPARTMENT!* MATTER OF FACT, THE *MADDER* HE GETS, THE *LESS* HE SEEMS TO PUT ANY *THOUGHT* BEHIND HIS ATTACKS!

HE JUST RELIES ON HIS POWERS TO FAST-FRY ANYTHING THAT GETS IN HIS WAY--

--AND I CAN'T *HELP* BUT GET IN HIS WAY HERE! HE'S TOO MUCH TO FIGHT IN THIS *CONFINED* SPACE! GOT TO GET HIM OUT INTO THE *OPEN* WHERE I CAN DO SOME *MANEUVERING!*

C'MON, GLOW-DOME...GIMME A *BREAK!* ALL YOUR RADIATION'S DOING IS GIVING MY COSTUME A GOOD CLEANING!

YOU GOT A REAL *SMART* MOUTH ON YOU, *BLONDIE...* AN' I DON'T LIKE THAT AT *ALL!* YOU WANNA GET HURT, I'M JUST THE GUY TO *DO IT!*

PROMISES, PROMISES! STOP FLAPPING YOUR BIG MOUTH AND LET'S SEE A LITTLE *ACTION!*

③

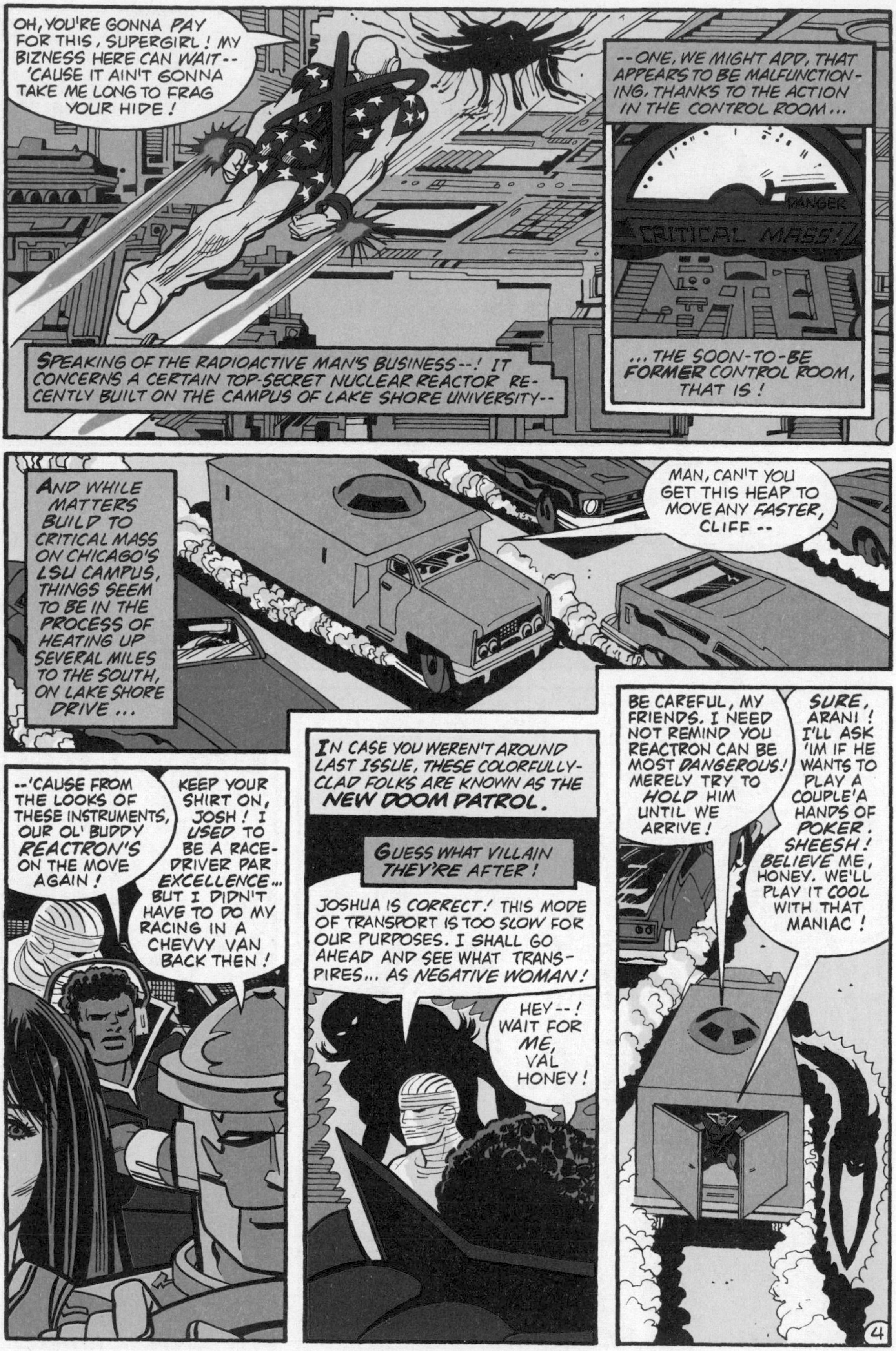
OH, YOU'RE GONNA PAY FOR THIS, SUPERGIRL! MY BIZNESS HERE CAN WAIT-- 'CAUSE IT AIN'T GONNA TAKE ME LONG TO FRAG YOUR HIDE!
--ONE, WE MIGHT ADD, THAT APPEARS TO BE MALFUNCTIONING, THANKS TO THE ACTION IN THE CONTROL ROOM...
DANGER
CRITICAL MASS!
SPEAKING OF THE RADIOACTIVE MAN'S BUSINESS--! IT CONCERNS A CERTAIN TOP-SECRET NUCLEAR REACTOR RECENTLY BUILT ON THE CAMPUS OF LAKE SHORE UNIVERSITY--
...THE SOON-TO-BE FORMER CONTROL ROOM, THAT IS!
AND WHILE MATTERS BUILD TO CRITICAL MASS ON CHICAGO'S LSU CAMPUS, THINGS SEEM TO BE IN THE PROCESS OF HEATING UP SEVERAL MILES TO THE SOUTH, ON LAKE SHORE DRIVE...
MAN, CAN'T YOU GET THIS HEAP TO MOVE ANY FASTER, CLIFF --
--'CAUSE FROM THE LOOKS OF THESE INSTRUMENTS, OUR OL' BUDDY REACTRON'S ON THE MOVE AGAIN!
KEEP YOUR SHIRT ON, JOSH! I USED TO BE A RACE-DRIVER PAR EXCELLENCE... BUT I DIDN'T HAVE TO DO MY RACING IN A CHEVVY VAN BACK THEN!
IN CASE YOU WEREN'T AROUND LAST ISSUE, THESE COLORFULLY-CLAD FOLKS ARE KNOWN AS THE NEW DOOM PATROL.
GUESS WHAT VILLAIN THEY'RE AFTER!
JOSHUA IS CORRECT! THIS MODE OF TRANSPORT IS TOO SLOW FOR OUR PURPOSES. I SHALL GO AHEAD AND SEE WHAT TRANSPIRES... AS NEGATIVE WOMAN!
HEY--! WAIT FOR ME, VAL HONEY!
BE CAREFUL, MY FRIENDS. I NEED NOT REMIND YOU REACTRON CAN BE MOST DANGEROUS! MERELY TRY TO HOLD HIM UNTIL WE ARRIVE!
SURE, ARANI! I'LL ASK 'IM IF HE WANTS TO PLAY A COUPLE'A HANDS OF POKER. SHEESH! BELIEVE ME, HONEY. WE'LL PLAY IT COOL WITH THAT MANIAC!
4

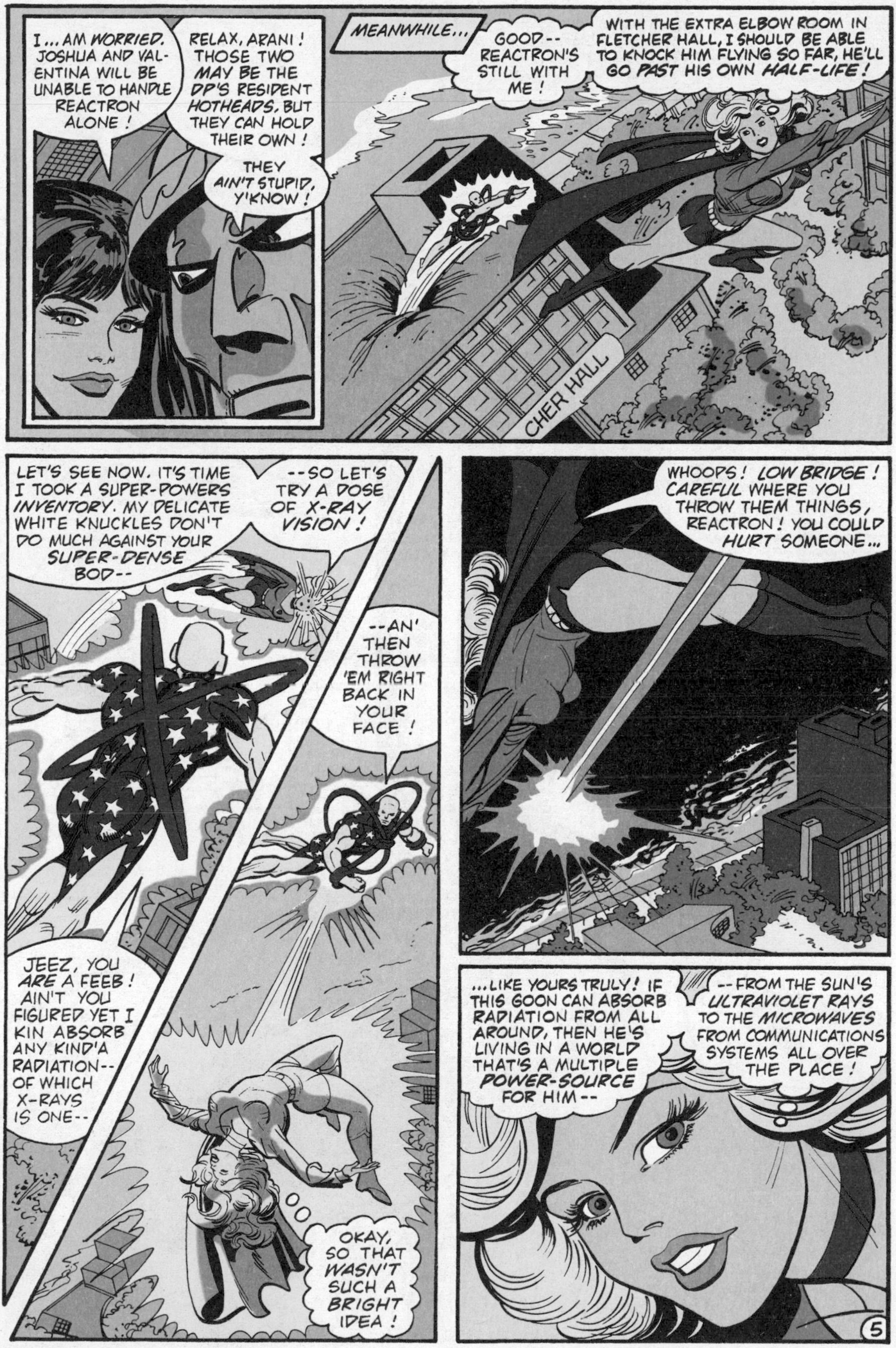
I... AM WORRIED. JOSHUA AND VALENTINA WILL BE UNABLE TO HANDLE REACTRON ALONE!
RELAX, ARANI! THOSE TWO MAY BE THE DP'S RESIDENT HOTHEADS, BUT THEY CAN HOLD THEIR OWN!
THEY AIN'T STUPID, Y'KNOW!
MEANWHILE...
GOOD-- REACTRON'S STILL WITH ME!
WITH THE EXTRA ELBOW ROOM IN FLETCHER HALL, I SHOULD BE ABLE TO KNOCK HIM FLYING SO FAR, HE'LL GO PAST HIS OWN HALF-LIFE!
CHER HALL
LET'S SEE NOW. IT'S TIME I TOOK A SUPER-POWERS INVENTORY. MY DELICATE WHITE KNUCKLES DON'T DO MUCH AGAINST YOUR SUPER-DENSE BOD--
--SO LET'S TRY A DOSE OF X-RAY VISION!
--AN' THEN THROW 'EM RIGHT BACK IN YOUR FACE!
JEEZ, YOU ARE A FEEB! AIN'T YOU FIGURED YET I KIN ABSORB ANY KIND'A RADIATION-- OF WHICH X-RAYS IS ONE--
OKAY, SO THAT WASN'T SUCH A BRIGHT IDEA!
WHOOPS! LOW BRIDGE! CAREFUL WHERE YOU THROW THEM THINGS, REACTRON! YOU COULD HURT SOMEONE...
...LIKE YOURS TRULY! IF THIS GOON CAN ABSORB RADIATION FROM ALL AROUND, THEN HE'S LIVING IN A WORLD THAT'S A MULTIPLE POWER-SOURCE FOR HIM--
--FROM THE SUN'S ULTRAVIOLET RAYS TO THE MICROWAVES FROM COMMUNICATIONS SYSTEMS ALL OVER THE PLACE!

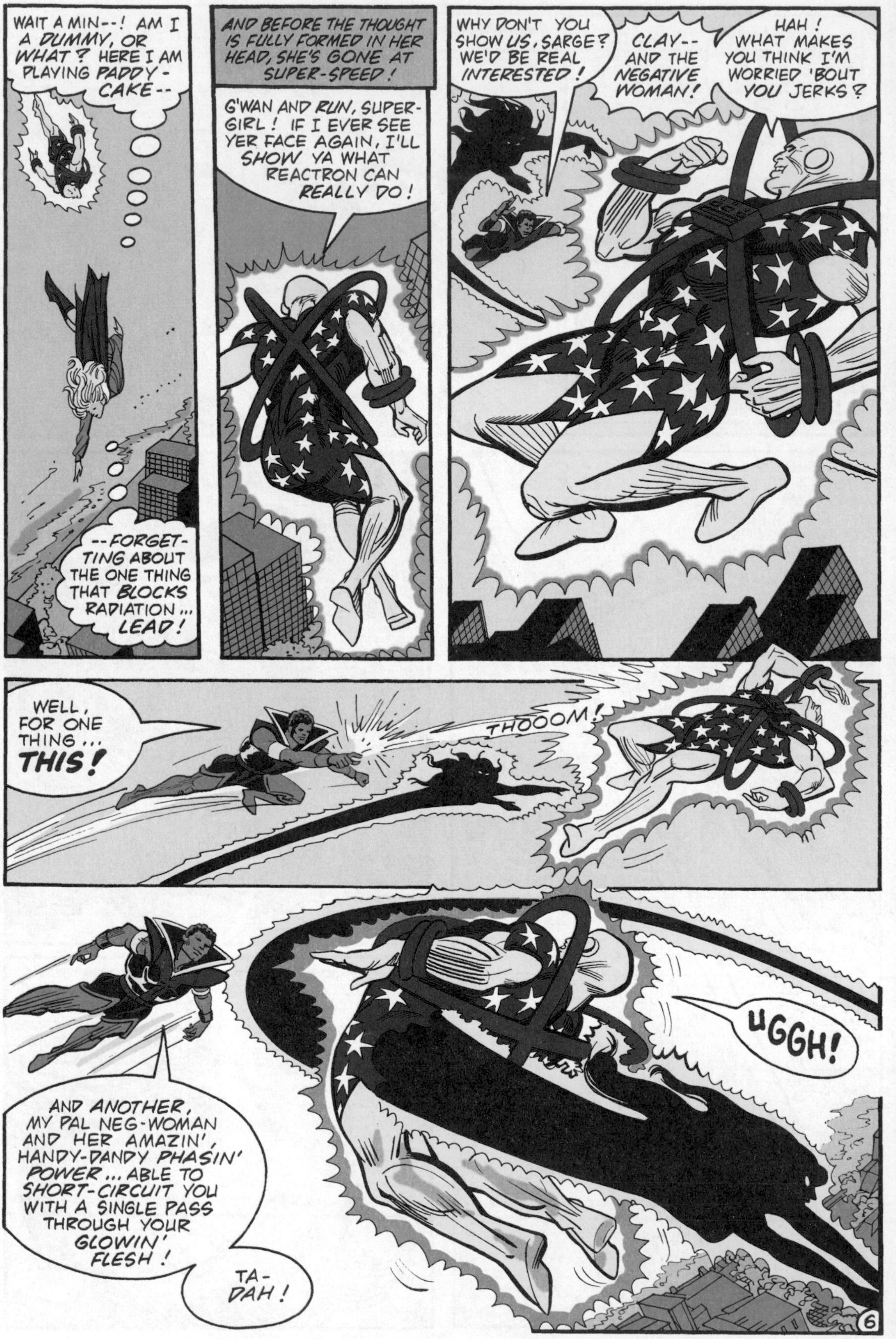

WAIT A MIN--! AM I A DUMMY, OR WHAT? HERE I AM PLAYING PADDY-CAKE--
--FORGETTING ABOUT THE ONE THING THAT BLOCKS RADIATION... LEAD!
AND BEFORE THE THOUGHT IS FULLY FORMED IN HER HEAD, SHE'S GONE AT SUPER-SPEED!
G'WAN AND RUN, SUPER-GIRL! IF I EVER SEE YER FACE AGAIN, I'LL SHOW YA WHAT REACTRON CAN REALLY DO!
WHY DON'T YOU SHOW US, SARGE? WE'D BE REAL INTERESTED!
CLAY-- AND THE NEGATIVE WOMAN!
HAH! WHAT MAKES YOU THINK I'M WORRIED 'BOUT YOU JERKS?
WELL, FOR ONE THING... THIS!
THOOOM!
AND ANOTHER, MY PAL NEG-WOMAN AND HER AMAZIN', HANDY-DANDY PHASIN' POWER... ABLE TO SHORT-CIRCUIT YOU WITH A SINGLE PASS THROUGH YOUR GLOWIN' FLESH!
TA-DAH!
UGGH!
6

Y-YA *HURT* ME! AIN'T *NOBODY* DOES THAT TO ME AND *LIVES!*

I WOULDN'T 'ZACTLY *COUNT* ON THAT HOLDIN' *TRUE*, SARGE! ME AN' MY PALS INTEND TO HURT YOU *BAD*...AND SPREAD THE NEWS FROM FORT DIX TO PENDLETON!

FHWOOM!

JUST *TRY* IT, CREEP! I GOT WHAT IT TAKES TO KEEP YER GIRL-FRIEND AWAY FROM ME--

--AN' MAYBE EVEN MAKE SURE SHE'S IN NO *SHAPE* TO DO NOTHIN' BUT *BLEED!*

MAN, I KNOWED YOU TO DO SOME MIGHTY *STUPID* THINGS SINCE WE SERVED TOGETHER IN 'NAM -- BUT *LAYIN'* HANDS ON MY LADY'S GOTTA BE THE *STUPIDEST* YET!

AS ALL HELL BREAKS LOOSE ON THE NORMALLY SEDATE COLLEGE CAMPUS, SUPER-GIRL REJOINS THE SCENE...

THE *DOOM PATROL--?!* I SUPPOSE I SHOULDN'T BE TOO SURPRISED TO SEE THEM! AFTER ALL, I SAW THEM BAT-TLING REACTRON *YESTERDAY!*

BUT JUDGING FROM THEIR SUCCESS-RATE THEN, THIS GIRL OF STEEL WILL BE A BIG *HELP* THIS TIME AROUND! *TEMPEST*... *NEGATIVE WOMAN* ... STAND CLEAR! I KNOW HOW TO STOP REACTRON!

SUPERGIRL! *NO* -- DON'T DO THAT!

7

SORRY IF I'M STEPPING ON YOUR SUPER-POWERED TOES BY BUTTING INTO THIS FIGHT -- BUT THIS IS MY HOME TURF THAT MANIAC'S TURNING INTO A RADIOACTIVE WASTELAND!

IT AIN'T *THAT*...IT'S JUST YOU DON'T KNOW WHAT YER DOIN'!

NO? BELIEVE ME, FRIEND...I'VE HAD *MORE* THAN ENOUGH EXPERIENCE WITH RADIATION TO KNOW IT TAKES *LEAD* TO CONTAIN IT... LIKE THESE OLD SEWER PIPES I PICKED UP FROM A JUNKYARD! KIND OF FITTING, HUH--

SEWAGE PIPES FOR HOLDING *HUMAN* SEWAGE!

BUT BEFORE THE MAID OF MIGHT CAN SEAL OFF THE RADIOACTIVE MENACE...

UNN!

THWOOOM

HEY--WHAT'S THE *DEAL*, TEMPEST? I THOUGHT WE WERE ON THE SAME SIDE!

WE *ARE*...BUT YOU SHOULD'A *LISTENED* TO YOUR TEAM-MATE!

LEAD'S THE *FIRST* THING WE TRIED ON THE SARGE...BUT IT DON'T *WORK*--! THAT DUDE PRODUCES SOME KIND'A ENERGY THAT EATS RIGHT *THROUGH* LEAD...AND CAUSES A REACTION--

--THE KIND THAT MAKES FOR A REAL *MOTHER* OF AN EXPLOSION!

GREAT KRYPTON!

YEAH, THAT'S ONE WAY OF PUTTIN' IT!

HAVE TO GET REACTRON *FAR* AWAY FROM THE GROUND BEFORE THIS GOES *BLOOIE*...AND WIPES OUT HALF OF THE CAMPUS!

8

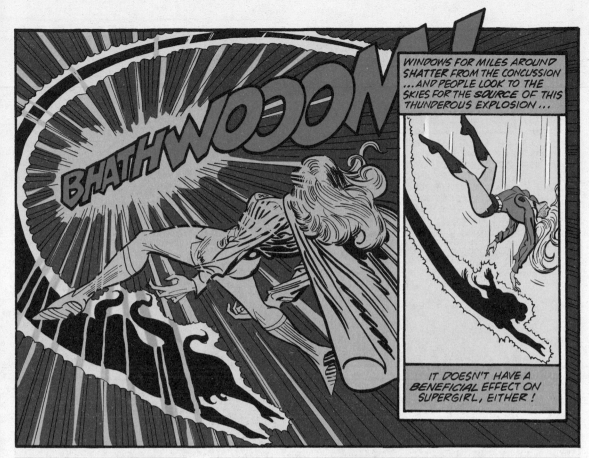

BHATHWOOOM!

WINDOWS FOR MILES AROUND SHATTER FROM THE CONCUSSION ...AND PEOPLE LOOK TO THE SKIES FOR THE *SOURCE* OF THIS *THUNDEROUS* EXPLOSION...

IT DOESN'T HAVE A *BENEFICIAL* EFFECT ON SUPERGIRL, EITHER!

AS FAST AS THOUGHT, THE ENERGY-BEING KNOWN AS *NEGATIVE WOMAN* CATCHES HER FALLING FORM, AND...

SORRY WE MISSED ALL THE *FUN*, JOSH, BUT A VAN AIN'T THE *QUICKEST* WAY TO TRAVEL IN *RUSH HOUR* TRAFFIC! WHAT *HAPPENED*?

LEAD HAPPENED, TIN-MAN!

OUCH! GLAD WHAT HAPPENED TO THAT STRETCH OF DESERT IN ARIZONA DIDN'T HAPPEN *HERE!* HEY... BACK WITH THE *LIVIN'*, I SEE, BLONDIE!

I...I'M FINE. WHERE'S *REACTRON*?

BEATS ME, SUPERGIRL! SAME THING HAPPENED LAST TIME HE MADE WITH THE BIG BANG-- HE JUST *DISAPPEARED!* BUT HE'LL SHOW *AGAIN*-- COUNT ON IT!

YOU PEOPLE *KNEW* THIS REACTRON -- *BEFORE* HE TURNED INTO A WALK-ING A-BOMB?

I DID! BUT IT'S A *LONG* STORY.

I'VE GOT *TIME*, TEMPEST. SPIN IT OUT!

"SURE! MY REAL NAME'S *JOSHUA CLAY* -- U.S. ARMY VET AND *MUTANT EXTRAORDINAIRE!*"

"I FIRST MET REACTRON WHEN WE WAS STILL GETTIN' OUR TAILS WHOPPED IN VIET NAM, ONLY HE WAS JUST PLAIN *SGT. BEN KRULLEN* BACK THEN."

9

"LOTSA THINGS WERE DIFFERENT THEN -- 'SPECIALLY ME! I DIDN'T KNOW IN THEM DAYS I WAS A FREAK! 'COURSE, ONE THING WAS THE SAME:

"ME AND KRULLEN HATED EACH OTHER SOMTHIN' FIERCE!

I DON'T KNOW HOW A JERK LIKE YOU MADE IT INTO TH' ARMY, CLAY! HOW DID YA GET US LOST?

CASE YOU'RE FORGETTIN', CRACKER, I WAS DRAFTED! AN' I DON'T SEE YOU PULLIN' US OUTTA THIS MESS!

I TOL' YA TO WATCH THAT MOUTH OF YOURS! THE LAST THING I WANT NOW IS TA LISTEN TA YOUR CRUD!

KRAK!

YOU LOUSY--!

COOL IT, JOSH! SAVE IT TILL WE'RE OUT OF THIS, OKAY?

HAH! I AIN'T WORRIED ABOUT HIM! NOW GET MOVIN'! I WANNA FIND OUR CAMP BEFORE TH' CONG FINDS US!

"OH YEAH, ME AND KRULLEN WANTED TO CHILL EACH OTHER MORE'N WE WANTED TO FIGHT THE CONG! THOUGH I GOTTA ADMIT, THE SARGE HAD IT IN FOR THEM TOO... ALMOST TOO MUCH...

WELL WELL! LOOKEE THERE -- A CONG VILLAGE!

YOU'RE CRAZY, MAN! THEM'S JUST OLD FOLKS AND KIDS. WE DON'T HAVE TO MESS WITH 'EM!

LIKE HELL, CLAY! I CAN SMELL COMMIES A MILE AWAY -- SO MOVE OUT -- WE'RE HITTIN' 'EM!

SARGE-- NO!

RATATATATAT!

"IT WAS TOO LATE. KRULLEN WAS TEARIN' INTO 'EM LIKE HE WAS THE INDIANS AFTER CUSTER'S SCALP --

"--AND ALL I COULD DO WAS WATCH HIM GET HIS JOLLIES BY MASSACRIN' A BUNCH OF HELPLESS OLD WOMEN AND BABIES.

"LEASTWAYS, THAT'S WHAT I THOUGHT --

"--BUT A SECOND LATER, I FOUND OUT OTHERWISE! I STARTED FEELIN' FUNNY. ALL HOT, LIKE I WAS BUSTIN' OUTTA MY SKIN --

"AND WHEN I TELL YOU I WAS SCARED, I AIN'T KIDDIN'!"

⑩

"THEN, IT WAS LIKE I WASN'T IN CONTROL NO MORE! ALL THIS STUFF STARTED SHOOTIN' OUTTA MY HANDS--"

"--AND I NAILED KRULLEN SQUARE IN THE BACK WITH IT!"

"'COURSE, THE SARGE WEREN'T ONE TO TAKE THAT LYIN' DOWN --HE FORGOT ALL ABOUT SLAUGHTERIN' THEM FOLKS--"

"--AND STARTED TO PLAY TARGET PRACTICE WITH MY HIDE! I STILL DIDN'T KNOW WHAT WAS GOIN' ON --AND I WASN'T ABOUT TO STOP THEN AND FIGGER IT OUT!"

"I ZAPPED HIM AGAIN--"

"--BUT MY AIM WAS AS LOUSY WITH MY POWER-BLASTS AS IT WAS WITH A RIFLE! STILL, MY METHOD MAY'A BEEN CRUDE--"

"--BUT IT WAS EFFECTIVE!"

"I TOOK OFF LIKE A JACKRABBIT INTO THE JUNGLE, AND I DIDN'T STOP RUNNIN'--"

--TILL MY FEET TOUCHED DOWN ON THE GOOD OLD U.S. OF A.! YEAH, THAT'S RIGHT, BLONDIE --I DESERTED FROM THE ARMY!

BEEN ON THE LAM EVER SINCE... TILL I LINKED UP WITH THE DOOM PATROL!

I...I'M NOT PASSING ANY JUDGMENTS, JOSHUA. IT MUST'VE BEEN AWFUL. BUT THAT STILL DOESN'T EXPLAIN HOW KRULLEN GOT TO BE REACTRON.

I WAS JUST GETTIN' TO THAT. I FOUND OUT LATER THAT THE SARGE WAS ONE'A THEM SOLDIERS IN THE EARLY 1950'S --WHO WITNESSED THE A-BOMB TESTS.

ONLY SOMETIMES THEY WERE STATIONED TOO CLOSE TO GROUND ZERO! ALL THAT RADIATION DID SOMETHIN' WEIRD TO KRULLEN'S BODY CHEMISTRY--

11

-- CAUSIN' SOME KINDA MUTATION... THAT'S HOW HE SURVIVED MY BLASTS IN 'NAM!

ONCE KRULLEN REALIZED WHAT HAD HAPPENED TO HIM, HE ALLIED HIMSELF WITH A GROUP CALLED THE COUNCIL...

WHOA, CELSIUS! I'VE HEARD OF THEM... IN FACT, I JUST HAD A RUN-IN WITH THEM MYSELF!*

*Actually, Supergirl had MORE than one encounter with them, not knowing they were behind things in issues 4 through 7! -- Julie

THEY'RE YOUR BASIC INTERNATIONAL CARTEL OF POWER-BROKERS AIMING FOR WORLD DOMINATION, IS ALL!

THEIR SCIENTISTS WORKED ON KRULLEN AN' MADE HIM THE SWEET, LOVIN' SOUL HE IS TODAY!

I TAKE IT REACTRON'S PRETTY MUCH UNSTOPPABLE, HUH?

YEAH, THAT'S THE WAY IT'S SHAPING UP! WE'VE BEEN TRYING NOW FOR WEEKS AND ALL WE'VE GOT TO SHOW FOR IT IS LUMPS!

WHAT SAY WE ALL WORK TOGETHER AND SEE IF... HUH?!

WHAT IS WRONG, SUPERGIRL? YOU LOOK AS IF YOU HAVE SPOTTED DANGER... YET I SEE NOTHING...

THAT'S BECAUSE YOU HAVEN'T GOT SUPER-EYEBALLS CAPABLE OF SEEING LIGHT-WAVE-LENGTH FREQUENCIES MOST PEOPLE CAN'T!

STAY PUT, FOLKS! I'VE GOTTA GO SEE A MAN ABOUT A NUCLEAR MELT-DOWN!

WHAT'S SHE TALKIN' ABOUT--?!

OH-OH! THESE PHOTO-ELECTRIC PEEPERS OF MINE'VE PICKED UP ON IT TOO, JOSH--

--INTENSE RADIATION FIELD PULSATIN' INTO THE AIR FROM SOMEWHERE DOWN BELOW! WANNA TAKE BETS REACTRON'S AT IT AGAIN?

YOU KIDDIN'? THE DP DON'T PAY ENOUGH I CAN AFFORD TO TAKE A LOSIN' PROPOSITION LIKE THAT!

12

THIS MUST BE MY DAY FOR STUPID MISTAKES! FIRST I IGNORE TEMPEST'S WARNING ABOUT USING LEAD ON REACTRON --

--AND THEN I FORGET THE NUCLEAR REACTOR THE SCIENCE DEPARTMENT BUILT UNDER THE CAMPUS ...AND A CHECK WITH MY SUPER-VISION SHOWS THAT IT WAS DAMAGED IN MY FIGHT WITH REACTRON!

DANGER CRITICAL MASS

AND THE NEWS GETS WORSE...INSTEAD OF MELTING DOWN, WHICH IS BAD ENOUGH, THIS DOOHICKEY'S RUNNING WILD--!

AND WITH THE CONTROLS LOOKING LIKE SOMETHING IN A JUNKYARD, I CAN'T SHUT DOWN THE SYSTEM IN TIME TO STOP IT!

...AT LEAST NOT FROM OUT HERE! MAYBE THERE'S SOMETHING I CAN DO IN THE HEART OF THE REACTOR ITSELF!

SOMEBODY, HOWEVER, HAS BEATEN YOU TO IT, SUPERGIRL, FOR WITHIN THE REACTOR'S CORE, AT THAT VERY MOMENT...

OH MAN, IF THERE'S ANYTHIN' BETTER'N ABSORBIN' THIS MUCH RADIATION, I DON'T THINK I COULD STAND IT!

REACTRON!

THAT'S THE NAME, SUPERGIRL! YER GONNA BE AWFUL SORRY YOU CAME BACK, 'CAUSE NOW I'M SO POWERFUL, I AIN'T GONNA JUST SEND YOU RUNNIN'--

--I'M GONNA KILL YOU!

13

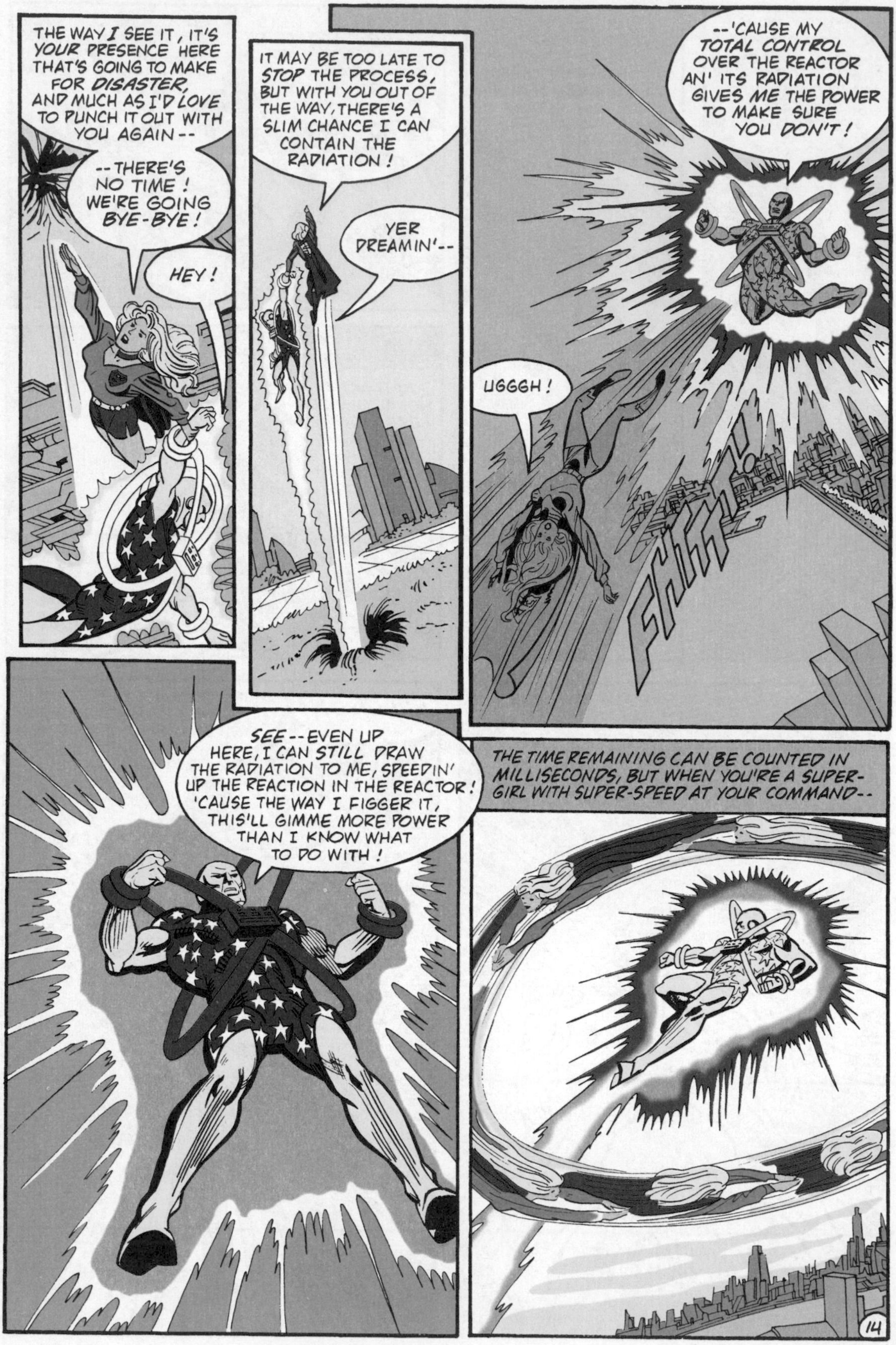

THE WAY I SEE IT, IT'S YOUR PRESENCE HERE THAT'S GOING TO MAKE FOR DISASTER, AND MUCH AS I'D LOVE TO PUNCH IT OUT WITH YOU AGAIN --
-- THERE'S NO TIME! WE'RE GOING BYE-BYE!
HEY!
IT MAY BE TOO LATE TO STOP THE PROCESS, BUT WITH YOU OUT OF THE WAY, THERE'S A SLIM CHANCE I CAN CONTAIN THE RADIATION!
YER DREAMIN'--
--'CAUSE MY TOTAL CONTROL OVER THE REACTOR AN' ITS RADIATION GIVES ME THE POWER TO MAKE SURE YOU DON'T!
UGGGH!
FHTTT!
SEE -- EVEN UP HERE, I CAN STILL DRAW THE RADIATION TO ME, SPEEDIN' UP THE REACTION IN THE REACTOR! 'CAUSE THE WAY I FIGGER IT, THIS'LL GIMME MORE POWER THAN I KNOW WHAT TO DO WITH!
THE TIME REMAINING CAN BE COUNTED IN MILLISECONDS, BUT WHEN YOU'RE A SUPER-GIRL WITH SUPER-SPEED AT YOUR COMMAND--
14

--AND THE ABILITY TO CREATE IN AN INSTANT A VORTEX OF SUCH POWER AND MAGNITUDE THAT NOTHING CAN ESCAPE IT...

...THEN THAT'S ABOUT AS GOOD AS HAVING ALL THE TIME IN THE WORLD.

WH-WHAT'RE YA DOIN'...?! I...I CAN'T GET OUTTA THIS WIND-FUNNEL...RADIATION'S TOO CONCENTRATED FOR ME TO ABSORB ALL AT ONCE...

LIKE WE SAID, NOTHING COULD ESCAPE THE MAID OF MIGHT'S VORTEX-- NOT EVEN THE AWESOME FORCE OF AN ATOMIC EXPLOSION--

--NOW DISPERSED AS IT SHOOTS SPACE-WARDS, RELEASING ITS DEADLY ENERGY HIGH ABOVE THE ATMOSPHERE, WHERE IT CAN HARM NO ONE --

--SAVE SUPERGIRL!

SHE'S OUT LIKE A LIGHT! BUT...I DIDN'T THINK EVEN A MINIATURE-A-BOMB'D BE ABLE TO KAYO HER!

IT DIDN'T, JOSH! BUT MY BUILT-IN SENSORS ARE PICKING UP SOMETHING THAT PROBABLY CAN... AND DID! RADIATION, FRIEND --

-- A POWERFUL--AND UNKNOWN KIND THAT SEEMS TO BE POISONING HER!

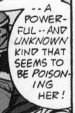

NEXT: A SICK SUPERGIRL V.S MATRIX-PRIME! "RADIATION FEVER" ON SALE MAY 19! IT'S A DATE!

Cover by **Ed Hannigan** & **Dick Giordano**

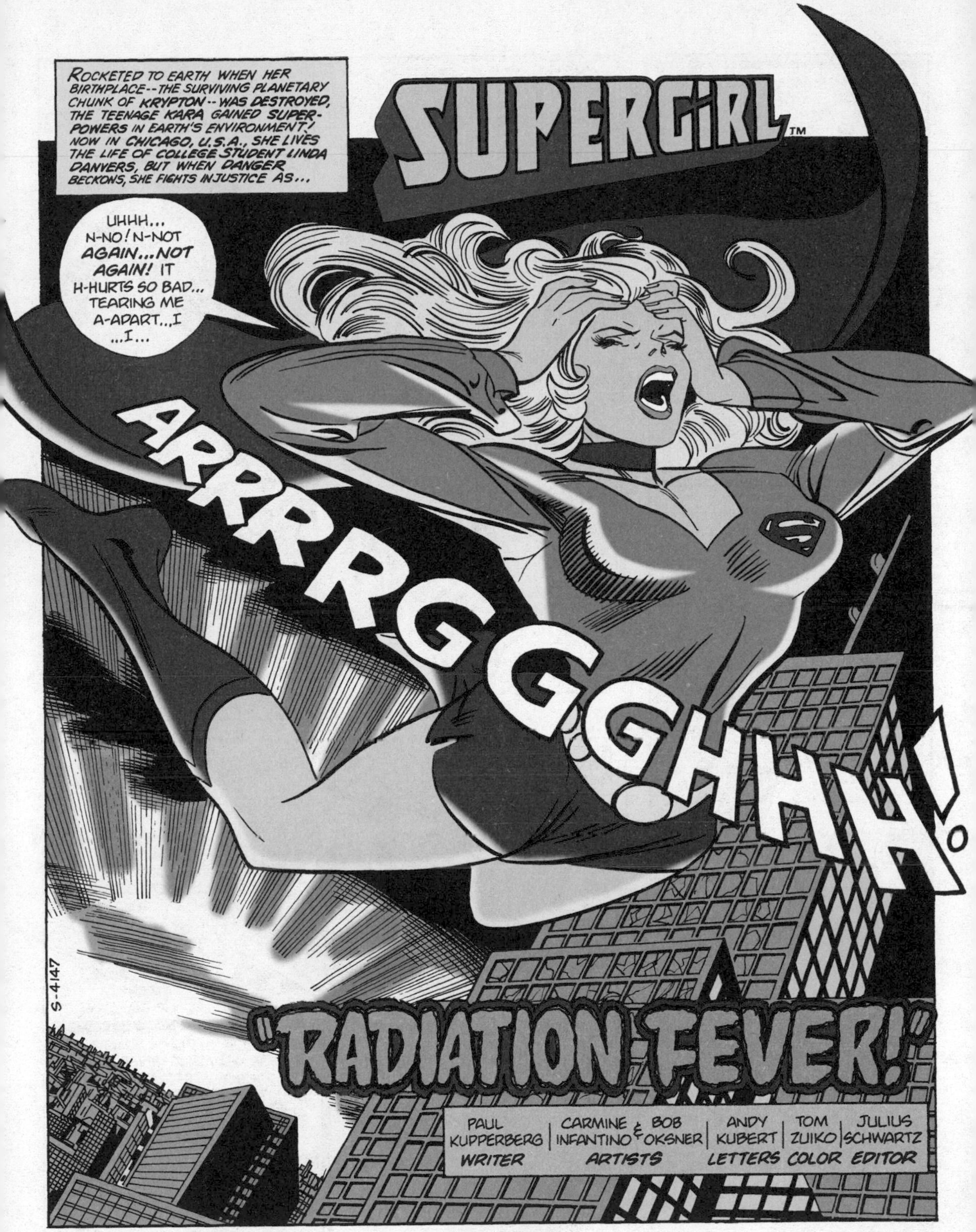

ROCKETED TO EARTH WHEN HER BIRTHPLACE--THE SURVIVING PLANETARY CHUNK OF KRYPTON--WAS DESTROYED, THE TEENAGE KARA GAINED SUPER-POWERS IN EARTH'S ENVIRONMENT! NOW IN CHICAGO, U.S.A., SHE LIVES THE LIFE OF COLLEGE STUDENT LINDA DANVERS, BUT WHEN DANGER BECKONS, SHE FIGHTS INJUSTICE AS...
SUPERGIRL™
UHHH... N-NO! N-NOT AGAIN...NOT AGAIN! IT H-HURTS SO BAD... TEARING ME A-APART...I ...I...
ARRRRGGGHHH!
"RADIATION FEVER!"
PAUL KUPPERBERG WRITER
CARMINE INFANTINO & BOB OKSNER ARTISTS
ANDY KUBERT LETTERS
TOM ZUIKO COLOR
JULIUS SCHWARTZ EDITOR
S-4147

THE AIR FOR *MILES* AROUND RE-VERBERATES WITH THE SOUNDS OF HER *AGONY*--*SHATTERING* WINDOWS...TRIPPING SENSITIVE ALARM DEVICES...

AT THE MOMENT, THOUGH, *THAT'S* THE *LEAST* OF HER WORRIES!

AND WITHOUT EVEN REALIZING IT HAS HAPPENED, THE MAID OF STEEL MAKES SUDDEN, *JARRING* CONTACT WITH THE GROUND...

THWOOPF!

SHE IS *UNCONSCIOUS* LONG BEFORE THAT HAPPENS.

SOUNDED LIKE SOMEONE DROPPED A *BOMB!* YOU PEOPLE STAY BACK TILL I SEE WHAT HIT!

OFFICER MARTIN APPROACHES *CAUTIOUSLY,* EXPECTING TO FIND THE *WORST* IMBEDDED IN ADAMS STREET--

THE WORLD STARTS TO *BLUR* AROUND HER, SHIFTING IN AND OUT OF FOCUS...

PAIN TEARS THROUGH EVERY FIBER OF HER BEING...

HER BODY IS *AFLAME* WITH FEVER...

THAT'S *EXACTLY* WHAT HE GETS!

SUPERGIRL...!?

DISPATCH! THIS'S MARTIN ON ADAMS AND THE TOWER... GET AN AM-BULANCE HERE ON THE *DOUBLE!* *SOME-THING'S* KAYOED SUPERGIRL--

--AND FROM THE LOOK OF HER, I HOPE TO HEAVEN *I* NEVER HAVE TO TANGLE WITH *WHATEVER* IT WAS THAT DID IT!

2

THE CHICAGO MEDICAL CENTER:

BWEE WOOPEE WOOPEE

SCREEECCHH!

GIVE ME A READING OF HER *VITALS!*

GET HER UPSTAIRS ...*STAT!*

I'M NOT GETTING ANY READINGS THAT MAKE *SENSE!*

SHE'S STOPPED *BREATHING,* DOCTOR!

LET'S GET HER ON THE RESPIRATOR!

WHAT'S HER *HEART?*

I...I CAN'T *TELL,* DOCTOR.

OKAY, *SHOCK* 'ER!

YEAH...BUT HOW MUCH *VOLTAGE* DO WE USE FOR HER?

HOW SHOULD I KNOW? THEY DIDN'T GIVE A COURSE IN *KRYPTONIAN BIOLOGY* AT MED SCHOOL!

GOOD LORD! HER TEMPERATURE...IT *BLEW* OUT THE THERMOMETER!

SHE'S *BURNIN'* UP! MUST BE 120° AT *LEAST...!*

SHE OUGHTTA BE *DEAD* WITH A TEMP LIKE THAT--!

OUR INSTRUMENTS AREN'T *GEARED* TO *THIS* KIND OF PATIENT, NURSE. FOR ALL WE KNOW, SHE *IS* DEAD!

3

SHE ISN'T.

--AND *TRIES* TO CRY OUT, TO REASSURE THEM OF THE LIFE THAT STILL SPARKS WITHIN HER...

BUT SHE'S AS *CLOSE* TO IT AS ANY BEING CAN COME AND STILL BE CONSIDERED AMONG THE *LIVING*. INDEED, SOMEWHERE IN THE DEEPEST RECESSES OF HER MIND, SHE *HEARS* THE EXCHANGE BETWEEN DOCTOR AND NURSE--

BUT SHE CAN'T. ALL SHE CAN DO IS *REMEMBER* THE EVENTS THAT LED UP TO THIS, BEGINNING THAT MORNING AT LAKE SHORE UNIVERSITY AND HER BATTLE WITH *REACTRON*.

REMEMBER HOW, ON THE *VERGE* OF BRINGING ABOUT *NUCLEAR* DESTRUCTION TO THE LAKEFRONT COLLEGE, SHE *TRAPPED* THE RADIOACTIVE MAN IN A *SUPER-SPEED* VORTEX--

--CONTAINING THE AWESOME RELEASE OF ENERGY, SENDING IT SHOOTING *HARMLESSLY* INTO SPACE...

THAAMHOOOOOOOMMM!

CHICAGO WAS *SAVED* FROM THE EFFECTS OF ATOMIC RADIATION.

SUPERGIRL WASN'T SO LUCKY!

SHE WASN'T ALONE, EITHER. THE SUPERBEINGS WHO MAKE UP THE *NEW DOOM PATROL* WERE ON HAND--

--BUT SHE DIDN'T HEED THEIR WARNINGS...

DON'T BE *SILLY!* HAVEN'T YOU HEARD THAT WE KRYPTONIANS ARE *IMMUNE* TO THAT SORT OF THING?

WHOA! TAKE IT *EASY*, KID! MY SENSORS ARE GOING *WILD* WITH READINGS OF *RADIATION*... ALL COMIN' OFF 'A *YOU!*

4

TELL ME *ANOTHER* ONE, WHY DON'TCHA? YOU'RE *HURTIN'!* REACTRON *DID* SOME-THIN' TO YOU!

I *APPRECIATE* YOUR CONCERN... BUT I'M FINE, REALLY, I...I'M...

..."*FINE!*

HEY! CALM *DOWN* THERE, SUPERGIRL! YOU SHOULDN'T BE JUMPING AROUND! YOU'RE ONE *SICK* LADY!

UHHH... WH-WHERE AM I? THE HOSPITAL--?

≈*WHEW!*≈ THAT WAS *SOME* SPILL I TOOK, DOC. BUT I'M ALL RIGHT, HONEST!

UH-*HUH!* LIKE HECK YOU ARE, SUPER-GIRL. MY BUSINESS IS *SICK PEOPLE*, AND YOU'RE ONE OF 'EM IF I'VE EVER SEEN ONE!

LOOK, I'VE JUST HAD A *TOUGH* EN-COUNTER WITH A WALKING, TALKING, HUMAN NUCLEAR REACTOR...IT JUST THREW ME FOR A LOOP IS ALL.

RADIATION, HUH? MAYBE YOU OUGHT TO SEE AN EXPERT IN...

FORGET IT, DOCTOR. IN CASE YOU HAVEN'T *HEARD*, MY BIOLOGY'S A BIT *DIFFERENT* THAN ...THAN...OOHH...

SURE, YOU'RE JUST THE *PIC-TURE* OF HEALTH! YOU CAN HARDLY STAND UP, LET ALONE...

P-PLEASE, DOCTOR. TH-THERE'S N-NOTHING *YOU* CAN DO FOR ME! I J-JUST NEED TO *REST*...

SUPER-GIRL! HOLD IT RIGHT *THERE--!*

THE NAME'S *PETERS*, SUPER-GIRL...*LT. PETERS* OF THE CHICAGO P.D.

SOUNDS LIKE A TELEVISION SERIES TO ME!

HEY, YOU'RE *REAL* FUNNY! TRY LAUGHING *THIS* OFF, SWEET-HEART...MY BOSS GOT IT IN HIS HEAD TO SLAP YOU WITH A CHARGE OF *RECKLESS ENDANGERMENT* FOR THAT STUNT YOU PULLED BEFORE!

⑤

Y-YOU'RE **KIDDING!**

KIDDING? SURE, WE JUST LOVE PEOPLE DROPPING OUT OF THE AIR LIKE BIG ROCKS AND MAKING **HOLES** IN THE SIDEWALKS **OR** THE PEOPLE WALKING ON 'EM!

NOW, SEEING WHAT YOU'VE BEEN DOING FOR THE CITY THESE LAST FEW WEEKS, I TALKED MY CAPTAIN INTO DROPPING THE IDEA--

--BUT HE'S **STILL** NOT THRILLED WITH HAVING CAPED DO-GOODERS FLYING AROUND MAKING **TROUBLE!** AND IF YOU WANT TO KNOW THE **TRUTH**... NEITHER AM I!

GEE, YOU'RE ALL **HEART,** LIEUTENANT! LISTEN, NEXT TIME A TEN-FOOT ROBOT OR A SUPER-POWERED BAD GUY STARTS TEARING UP THE PLACE, I'LL GIVE YOU AND YOUR CAPTAIN A CALL, OKAY?

NOW, IF YOU'LL **EXCUSE** ME...

JUST BE **COOL,** LADY. WE'RE GONNA BE **WATCHING** YOU!

THE **NERVE** OF THAT GUY! I SAVE HALF OF CHICAGO FROM BECOMING ANOTHER **HIROSHIMA,** AND **HE** THREATENS TO HAVE ME **BUSTED!**

IF I DIDN'T FEEL SO MESSED UP RIGHT NOW, I'D HAVE DONE SOME RECKLESS ENDANGERING ON HIS...HIS...?WHEW? **FORGET** THE HOSTILITY ...JUST TRYING TO **FLY'S** HARD ENOUGH!

BUT FLY SHE DOES, AT LEAST AS FAR AS 1537 WEST FARGO AVENUE IN THE CITY'S ROGER'S PARK SECTION, TO THE HOME OF...

DANVERS! HEY, YOU **IN** THERE, LINDA?

C'MON, KIDDO, IT'S **DRAFTY** OUT HERE! OPEN UP!

?GROAN? I **MUST** BE IN **BAD** SHAPE--! I ALMOST SLEPT THROUGH **THAT** RACKET!

HOLD YOUR **HORSES!** I'M COMING!

WHAT TOOK YOU SO LONG? I DIDN'T SEE YOU IN CLASSES TODAY, SO I THOUGHT I'D STOP BY.

SAY, WHAT'S THE MATTER WITH **YOU,** LIN? YOU LOOK LIKE SOMETHING THE CAT DRAGGED IN!

MUST'VE BEEN AN AWFUL **BIG** CAT DOIN' THE DRAGGING! HIYA, GORGEOUS!

6

HI, GUYS. OH, IT'S NOTHING. JUST A COLD, I GUESS.

COLD MY *FOOT!* LOOKS MORE LIKE *PNEUMONIA!* YOU SEEN A DOCTOR YET?

MMMM? OH, YEAH. HE TOLD ME TO REST, DRINK PLENTY OF FLUIDS, ALL THAT STUFF.

SOUNDS LIKE THE KIND OF DOCTOR THAT'D PRE-SCRIBE *ASPIRIN* FOR A BROKEN LEG! THIS'S MORE'N A *COLD* YOU'VE GOT, SWEETIE!

APPEARS OUR LIN'S BEEN RUN-NING HERSELF *RAGGED,* HUH, JOHNNY?

≈WHEW!≈ HAVE YOU GOT ONE HECK OF A *TEMPER-ATURE!*

C'MON, JOAN, STOP PLAYING *MOTHER HEN!* LOOK-- I PLAN ON JUST SITTING HERE WITH SOME CHICKEN SOUP AND VEGING OUT IN FRONT OF THE TUBE TILL I'M BETTER, OKAY?

IN *OTHER* WORDS, YOU VANT TO BE *ALONE,* HUH? HO-KAY, KIDDO, BUT IF YOU NEED ANYTHING, I'M RIGHT UPSTAIRS.

WAITAMINNIT! DON'TCHA WANT ME TO STICK AROUND AND *SOOTHE* YOUR FEVERED BROW...?

SHE *SAID* BYE-BYE, CASANOVA! LET'S *SPLIT!*

WOOF! THEY *MEAN* WELL... BUT I THOUGHT THEY'D *NEVER* LEAVE. I CAN BARELY *SEE* STRAIGHT! REACTRON MUST'VE DONE SOME NUMBER ON ME TO MAKE ME FEEL *THIS* WAY!

...AND A SPOKESMAN AT THE CHICAGO MEDICAL CENTER HAS *CONFIRMED* THAT SUPER-GIRL WAS BROUGHT TO THE *EMER-GENCY* WARD THIS AFTER-NOON--

--ALTHOUGH THEY DECLINE TO SAY *WHAT* SHE WAS BEING TREATED FOR. HOWEVER, SOURCES AT THE HOSPITAL *DO* TELL US THAT SHE WAS IN "A *BAD* WAY," EVEN THOUGH SHE LATER CHECKED HERSELF OUT!

WELL, WELL! LOOK WHO MADE THE SIX P.M. NEWS!

RUMOR HAS IT SHE'S SUFFERING FROM *RADIA-TION* POISONING AS A RESULT OF AN EARLIER BATTLE WITH...

SIX O'CLOCK-!?

I ALMOST *FORGOT!* I'VE GOT A *DATE* TONIGHT--!

7

...AND A *FIRST* DATE, AT THAT! THAT'D BE A *GREAT* WAY TO START OFF WITH PHILIP DECKER--BEING *SICK!* MAYBE I DON'T FEEL UP TO LEAP-ING TALL BUILDINGS IN A SINGLE BOUND--

--BUT I'M *SURE* I CAN GET IT TOGETHER ENOUGH FOR DINNER AND A CONCERT!

SO THE INCIDENT REMAINS SHROUDED IN *MYSTERY.*

HAS CHICAGO'S NEW RESIDENT SUPER-HERO BEEN *STRICKEN* WITH SOME FATAL SICKNESS...OR ARE THE WAYS OF SUCH PEOPLE SO *DIFFERENT* THAN OURS THAT WE'RE *NEVER* TO KNOW?

HOW VERY *INTER-ESTING!*

SUPERGIRL HAS SHOWN HERSELF TO BE QUITE THE *NUI-SANCE* TO MY OPERA-TIONS SINCE HER ARRIVAL ON THE SCENE. PERHAPS *NOW* IS THE TIME TO *END* THAT BIT OF ANNOYANCE--

--WHILE WORKING THE SITUATION VERY MUCH TO MY ADVANTAGE!

PROFESSOR *DRAKE!*

AH YES, I AM, ER...HERE, *CHAIRMAN!* HOW CAN I BE OF, UMM..., SERVICE TO YOU?

YOUR *PROJECT-REDUNDANT,* DRAKE. IT IS READY FOR IMPLEMENTA-TION?

YES, SIR. ALL READY!

VERY GOOD. THEN LET US *PRE-PARE* FOR YOUR FIRST *SUBJECT* OF THE PROJECT!

8

AND SO, A SHORT WHILE LATER...

RIGHT ON *TIME*, LINDA... ALTHOUGH I MUST SAY, THIS SIGHT WOULD'VE BEEN *WORTH* WAITING FOR!

WHY, THANK YOU! I'VE BEEN SAVING IT FOR A SPECIAL OCCASION LIKE THIS!

I GUESS HAVING DINNER WITH A *WORLD-FAMOUS* SYMPHONY ORCHESTRA CONDUCTOR'S ISN'T JUST *ROUTINE* WITH YOU?

LISTEN, IF I CAN'T GET A DATE WITH BERNSTEIN AND WILLIAMS, I CAN SETTLE FOR *YOU!*

HMMM. I'M GOING TO HAVE TO *WATCH* MYSELF AROUND YOU, MS. DANVERS! YOUR *NOT* JUST AN *AVERAGE* COLLEGE STUDENT, ARE YOU?

WELL, I LIKE TO *THINK* I'M NOT. THEN AGAIN, PHILIP DECKER'S NOT EXACTLY THE GUY I'D ENVISION AS THE ONE THEY'D HAND OVER THE REIGNS OF THE CHICAGO SYMPHONY TO, EITHER!

YOU MEAN, "HOW'D SOMEONE THAT *YOUNG* AND THAT *AWESOMELY HIP* EVER GET SO *TALENTED,*" HUH?

WELL, IT'S A *LONG* STORY, LADY... AND YOU'RE GONNA HEAR EVERY *BIT* OF IT! HECK, YOU DIDN'T THINK THIS DINNER WAS FOR *FREE*, DID YOU?

LINDA DANVERS FORCES HERSELF TO LAUGH, IN SPITE OF THE DULL ACHE SHE FEELS THROUGHOUT HER BODY.

SHE *WANTS* TO ENJOY THIS MAN, THIS NIGHT. SHE *CAN'T.*

SOUTH SHORE DRIVE

AND AS THE EVENING WEARS ON, THE PAIN *INCREASES*--AND THE MAID OF MIGHT BEGINS TO *WORRY!*

...AND THAT'S WHEN I GOT TAPPED TO LEAD THE BALTIMORE SYMPHONY. IT WASN'T WHAT YOU CALL ONE OF THE "A" ORCHESTRAS AT THE TIME, BUT I FIGURED WITH WORK, IT...

HEY! YOU STILL *WITH* ME, LINDA?

I...I'M SORRY, PHILIP. I GUESS I SHOULDN'T HAVE COME OUT TONIGHT. I'M REALLY NOT *WELL*...

I... SUPPOSE I DIDN'T WANT TO *MISS* OUR DATE...

YEAH, WOW, I CAN *SEE* THAT. WHY DIDN'T YOU SAY SOMETHING *BEFORE?*

9

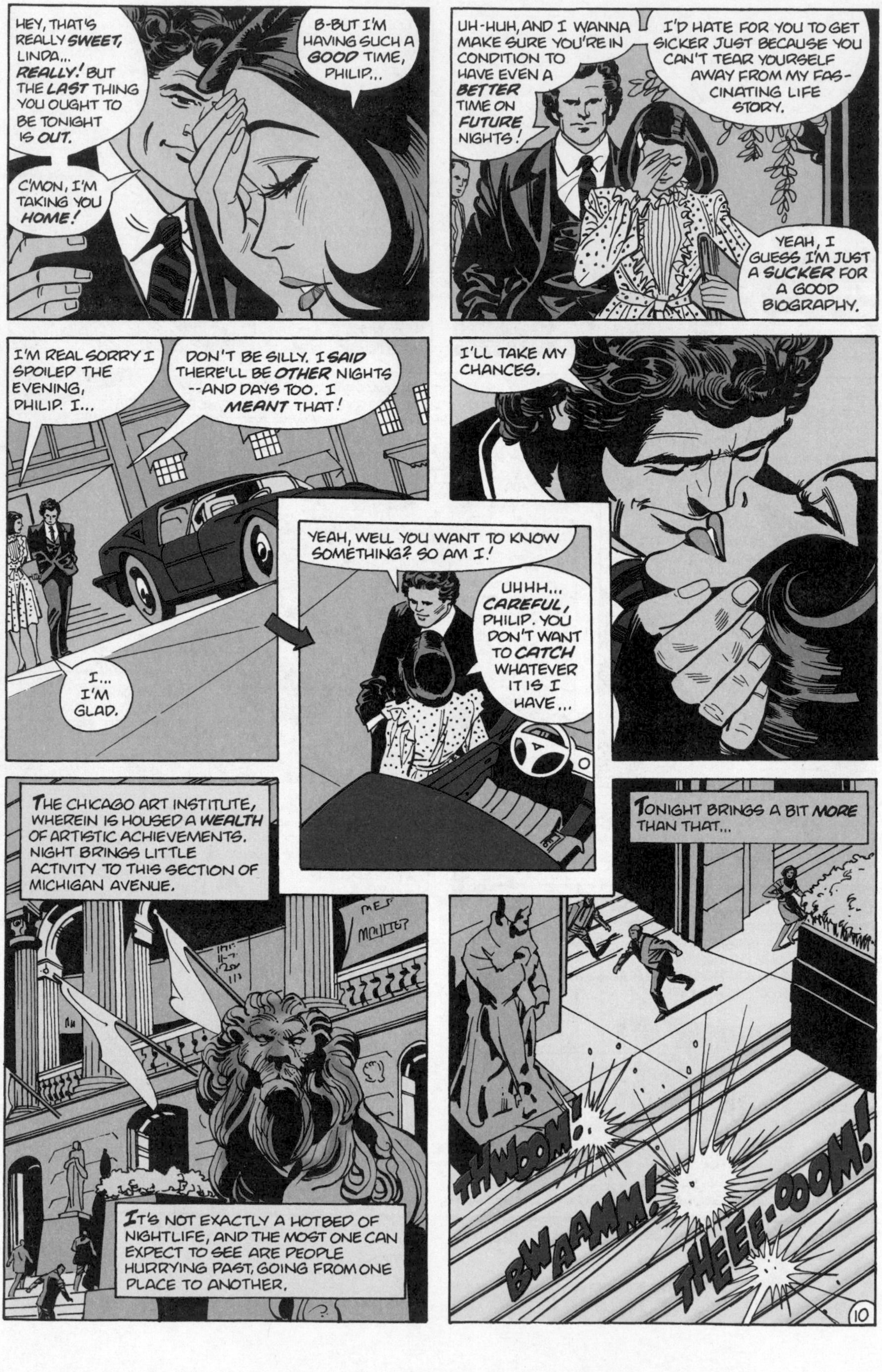
HEY, THAT'S REALLY SWEET, LINDA... REALLY! BUT THE LAST THING YOU OUGHT TO BE TONIGHT IS OUT.
B-BUT I'M HAVING SUCH A GOOD TIME, PHILIP...
C'MON, I'M TAKING YOU HOME!
UH-HUH, AND I WANNA MAKE SURE YOU'RE IN CONDITION TO HAVE EVEN A BETTER TIME ON FUTURE NIGHTS!
I'D HATE FOR YOU TO GET SICKER JUST BECAUSE YOU CAN'T TEAR YOURSELF AWAY FROM MY FASCINATING LIFE STORY.
YEAH, I GUESS I'M JUST A SUCKER FOR A GOOD BIOGRAPHY.
I'M REAL SORRY I SPOILED THE EVENING, PHILIP. I...
DON'T BE SILLY. I SAID THERE'LL BE OTHER NIGHTS --AND DAYS TOO. I MEANT THAT!
I... I'M GLAD.
YEAH, WELL YOU WANT TO KNOW SOMETHING? SO AM I!
UHHH... CAREFUL, PHILIP. YOU DON'T WANT TO CATCH WHATEVER IT IS I HAVE...
I'LL TAKE MY CHANCES.
THE CHICAGO ART INSTITUTE, WHEREIN IS HOUSED A WEALTH OF ARTISTIC ACHIEVEMENTS. NIGHT BRINGS LITTLE ACTIVITY TO THIS SECTION OF MICHIGAN AVENUE.
IT'S NOT EXACTLY A HOTBED OF NIGHTLIFE, AND THE MOST ONE CAN EXPECT TO SEE ARE PEOPLE HURRYING PAST, GOING FROM ONE PLACE TO ANOTHER.
TONIGHT BRINGS A BIT MORE THAN THAT...
THWOOM!
BWAAMM!
THEEE-OOOM!

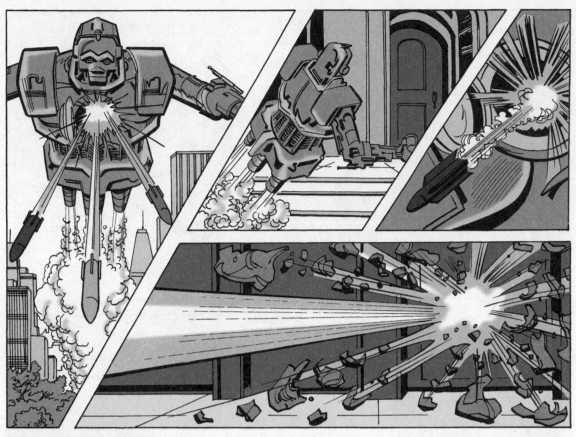

THANKS FOR EVERYTHING, PHILIP. I'LL TALK TO YOU TOMORROW, OKAY?

COUNT ON IT, LINDA! YOU *SURE* YOU DON'T NEED HELP GETTING UPSTAIRS?

POSITIVE. BESIDES FINDING A PARKING SPOT AROUND HERE AT THIS HOUR'S ABOUT AS EASY AS CLIMBING THE HIMALAYAS IN SANDALS!

G'NIGHT THEN, MA'AM. AND GET PLENTY OF *REST,* RIGHT?

THAT'S ABOUT *ALL* I'VE GOT THE STRENGTH FOR *ANYWAY!*

11

*Supergirl tangled with Matrix-Prime in issues #6 & 7 - Julie

12

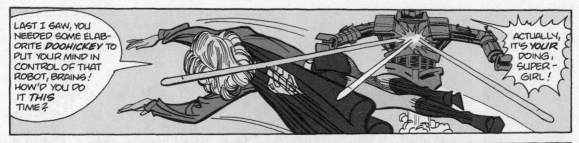

LAST I SAW, YOU NEEDED SOME ELABORITE *DOOHICKEY* TO PUT YOUR MIND IN CONTROL OF THAT ROBOT, BRAINS! HOW'D YOU DO IT *THIS* TIME?

ACTUALLY, IT'S *YOUR* DOING, SUPERGIRL!

WHEN YOU ATTEMPTED TO *DESTROY* MATRIX-PRIME WHILE MY PERSONA WAS IN CONTROL, YOU CAUSED SOME MANNER OF *FEEDBACK* BETWEEN MY MIND AND MATRIX'S--

THWAK

UNNNHHH!

--IN EFFECT *FUSING* OUR CONSCIOUSNESSES INTO *ONE!* THUS, I WAS ABLE TO *TELEPATHICALLY* ACTIVATE OUR INTERNAL SELF-REPAIR FUNCTIONS--

--AND *SUMMON* THIS BODY TO...AH, *RELEASE* ME FROM CUSTODY!

UGH! W-WONDERFUL! ALL OF A S-SUDDEN, I FEEL D-*DIZZY*...ANOTHER OF THOSE *ATTACKS...*

OF COURSE, I CHOSE TO ONCE AGAIN ALLY MYSELF WITH THE *COMMITTEE*--AND *THAT,* SUPERGIRL, IS YOUR SAD MISFORTUNE!

FEVERISH ...CAN'T SEE STRAIGHT ...*PAIN...!*

DRONE MISSILES... GOTTA...*AVOID* THEM...!

SHE *TRIES,* SUPERGIRL DOES, BUT DESPITE HER BEST EFFORT--

--IT'S JUST NOT *ENOUGH.*

WOOOOOOOOM

13

TIME-SHIFT:

SHE DOESN'T KNOW HOW *LONG* SHE'S BEEN UNCONSCIOUS.

SHE DOESN'T *CARE.*

THE DARKNESS HAS BROUGHT RESPITE FROM THE PAIN. A RELEASE FROM NEAR UNBEARABLE AGONY.

BESIDES--

--SUPERGIRL *KNOWS* SHE'S IN FOR TROUBLE WHENEVER SHE WAKES UP!

HUH--? WHERE...?!

HOW ARE YOU SUPER-GIRL? I'VE BEEN *WONDERING* WHEN YOU'D *RETURN,* AH...AS IT WERE!

I...I'M BACK...AND NOT IN TH--THE LEAST BIT *HAPPY,* EITHER...!

NOW, NOW, MY DEAR. NEITHER ARE YOU, AHHH...WELL. DON'T STRAIN YOURSELF. YOU'RE, ER...NOT GOING ANY- WHERE.

H--HE'S RIGHT...! I FEEL WEAK AS A K-KITTEN...!

YES, YOU, ER...SEE, I'VE RUN SOME *TESTS* ON YOU, MY DEAR AND, AHHH...FOUND THAT YOU'RE SUFFERING FROM SOME FORM OF, AHH... *RADIATION* POISONING.

QUITE *SURPRISING,* ACTUALLY.

14

I'D ALWAYS, AH... ASSUMED YOU WERE *INVULNERABLE* TO SUCH ENERGIES. APPARENTLY OUR FRIEND *REACTRON* WAS ABLE TO GENERATE SOME, ER... *NEW* TYPE OF RADIATION CAPABLE OF AFFECTING EVEN *YOU.*

WELL, ER... BE THAT AS IT MAY, THE *UP-SHOT* IS THAT FOR THE MOMENT, AT LEAST, YOU ARE QUITE *POWER-LESS*--

--RENDERING YOU MOST, ER... VULNER-ABLE TO WHAT WE'VE IN MIND FOR YOU, NOW, AHH... JUST *RELAX.* THIS SHAN'T HURT.

WH-WHAT ARE YOU...?

AHHH, YOU WISH TO KNOW MY ER... *INTEN-TIONS?* OF COURSE, DEAR WOMAN.

DESPITE YOUR CURRENT, AHH... ILLNESS, YOU ARE *STILL* A MOST *REMARKABLE* HUMAN BEING. *IMAGINE* THE POWER ONE WOULD WIELD WITH AN EN-TIRE *ARMY* OF SUCH BEINGS AT HIS DISPOSAL, HMM?

YOU MEAN... *CLONING*--?!

UMMM... SOMETHING *LIKE* THAT, BUT NOT *QUITE.* AHH, YOU SEE, *TRUE* CLONING REQUIRES THAT THE REPLICATED CELLS BE NURTURED, BIRTHED AND *RAISED* AS WERE THE PAR-ENT CELLS.

THAT TAKES FAR *TOO* LONG. NO, WITH, ER... *MY* PROCESS, THE REPLI-CATION IS NEAR *INSTANTAN-EOUS*--

--RESULTING IN *PERFECT,* AHH... DUPLICATES OF THE HOST BEING. THE, ER... *TRICK'S IN THE SOLUTION*-- MORE OF A *LIQUID* COMPUTER, ACTUALLY--

--WHICH *READS* THE *DNA CODE* OF THE SUBJECT AND *DU-PLICATES* IT FROM THE RAW ORGANIC MATERIALS FOUND IN THE SECOND VAT.

I'M REALLY, ER... QUITE *PROUD* OF MY ACCOMP-LISHMENT. IT TAKES ONLY *SECONDS* TO CREATE AS MANY AS, AHHH... HALF A DOZEN DUPLICATES.

OF, ER... COURSE, I WOULD BE MOST *REMISS* IF I WERE TO CLAIM MY PRO-CESS TO BE, AHH... PERFECT. IT HAS ITS *SLIGHT* DRAWBACKS.

15

FOR ONE THING, WHILE THE DUPLICATES POSSESS, AHH... *IDENTICAL* PROPERTIES TO THE ORIGINAL, THEY TEND TO BE ON A SLIGHTLY, ER...*SMALLER* SCALE...

BUT THAT'S NOT THE, UHHH... *WORST* OF IT, I'M AFRAID.

INDEED NOT. NO, FOR, AH... ONCE THE COMPUTER HAS PUT THE SUBJECTS THROUGH THEIR, UHH... EXAMINATIONS, THEY HAVE AN UNFORTUNATE TENDENCY--

--TO, ER.... DIE.

NEXT ISSUE: *SUPERGIRL* VERSUS HER *SIX DUPLICATES* IN **"A DARK AND FROZEN PURGATORY!"** ON SALE JUNE 16! IT'S A *DATE!*

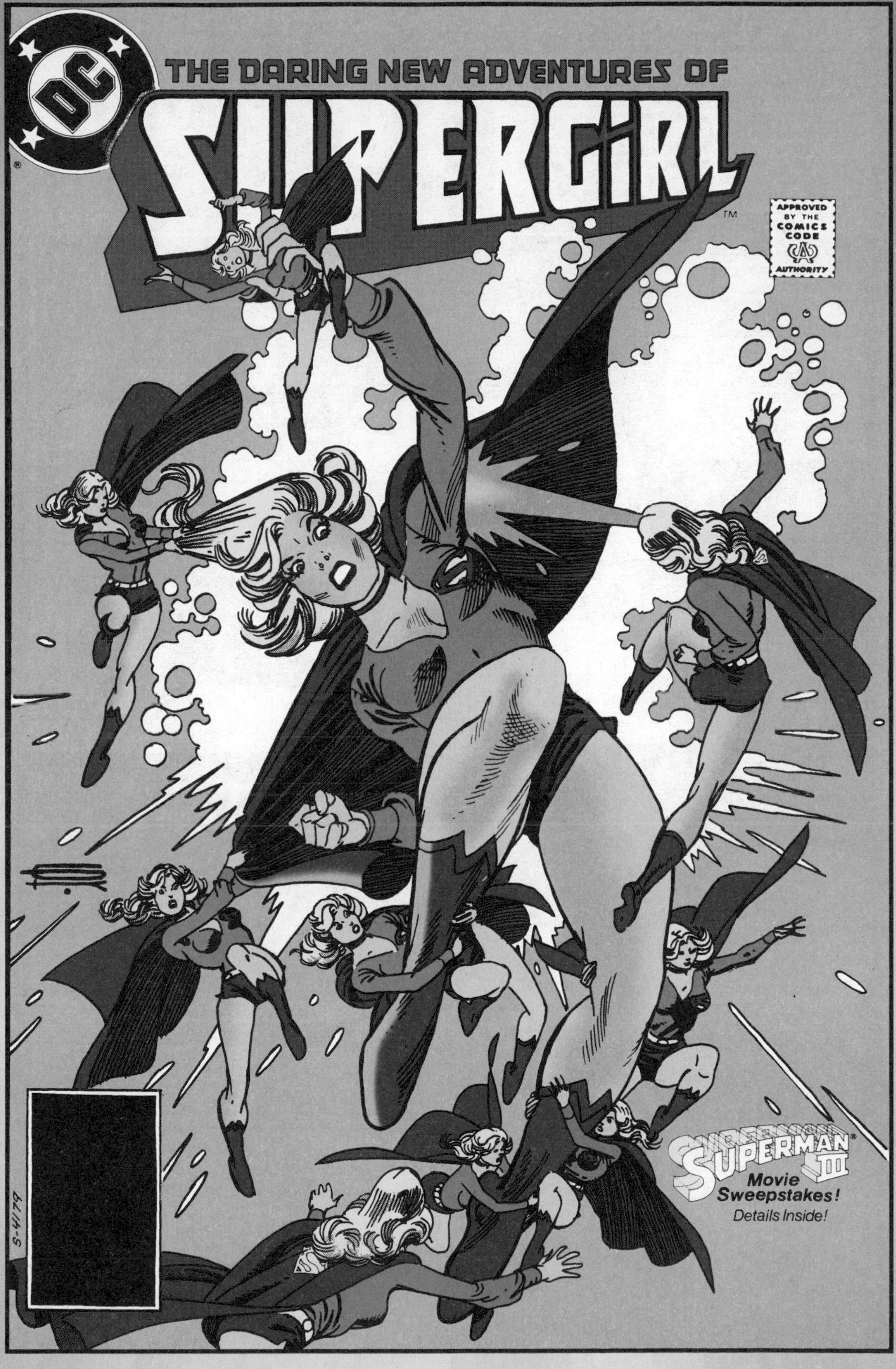
THE DARING NEW ADVENTURES OF
SUPERGIRL
APPROVED BY THE COMICS CODE AUTHORITY
SUPERMAN III
Movie Sweepstakes!
Details Inside!

Cover by **Gil Kane**

ROCKETED TO EARTH WHEN HER BIRTHPLACE--THE SURVIVING PLANETARY CHUNK OF *KRYPTON*--WAS DESTROYED, THE TEENAGE *KARA* GAINED SUPER-POWERS IN EARTH'S ENVIRONMENT! NOW IN *CHICAGO, U.S.A.*, SHE LIVES THE LIFE OF COLLEGE STUDENT *LINDA DANVERS*, BUT WHEN DANGER BECKONS, SHE FIGHTS INJUSTICE AS...

SUPERGIRL™

SOMEWHERE IN CHICAGO:

A COOL, METALLIC DRYNESS FILLS THIS CHAMBER, SHROUDED BENEATH THE SOFT, PERSISTENT HUM OF COMPLEX ELECTRONICS.

CLICK... WHIRRR... CLICK... WHRRR-CL'C

THIS IS THE HEAD-QUARTERS OF THE ORGANIZATION KNOWN ONLY AS THE *COUNCIL*. IT'S ALSO THE PLACE WHERE SUPERGIRL *DIED!*

YOU ARE *CERTAIN*, PROFESSOR DRAKE? THERE CAN BE NO ROOM FOR *ERROR!*

OH, ER...YES, CHAIRMAN. SEE FOR YOURSELF. ACCORDING TO EVERY, AHH.... TEST I'VE CONDUCTED, SUPERGIRL HAS MOST DECIDEDLY, ER.... *DECEASED!*

A DARK and FROZEN PURGATORY!

S-4148

PAUL KUPPERBERG, *WRITER* ★ CARMINE INFANTINO, ★ BOB OKSNER, ★ MILT SNAPINN, *LETTERER* *ARTISTS* TOM ZIUKO, *COLORIST* ★ JULIUS SCHWARTZ, *EDITOR*

OF COURSE, SIR, SHE DIDN'T DIE IN *VAIN*, AHH...AT LEAST NOT AS FAR AS *WE* ARE CONCERNED, HMMM? FROM ALL, ER...INDICATIONS, *PROJECT REDUNDANT* WAS A SUCCESS!

AS YOU SEE, CHAIRMAN, BEFORE THE PROCESS, ER...KILLED HER, I WAS ABLE TO CREATE SIX *NEAR-PERFECT DUPLICATES* OF SUPERGIRL--

--ALL OF WHICH ARE NOW AWAITING *ACTIVATION!*

"NEAR-PERFECT", PROFESSOR? YOU SAID YOUR CLONING PROCESS WAS *FAULTLESS* IN ITS ABILITY TO REPLICATE HUMANS!

OH, IT *IS*, SIR...EXCEPT FOR, ER...*ONE TINY DETAIL.* YOU SEE, DUE TO CERTAIN, AH...*LIMITATIONS* IN AVAILABLE MATERIALS--

--I'M ONLY ABLE TO REPRODUCE THEM AT, ER...APPROXIMATELY *ONE-FIFTH* THE SIZE OF THE ORIGINAL.

WHAT!? YOU'RE NOT *SERIOUS*, DRAKE! WHAT *USE* COULD WE POSSIBLY *HAVE* FOR 12-INCH SUPERGIRLS?

I...I, AH...*ASSURE* YOU, SIR...TH-THE REPLICANTS POSSESS EVERY *BIT* OF POWER CONTAINED IN THE, ER...*ORIGINAL.*

INDEED, CONSIDERING, AH...SUPERGIRL'S CONDITION WHEN I, ER...GOT HER--WEAKENED BY SEVERE, ER...*RADIATION-POISONING*, THESE CLONES ARE, AH...*BETTER* TH...,

THAT'S *NOT* THE *POINT*, YOU *FOOL!*

I'M FULLY AWARE THAT *REACTRON* SOMEHOW MANAGED TO POISON HER WITH RADIATION, THUS ENABLING US ULTIMATELY TO *CAPTURE* HER--

--BUT I HAD EXPECTED *RESULTS* FROM YOU, DRAKE! I AM *MOST* DISAPPOINTED!

2

"I SHOULD DISLIKE MOST INTENSELY FINDING OF FURTHER FAILURES ON YOUR PART."

SILENCE.

THERE'S ALMOST A SOUND TO SILENCE-- A DEEP, EERIE ROAR OF THE BODY'S OWN FUNCTIONS, HEARD AS AN INTERNAL NOISE.

THERE IS NO SUCH NOISE HERE.

IT'S VERY STILL-- DEATHLY SO, MORE LIKE A MORTUARY THAN A PLACE OF SCIENTIFIC INQUIRY.

AT THE MOMENT, IT IS BOTH. THEY HAVE CONCLUDED SHE IS DEAD--

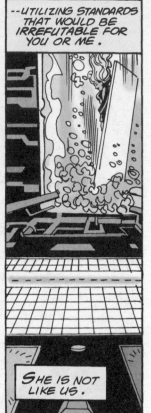

--UTILIZING STANDARDS THAT WOULD BE IRREFUTABLE FOR YOU OR ME.

SHE IS NOT LIKE US.

HER NAME IS SUPER-GIRL, NATIVE OF ARGO CITY, THE LAST SURVIVING CHUNK OF THE DEAD WORLD KRYPTON...POSSESSOR OF POWERS AND ABILITIES FAR BEYOND THOSE OF MORTAL BEINGS.

YET THAT DOES NOT MAKE HER BY DEFI-NITION IMMORTAL. AS WITH US, WHEN DEATH DOES COME, IT WILL BE FINAL.

IT'S ALL A MATTER OF KNOWING HOW TO ACCURATELY JUDGE THE CESSATION OF LIFE IN SUCH A BEING.

BEEP...

BEEP...

BEEP...

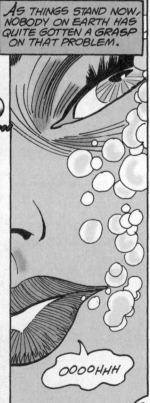

AS THINGS STAND NOW, NOBODY ON EARTH HAS QUITE GOTTEN A GRASP ON THAT PROBLEM.

OOOOHHH

3

OF COURSE, AS THE SIGNS WE INTERPRET AS LIFE BEGIN PULSATING AGAIN THROUGH THE MAID OF MIGHT'S BODY, THAT POINT BECOMES DECIDEDLY *MOOT* --

--BECAUSE IF SHE *DOESN'T* FREE HERSELF IN, SAY, THE NEXT *TEN SECONDS,* SHE *WILL* INDEED BE *DEAD* --

--BY *ANYONE'S* DEFINITION!

AND THEN THERE'S THE MATTER OF *FREEDOM* ITSELF, AS IT APPEARS TO BE A *RELATIVE* TERM ON ITS OWN.

FOR INSTANCE, THOUGH *SUPERGIRL'S* HANDS ARE NO LONGER BOUND, SHE IS FAR FROM BEING *FREE.*

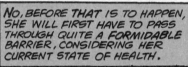

NO, *BEFORE* THAT IS TO HAPPEN, SHE WILL FIRST HAVE TO PASS THROUGH QUITE A FORMIDABLE *BARRIER,* CONSIDERING HER CURRENT STATE OF HEALTH.

BUT DEEP DOWN, THE YOUNG LADY NAMED *KARA* HAS ALWAYS HELD A *SECRET,* UNSPOKEN BELIEF....

IT'S NOT THE *POWERS* THAT MAKE THE *WOMAN* --

KRAAM!

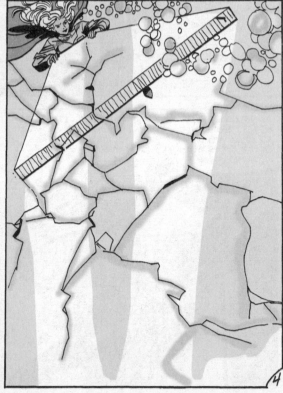

4

--IT'S THE WOMAN WITHIN!

SWARRKK!

;SPUTTER;

N-NOW...I KNOW...HOW A GOLDFISH FEELS...

...AND I DON'T LIKE IT... AT ALL!

I H-HURT ALL *OVER*...FEELS LIKE MY INSIDES ARE ON A ROLLER-COASTER RIDE. BEEN TRYING TO DENY IT, BUT FACTS ARE *FACTS*--

--I MAY BE A *SUPER* PERSON, BUT I'M *SICK*, NEVERTHELESS. ASIDE FROM MY BRIEF BOUT WITH *VIRUS X*-- WHICH SUPER-MAN EASILY CURED--I HAVEN'T BEEN REALLY *SICK* SINCE I LEFT ARGO CITY, YEARS AGO.

BUT REACTRON *ZAPPED* ME WITH *SOMETHING* I'VE NEVER BEEN ZAPPED WITH BEFORE--

--AND LIKE IT OR NOT, IT'S GOING TO *KILL* ME IF I DON'T DO SOME-THING..*FAST!*

;UNGH; R-REAL SMOOTH, KARA. HOW'RE YOU GONNA HELP YOURSELF WHEN *STANDING'S* A MAJOR EFFORT...?

THRWHAMP

5

WAZZAT? AIN'T SUPPOSED TO BE NOBODY IN THERE NOW!

NOBODY *AUTHORIZED*, Y'MEAN! WE BETTER CHECK IT OUT! THE CAP'N WOULD HAVE OUR BUTTS IF SOMEONE WAS MESSIN' AROUND WITH THE PROFESSOR'S STUFF!

AWRIGHT! LET'S JUST *HOLD* IT RIGHT *NOW* BEFORE WE....HEY! AIN'T THAT *SUPERGIRL*...?

WHAT *IS* THIS?! A *SOCIAL TEA?* LET'S BLAST HER!

THAT'S THE NAME, FRIEND. SORRY FOR MAKING SO MUCH NOISE--IN FACT, YOU DON'T KNOW JUST *HOW* SORRY!

÷OOFF!÷ I...I FELT THAT! THANK RAO I STILL HAVE MY *INVULNERABILITY*, OR I'D BE AUDITIONING FOR THE LEAD IN A *SWISS CHEESE* COMMERCIAL!

CHWRAAAM!

RAT-A-AT-TAT-A-TAT-TAT

MMMMHH....IT'S AN EFFORT JUST USING MY *HEAT VISION* ON THESE GOONS..., AND FRANKLY, I *HATE* IT!

YEEE--

--OUCH!

I CAN LIVE *WITHOUT* SUPER-POWERS, I SUPPOSE. LORD KNOWS I SURVIVED THE FIRST FIFTEEN YEARS OF MY LIFE AS A NORMAL KID AND CAN DO IT *AGAIN*--

--BUT THIS THING'S NOT JUST AFFECTING MY *POWERS!*

KRAK!

6

IT'S EATING ME UP INSIDE... BRINGING ON *BLACKOUTS*... LOWERING MY RESISTANCE TO ATTACK! DRAKE'S CLONING DEVICE *DIDN'T* KILL ME --

--BUT IT SURE CAME *CLOSE*... CLOSER THAN I WANT TO BE *AGAIN!*

TIME I MADE MYSELF *SCARCE* HERE --

KRAK!

--'CAUSE MUCH AS I WANT TO PUT THIS OPERATION OUT OF BUSINESS, IT'S NOT *WORTH* MY LIFE TO DO IT RIGHT NOW!

BUT I'LL BE *BACK*...

...RAO WILLING!

WITHIN SECONDS, THE ONLY EVIDENCE OF HER PRESENCE IS A SIZABLE HOLE WHERE THE CEILING USED TO BE --

--AND ONE IRATE "CHAIRMAN"!...

DEAD, PROF. DRAKE?!

THIS IS GETTING MOST *TEDIOUS!* EVERY TIME SUPERGIRL *SEEMS* TO BE IN OUR GRASP, SHE MANAGES TO *THWART* US! WHY IS THAT, PROFESSOR?

R-REALLY, SIR.... Y-YOU *CAN'T*, ER... BE SUGGESTING *I* AM TO BLAME FOR, AHH... THOSE *PAST* FAILURES...?

SIR, PLEASE ALLOW ME TO, ER...DEMONSTRATE A METHOD THAT WILL, ER...ALLOW FOR HER *RECAPTURE* --

7

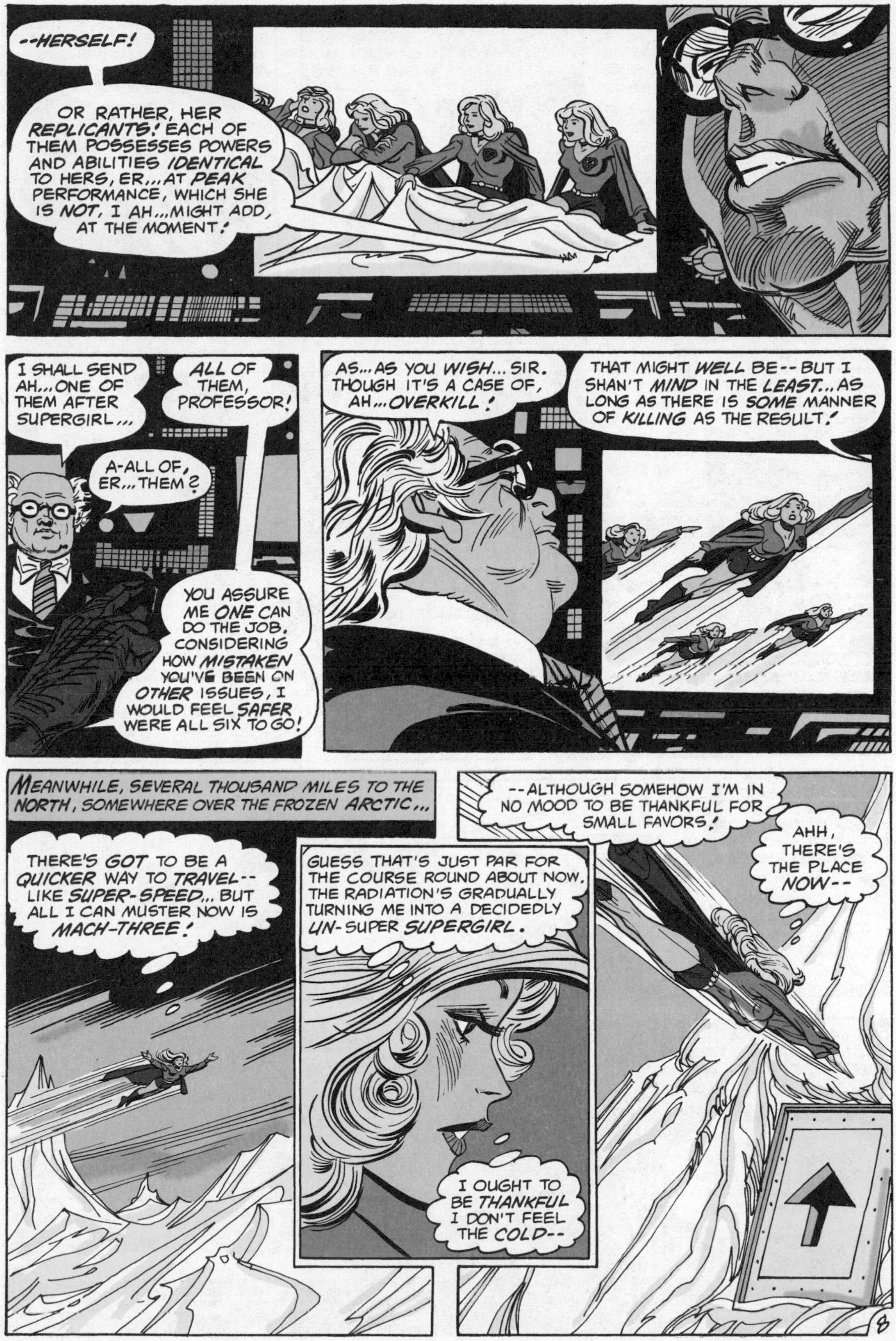
--HERSELF!
OR RATHER, HER REPLICANTS! EACH OF THEM POSSESSES POWERS AND ABILITIES IDENTICAL TO HERS, ER... AT PEAK PERFORMANCE, WHICH SHE IS NOT, I AH... MIGHT ADD, AT THE MOMENT!
I SHALL SEND AH... ONE OF THEM AFTER SUPERGIRL...
ALL OF THEM, PROFESSOR!
A-ALL OF, ER... THEM?
YOU ASSURE ME ONE CAN DO THE JOB. CONSIDERING HOW MISTAKEN YOU'VE BEEN ON OTHER ISSUES, I WOULD FEEL SAFER WERE ALL SIX TO GO!
AS... AS YOU WISH... SIR. THOUGH IT'S A CASE OF, AH... OVERKILL!
THAT MIGHT WELL BE-- BUT I SHAN'T MIND IN THE LEAST... AS LONG AS THERE IS SOME MANNER OF KILLING AS THE RESULT!
MEANWHILE, SEVERAL THOUSAND MILES TO THE NORTH, SOMEWHERE OVER THE FROZEN ARCTIC...
THERE'S GOT TO BE A QUICKER WAY TO TRAVEL-- LIKE SUPER-SPEED... BUT ALL I CAN MUSTER NOW IS MACH-THREE!
GUESS THAT'S JUST PAR FOR THE COURSE ROUND ABOUT NOW. THE RADIATION'S GRADUALLY TURNING ME INTO A DECIDEDLY UN-SUPER SUPERGIRL.
I OUGHT TO BE THANKFUL I DON'T FEEL THE COLD--
--ALTHOUGH SOMEHOW I'M IN NO MOOD TO BE THANKFUL FOR SMALL FAVORS!
AHH, THERE'S THE PLACE NOW--
8

--SUPERMAN'S *FORTRESS OF SOLITUDE!* I DOUBT IF COUSIN *KAL* WILL BEGRUDGE ME THE USE OF THE FACILITIES--

--PROVIDED I...*UHHNN*...CAN GET *IN* THE PLACE!

CAN'T LIFT THE *KEY!*

GUESS I WAS WRONG WHEN I FIGURED HE PUT THAT THING THERE AS A STUNT! THERE AREN'T A LOT OF PEOPLE WHO ARE GOING TO BREAK IN *HERE*--

--CONSIDERING ALL THE *SENSORS* AND DEFENSE GIZMOS PUT INTO THIS THING!

MY NOT FIGHTING ANY GIZMOS RIGHT *NOW* MEANS THE SENSORS HAVE MY *SCENT*--

--AND THEY DON'T *LIKE* WHAT THEY *SMELL!* THESE *DECONTAMINATION MISTS* ARE EMPLOYED AUTOMATICALLY WHEN THEY SENSE UNKNOWN RADIATION OR BACTERIA IN THE AIR!

ONLY PROBLEM IS, THEY'RE NOT GOING TO HELP ME --

--'CAUSE WHAT I'VE GOT WILL TAKE A BIT *MORE* THAN SOME INDUSTRIAL-STRENGTH *LYSOL* TO KNOCK OUT!

FUNNY... I USED TO THINK I WAS *INVULNERABLE* TO JUST ABOUT *EVERY-THING* EXCEPT *KRYPTO-NITE* AND *MAGIC*--

--AS IF I'D ACTUALLY RUN INTO *EVERYTHING* IN THE UNIVERSE!

THERE ARE FORCES OUT THERE I DON'T KNOW ABOUT THAT *CAN* KNOCK ME FOR A LOOP...

9

...THOUGH I COULD'VE LIVED WITHOUT REACTRON PROVING THAT TO ME!

WELL, LET'S SEE WHAT KAL'S MEDI-COMPUTER HAS TO SAY ABOUT WHAT AILS ME.

HER EYES CLOSE, HER BREATH GROWS SHALLOW AS SHE ALLOWS THE GENTLE ELECTRONIC HUM TO SWAY HER WEARY BODY TO SLEEP--

--UNAWARE THAT SHE HAS BEEN FOLLOWED TO THIS PLACE IN THE HEART OF NOWHERE--

--TRAILED BY BEINGS WHOSE THOUGHTS REFLECT HERS DOWN TO THE LAST SYNAPSE!

THE REPLICANTS DIVE THROUGH THE FORTRESS DOORWAY, KNOWING THEIR PRESENCE WILL BE ACCEPTED BY THE SENSORS LOCATED WITHIN --

--FOR DESPITE THEIR DIMINUTIVENESS, AREN'T THEY, EACH AND EVERY ONE, AS MUCH SUPERGIRL AS THE ORIGINAL?

WITHIN EACH DUPLICATE'S MIND IS IMPLANTED THE ENTIRE MEMORY OF KARA ZOR-EL! EVERYTHING SUPERGIRL KNOWS, THEY KNOW!

WHAT SHE FEELS, THEY CAN ANTICIPATE!

10

WHAT SHE FEARS--

--THEY CAN MAKE REAL!

WEIRD-- SUDDENLY I GET THE FEELING--

--I'M NOT ALONE!

THWONK!

GREAT....JUST *GREAT!* HOW COULD I HAVE *FORGOTTEN* ABOUT THAT MAD SCIENTIST'S *CLONES* ...*ESPECIALLY* WHEN THEY'RE CLONES OF *ME!?*

SHOULD'VE FIGURED THEY WOULD SEND ONE OF, ER... *ME!* THEN AGAIN, I DON'T THINK I REALLY EXPECTED 'EM TO *WORK!*

MY *MISTAKE*--!

BUT NOT *SERIOUS!* AT *THIS* SIZE, HOW MUCH OF A PROBLEM--

--CAN *TINY* CLONES OF ME BE--?

A *BIG* PROBLEM! SHE HAS EVERY *BIT* OF MY POWERS!...

...WHICH IS MORE THAN I CAN SAY FOR *MYSELF* AT THE MOMENT!

11

﹔UGH!﹔

BAD ENOUGH I'VE GOT TO FIGHT MYSELF LIKE THIS... BUT *SIX* OF ME AGAINST ONE?! IT'S NOT *FAIR!*

WHAT AM I *SAYING?!* OF *COURSE* IT'S NOT FAIR, YOU *DUNCE...* 'CAUSE EVEN THOUGH THEY *LOOK* LIKE YOU, THEY *AREN'T...* THEY'RE JUST *COPIES--*

--AND *UNAUTHORIZED* ONES AT THAT!

CAN'T HOLD BACK JUST BECAUSE THESE THINGS WERE ONCE *PART* OF ME! THEY'RE *SEPARATE ENTITIES...* NOT TO MENTION *HOSTILE* ONES!

CAN'T TREAT THEM ANY DIFFERENT THAN ANY PESKY *INSECT!*

WHOOSSSSSHHHH!

ISN'T THAT *RIGHT, SMALL GIRL?* I MEAN, YOU DIDN'T COME AROUND TO TALK ABOUT THE LATEST FASHION NEWS, DID YOU?

GUESS NOT. YOU DON'T SEEM ALL THAT *TALKA-TIVE,* PERIOD!

THAT'S OKAY-- I'D HATE HAVING COMPETITION IN THE *SPARKLING REPARTEE* DEPARTMENT *ANYWAY!* I....OOOOFFF!

THWOOM!

THWAAAK!

UNHHH! STARTING TO ACHE ALL OVER...GETTING DIZZY--! BETWEEN THE RADIATION POISONING...AND CLONING PROCESS, I'M IN NO SHAPE FOR THIS...!

THOSE LI'L GIRLS OF STEEL...AREN'T LETTING UP JUST BECAUSE I'M NOT UP FOR THIS FIGHT--

--BUT THEY'VE FORGOTTEN I CAN STILL GO DOWN!

13

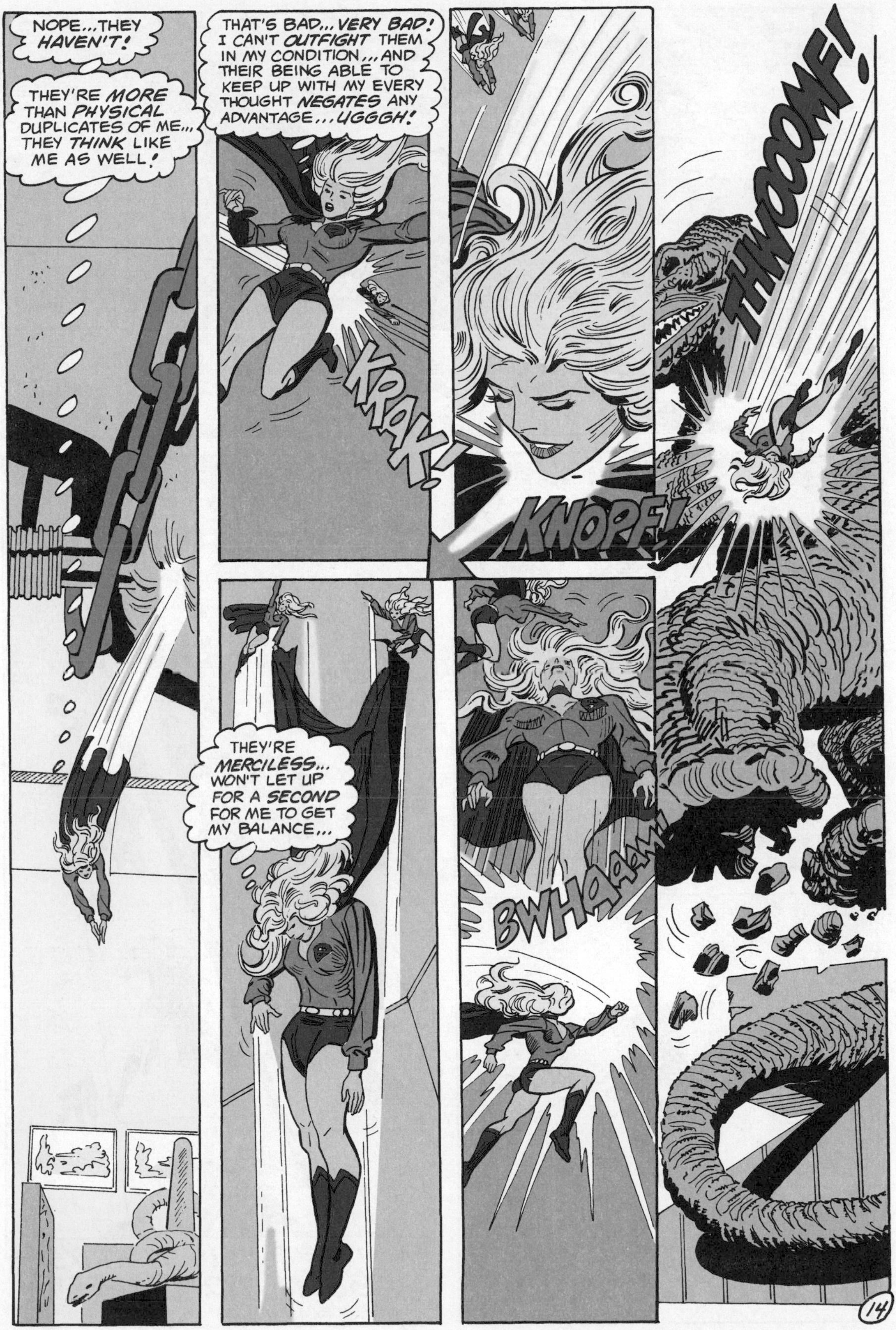
NOPE...THEY HAVEN'T!
THEY'RE MORE THAN PHYSICAL DUPLICATES OF ME... THEY THINK LIKE ME AS WELL!
THAT'S BAD... VERY BAD! I CAN'T OUTFIGHT THEM IN MY CONDITION... AND THEIR BEING ABLE TO KEEP UP WITH MY EVERY THOUGHT NEGATES ANY ADVANTAGE... UGGGH!
KRAK!
KNOPF!
THWOOOMF!
THEY'RE MERCILESS... WON'T LET UP FOR A SECOND FOR ME TO GET MY BALANCE...
BWHAAAM!
14

NEXT ISSUE: "GUESS WHO'S ABOUT TO DIE!" ON SALE JULY 21st! IT'S A DATE!

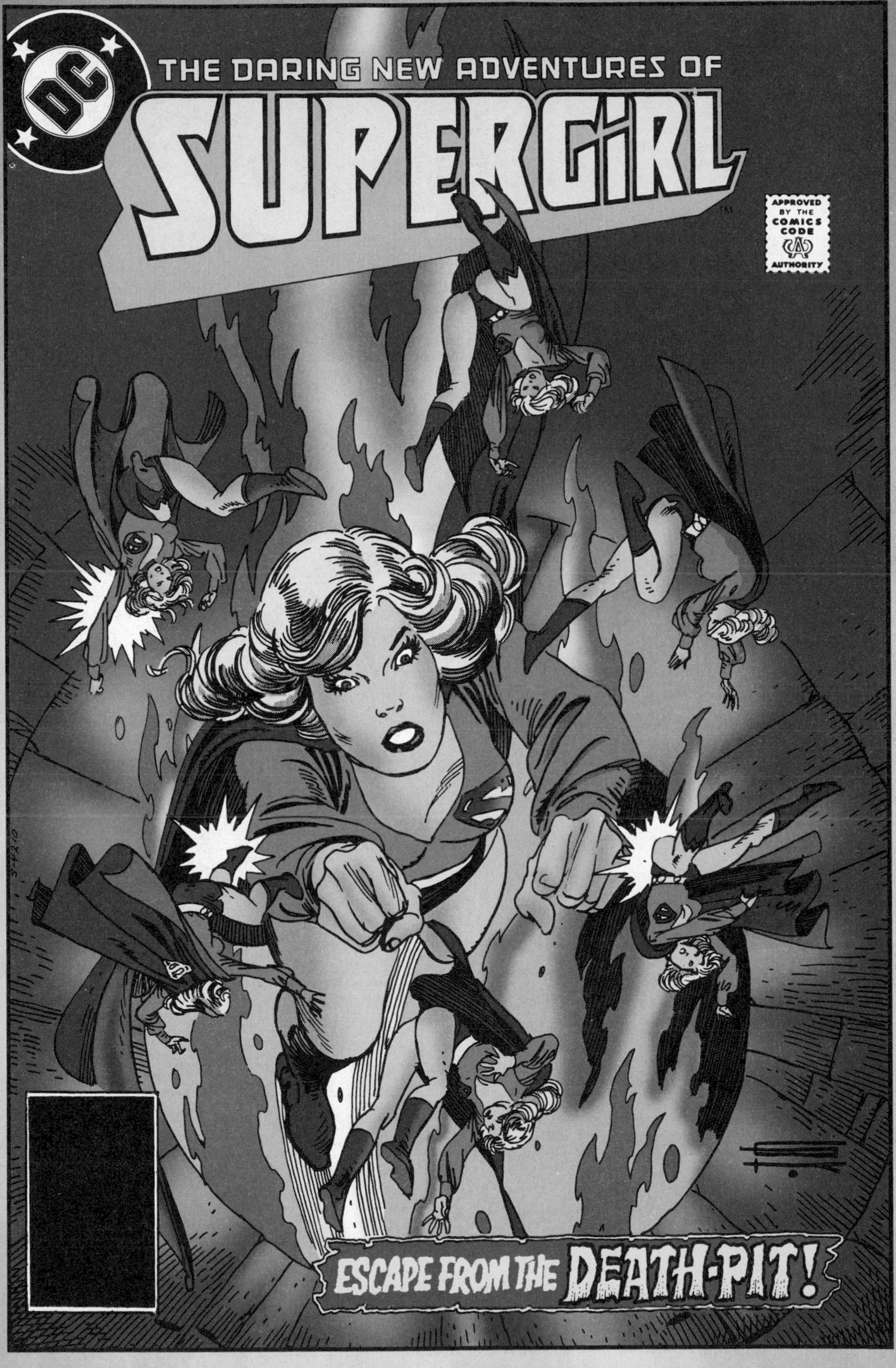

DC
THE DARING NEW ADVENTURES OF
SUPERGIRL
APPROVED BY THE COMICS CODE AUTHORITY
ESCAPE FROM THE DEATH-PIT!

Cover by **Gil Kane**

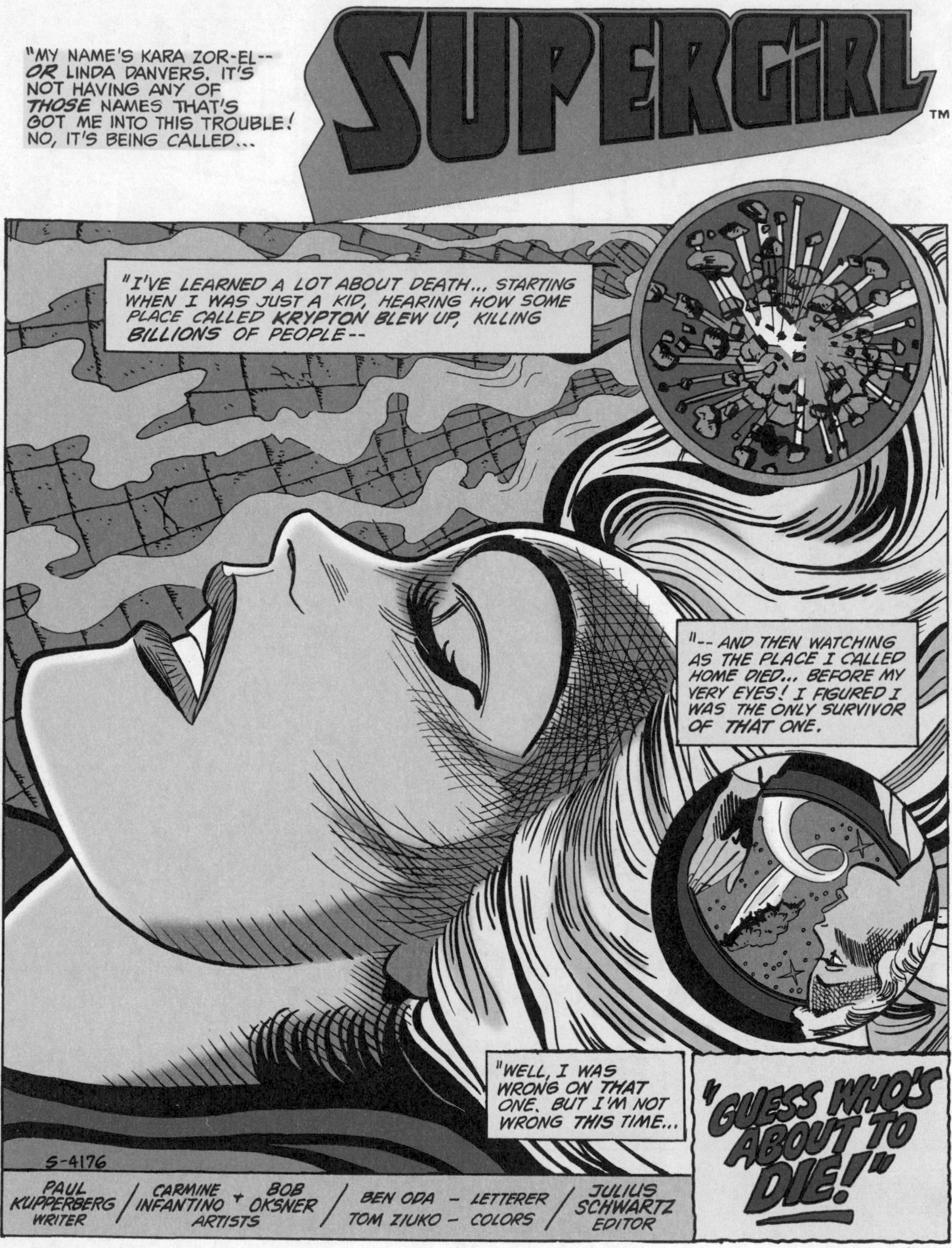
"MY NAME'S KARA ZOR-EL-- OR LINDA DANVERS. IT'S NOT HAVING ANY OF THOSE NAMES THAT'S GOT ME INTO THIS TROUBLE! NO, IT'S BEING CALLED...
SUPERGIRL™
"I'VE LEARNED A LOT ABOUT DEATH... STARTING WHEN I WAS JUST A KID, HEARING HOW SOME PLACE CALLED KRYPTON BLEW UP, KILLING BILLIONS OF PEOPLE--
"-- AND THEN WATCHING AS THE PLACE I CALLED HOME DIED... BEFORE MY VERY EYES! I FIGURED I WAS THE ONLY SURVIVOR OF THAT ONE.
"WELL, I WAS WRONG ON THAT ONE. BUT I'M NOT WRONG THIS TIME...
"GUESS WHO'S ABOUT TO DIE!"
S-4176
PAUL KUPPERBERG WRITER / CARMINE INFANTINO + BOB OKSNER ARTISTS / BEN ODA - LETTERER TOM ZIUKO - COLORS / JULIUS SCHWARTZ EDITOR

"I TRY TO FIGHT THEM, BUT LET'S FACE IT -- THE ODDS AGAINST ME ARE SIX-TO-ONE! HERE I AM, MY MUSCLES TURNED TO THE CONSISTENCY OF WARM JELLO --

"-- UP AGAINST HALF A DOZEN REPLICAS OF MYSELF... EACH WITH POWER EQUAL TO ME AT FULL STRENGTH!

"'BOUT TIME I GIVE UP AND CASH IN MY CHIPS, HUH? I MEAN, THAT RADIATION I ABSORBED ISN'T ABOUT TO MAGICALLY DISAPPEAR!*

*Courtesy of REACTRON in TDNAOS #9! --Julie

"AND THE GUY THAT CREATED THESE REPLICAS... HE KNEW WHAT HE WAS DOING ... FIGURED I WAS HALF-DEAD FROM THE RADIATION POISONING --

"-- SO WHY NOT FINISH THE JOB?

"I WANT TO RAISE MY HANDS... WANT TO TURN WHATEVER POWER I STILL HAVE ON THESE THINGS -- BUT I CAN'T...

"I DON'T HAVE THE STRENGTH TO DO ANYTHING --

"-- EXCEPT DIE.

"IT'S A LONG WAY DOWN... EVERY MOMENT OF THE FALL SEEMS LIKE AN ETERNITY.

"THE HEAT RISING AROUND ME! I CAN FEEL IT SEARING MY FLESH EVEN AS THE FALL BEGINS--

"DON'T KNOW WHEN I'VE FELT SUCH AGONY! WHAT'S IT GOING TO FEEL LIKE WHEN I HIT BOTTOM... INTO THAT SOUP OF RADIOACTIVE KRYPTONIAN ELEMENTS--?

"NO! MUSTN'T EVEN THINK ABOUT THAT!

"IT'LL ALL BE OVER IN SECONDS AND THE PAIN... THE FEAR... WILL BE DONE WITH.

"AND SO WILL I.

"RAO! ARE YOU CRAZY, KARA...?!

"YOU'RE NOT GONNA GIVE UP! C'MON-- THINK FAST! FIGURE SOMETHING OUT! AND WHATEVER IT IS--

3

"--IT'D BETTER BE GOOD!

KRMPF!

YEE-AARRGGHHH!

"NO! NOW NOW... NOT ANOTHER SPASM FROM THE RADIATION POISONING!

"GASPING...CAN'T HELP MYSELF --GONNA INHALE *UGH* FUMES... BURNING MY LUNGS...

"I DID IT! A HANDHOLD!!

"NOW... WHAT FALLS DOWN... CAN GO UP...

"...HUH?

"CHOKING! HURTS SO BAD... LIKE MY LUNGS ARE ON FIRE!

"I DON'T GET IT--

"OKAY! KEEP CALM -- THAT STUFF'S STILL HOT ENOUGH TO FRY EVEN A SUPER-KRYPTONIAN!

"DON'T EVEN INHALE ANY OF THE FUMES -- OR...

"--BUT MY BREATHING IS WORKING WONDERS!

"SOMETHING IN THE FUMES...? COULD IT BE DOING SOMETHING TO FIGHT THE RADIATION IN ME?

"ALL I KNOW IS I BETTER KEEP SUCKIN' IN THAT AIR! IT MAY SMELL WORSE THAN BAYONNE ON A HOT DAY--

4

"BUT I'M NOT COMPLAINING ABOUT THE RESULTS!"

SURPRISE, *SURPRISE,* LITTLE LOOK-ALIKES! GUESS WHO'S DECIDED SHE'S NOT UP TO BEING DISINTEGRATED TODAY...?

THAT'S RIGHT... I ALMOST *FORGOT* YOU AREN'T *MUCH* ON THE BATTLE CHATTER!

NO PROBLEM. I'LL DO THE TALKING FOR ALL OF US... OR IS THAT ALL OF *ME?*

DON'T ALL ANSWER AT *ONCE*--LET'S JUST START WITH YOU, SHORT-STUFF!

"SURE FEELS *STRANGE* FIGHTING MYSELF... EVEN MINIATURE DUPLICATES OF *ME*--

"--BUT THAT WON'T STOP ME FROM FIGHTING TO *WIN!* THESE LITTLE BUGGERS ARE HERE TO *KILL*--

"--AND EVEN IF I'M *NOT* ABOUT TO RETURN THE COMPLIMENT, THEY'VE GOT TO BE STOPPED! HAVE TO REMEMBER THEY'RE NOT *ME*--

"--NO MATTER WHAT THEY LOOK LIKE... NO MATTER THAT IN SOME STRANGE AND TWISTED WAY, THEY'RE A PART OF ME!

FORGET IT, GIRLS! THANKS TO THE MIRACLE OF MODERN, ER... SOMETHING OR OTHER, I'M A *CHANGED* PERSON-- CHANGED *BACK* TO WHAT I WAS *BEFORE* REACTRON GOT TO ME!

"THEY'RE NOT IMPRESSED.

"AND TRUTH TO TELL, I *DON'T KNOW* IF I REALLY BLAME THEM. EVEN AT *FULL* STRENGTH, THE ODDS ARE STILL SIX-TO-ONE--

"--AND THE *SURPRISES* JUST KEEP ON COMIN'! I FIGURED HEAT VISION WOULD SLOW THEM *DOWN*... BUT THEY'RE *AVOIDING* IT EVEN BEFORE I TURN IT ON THEM."

5

"GREAT!-- NOT ONLY DO THEY *LOOK* LIKE ME AND POSSESS ALL MY POWERS --THEY ALSO THINK LIKE ME!

"THEY'RE ANTICIPATING MY EVERY MOVE, TURNING MY STRATEGIES RIGHT BACK AT ME--

"-- THINKING MY OWN THOUGHTS EVEN AS *I* THINK THEM!"

C'MERE, YOU TWO LITTLE...

UGHH! DOUBLE-TEAMING ME!

YOU GUYS DEFINITELY AREN'T UP ON THE CONCEPTS OF *FAIR PLAY!*

LET'S TAKE THIS FIGHT WHERE THERE'S MORE SPACE TO *MANEUVER!*

OH... YOU ALREADY *THOUGHT* OF THAT! NOT SURPRISING ALL THINGS CONSIDERED--

--BUT I'M *STILL* GONNA HAVE TO *INSIST!*

THWAMM!

6

INTERLUDE:

A QUIET STREET IN A NORTH-EASTERN CHICAGO NEIGHBORHOOD. IDA BERKOWITZ HAS CALLED THIS STREET HOME FOR NEARLY 35 YEARS--

--FINDING THERE A PEACE, A SECURITY SHE HAS NOT KNOWN SINCE HER CHILDHOOD IN POLAND. THERE IS A SENSE OF PLACE FOR HER IN THIS BUILDING, ON THIS STREET.

THAT PEACE IS ABOUT TO BE SHATTERED. THE PLACE IS ABOUT TO BE TAINTED--

····OY····
MY GOD····!

--WITH A LITTLE BIT OF NIGHTMARE!

A SIMPLE SWEEP OF AN ARM HOLDING A SPRAYCAN... AND IDA BERKOWITZ'S SECURITY IS GONE, NEVER TO BE REPLACED.

AND THE TRUE HORROR OF IT IS THAT THERE ARE THOSE WHO TAKE SATISFACTION FROM THAT!

7

"THEY JUST WON'T GIVE UP! THEY'RE OUT AFTER SOME KRYPTONIAN BLOOD... AND THEY AIM TO *GET IT!* WELL, I WISH 'EM *LUCK*--"

"--'CAUSE THEY'RE GONNA *NEED IT!*"

YOU *KNEW* I WAS HEADED THIS WAY, DIDN'T YOU--

--BUT DID YOU KNOW I WAS GONNA DO *THIS?*

"I HAVE A PLAN, I THINK... OR MAYBE IT'S BETTER *NOT* TO THINK! ANYTHING I DO, THEY'RE GOING TO KNOW ABOUT -- BUT MAYBE, JUST MAYBE, THIS ONE'S SO *OUTRAGEOUS*--"

"--SO MUCH AN ACT OF *DESPERATION*, MY TINY REPLICAS WON'T REALIZE WHAT I'M UP TO UNTIL IT'S TOO LATE!"

CONSIDERING HOW MUCH OF *ME* YOU ARE, YOU PROBABLY *KNOW* ALL ABOUT SUPERMAN'S *INTERPLANETARY ZOO* COLLECTION--

SKREEEK!

EEARRK

-- AND THESE BEASTIES FROM OTHER WORLDS THAT PREY ON OTHER SPECIES ABOUT *YOUR* SIZE! HAVE FUN, KIDDIES--

--BECAUSE LIKE *GROUCHO* USED TO SAY... "HELLO, I MUST BE *GOING*...!"

"SO FAR, SO GOOD! I KNEW THE CRITTERS COULDN'T HURT MY DOUBLES, BUT THEY *CAN* SLOW 'EM DOWN--"

"--KEEP THEM OFF *BALANCE* ENOUGH FOR ME TO GET WHERE I'M GOING!"

WHOOOOSSHH

8

"CONSIDERING HOW NEW THEY ARE TO THE GAME, THOSE LITTLE FOLK AREN'T BAD AT SUPER-POWERED STUFF. OF COURSE, THEY HAVE MY YEARS OF EXPERIENCE TO DRAW ON--

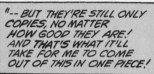

KHLWHAAM!

"-- BUT THEY'RE STILL ONLY COPIES, NO MATTER HOW GOOD THEY ARE! AND THAT'S WHAT IT'LL TAKE FOR ME TO COME OUT OF THIS IN ONE PIECE!

THWAAM!

"FRIENDS--

"-- YOU'VE JUST BEEN SUCKERED!

9

"GOLD KRYPTONITE GIVES ME THE CREEPS! IT'S SPOOKY KNOWING THERE ARE GLOWING ROCKS AROUND THAT CAN TAKE AWAY MY POWERS IN A SECOND--

"--BUT RIGHT NOW, I'M NOT COMPLAINING!

"CREEPY OR NOT, A GAL'S GOTTA DO WHAT A GAL'S GOTTA DO...

DON'T EVEN BOTHER TRYING, KIDDIES--YOUR DAYS AS MINI-SUPER-MES ARE OVER... FOR GOOD!

ONLY PROBLEM NOW IS... WHAT AM I SUPPOSED TO DO WITH HALF A DOZEN FOOT-TALL REPLICAS OF MYSELF?

"ALL RIGHT...SO NO ONE EVER PROMISED ME EVERY PROBLEM WOULD HAVE AN EASY ANSWER!"

THE SOUTH SIDE OF CHICAGO. LIKE THE SONG SAYS, IT'S THE BADDEST PART OF TOWN--

--ALTHOUGH WHEN HE PENNED THOSE WORDS, THE WRITER HAD NO WAY OF KNOWING JUST HOW BAD IT WAS...

NO...! IT... IT CAN'T BE--!

--NOT POSSIBLE AT ALL!

"I MAY NOT HAVE BEEN IN THE BEST SHAPE WHEN I LEFT HERE EARLIER, BUT I STILL REMEMBER WHERE I WAS LEFT FOR DEAD--

I'VE LOST ALL CONTACT WITH MY REPLICANTS! PERHAPS IT'S JUST, AH...A COMPUTER MALFUNCTION?!

YES! THAT MUST BE IT! IT WOULD NOT BE POSSIBLE FOR SUPERGIRL, IN HER WEAKENED STATE, TO DEFEAT THEM--

10

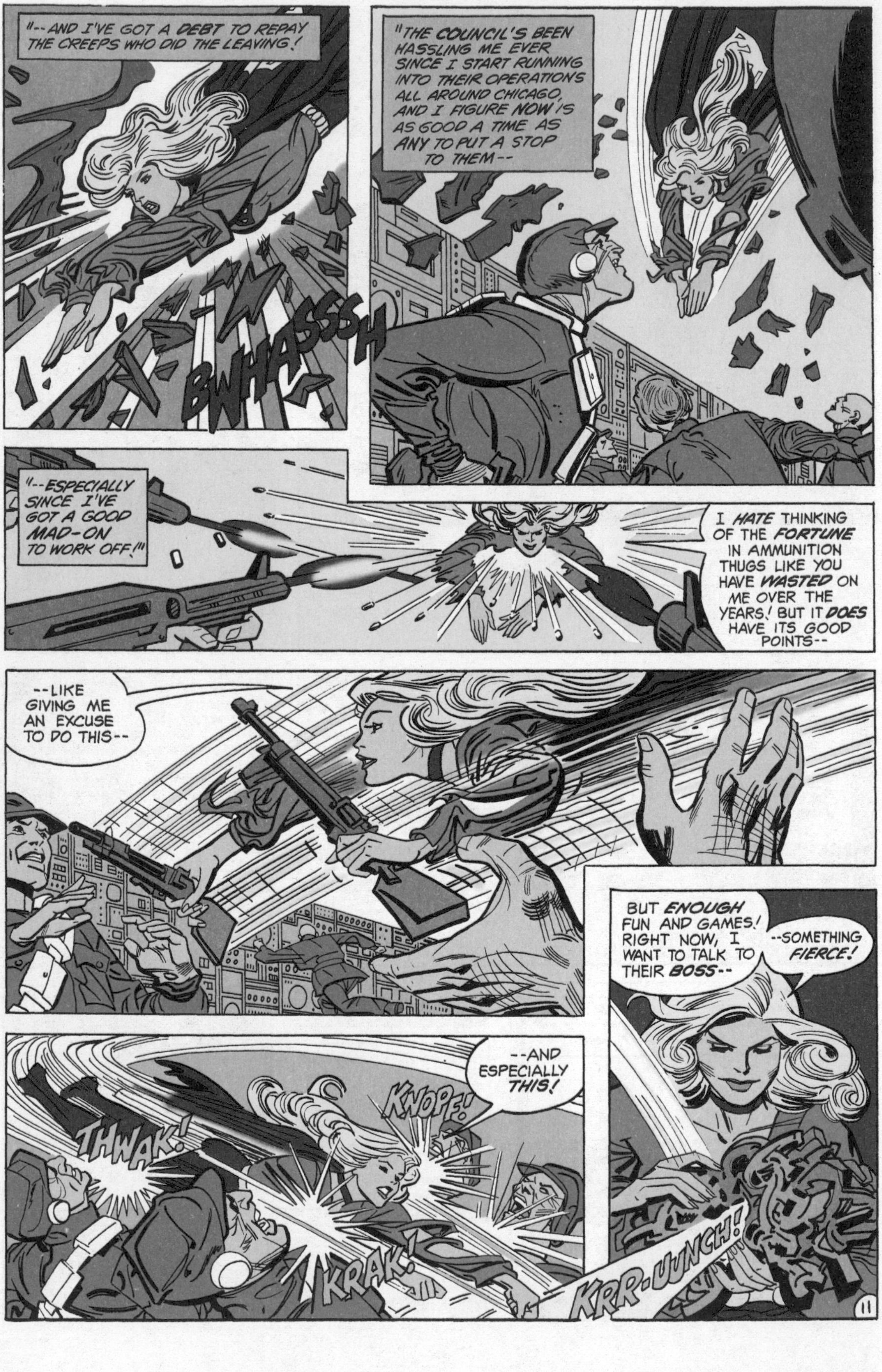
"--AND I'VE GOT A DEBT TO REPAY THE CREEPS WHO DID THE LEAVING!
BWHASSSSH
"THE COUNCIL'S BEEN HASSLING ME EVER SINCE I START RUNNING INTO THEIR OPERATIONS ALL AROUND CHICAGO, AND I FIGURE NOW IS AS GOOD A TIME AS ANY TO PUT A STOP TO THEM--
"--ESPECIALLY SINCE I'VE GOT A GOOD MAD-ON TO WORK OFF!"
I HATE THINKING OF THE FORTUNE IN AMMUNITION THUGS LIKE YOU HAVE WASTED ON ME OVER THE YEARS! BUT IT DOES HAVE ITS GOOD POINTS--
--LIKE GIVING ME AN EXCUSE TO DO THIS--
--AND ESPECIALLY THIS!
KNOPF!
THWAK!
KRAK!
BUT ENOUGH FUN AND GAMES! RIGHT NOW, I WANT TO TALK TO THEIR BOSS--
--SOMETHING FIERCE!
KRR-UUNCH!
11

OH....! FIRST I LOSE CONTACT WITH, AH....THE *REPLICANTS* AND THEN THE *ALERT* IS, ER....SOUNDED....?! C-COULD IT *BE*....?

I'M....EH....ALMOST *AFRAID* TO LOOK!

AS WELL YOU *SHOULD* BE, YOU DOD'DERING OLD *FOOL!*

TH-THE *CHAIRMAN!* THEN IT....IT, AH....IS HER--ER....*SHE?!*

YOU *REALIZE* WHAT THIS *MEANS*, DRAKE? NOT ONLY HAVE YOUR CLONES *FAILED* -- OUR ENTIRE OPER-ATION HAS BEEN PUT IN DIRE *JEOPARDY!*

I....AH, I....

SAY *NOTHING!* YOU FAILED ME....AND *THAT* I WILL NOT *TOLERATE!* YOU WERE GIVEN A CHANCE--

SUPERGIRL! WHO YOU *SWORE* TO ME WOULD *DIE* BEFORE SHE COULD RETURN HERE AND INTERFERE AGAIN!

--AND *ONE* IS ALL I WILL *ALLOW!*

PROFESSOR *DRAKE* TREMBLES, HIS VOICE A DRY CROAK IN HIS PARCHED THROAT. HE TRIES TO PLEAD FOR *MERCY.*

HE KNOWS IT WILL DO NO *GOOD.*

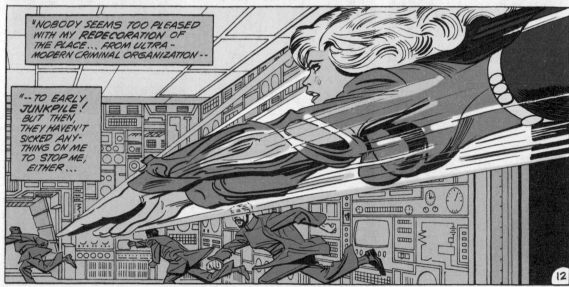

"*NOBODY* SEEMS TOO PLEASED WITH MY *REDECORATION* OF THE PLACE... FROM ULTRA-MODERN CRIMINAL ORGANIZATION --

"-- TO EARLY *JUNKPILE!* BUT THEN, THEY HAVEN'T *SICKED* ANY-THING ON ME TO *STOP* ME, EITHER...

12

"I DON'T KNOW IF ANY OF THIS'LL DO ANY GOOD! LAST TIME I TRASHED ONE OF THE COUNCIL'S SET-UPS, THEY WERE BACK IN BUSINESS IN NO-TIME FLAT!"

THWAAM

"STILL, YOU CAN'T BLAME A GIRL FOR TRYING!"

KREEEIIIIPP!

"A SCREAM--!"

"--THE KIND THAT MEANS SOMEONE'S GETTING KILLED--"

"--THE KIND YOU EITHER LOCATE REAL FAST--"

BLAMM!

"--OR WHAT YOU FIND WHEN YOU DO TRACK IT DOWN--"

RRR-RIIP!

"--IS DEATH!"

"NO PULSE... NO NOTHING. WHOEVER DID THIS DID A THOROUGH JOB-- CRUSHED HIS SKULL LIKE AN EGGSHELL."

13

"YOU'VE GOT TO BE AWFULLY *POWERFUL* TO DO THIS TO A MAN... MAYBE *MORE* POWER-FUL THAN IS POSSIBLE! IT LOOKS MORE LIKE THE WORK OF A ROBOT... OR--?"

YOUR DOING, SUPERGIRL?

WHO--? OH.

LT. PETERS, ISN'T IT?

YEAH, GABE PETERS, C.P.D. LAST TIME WE MET, YOU WERE PRAC-TICING TO BE *POSTER CHILD* FOR NATIONAL *DEAD* WEEK!

SOMETHING LIKE THAT, BUT I'M *BETTER* NOW.

SO I SEE, BUT IT LOOKS LIKE YOU WERE TRAINING *THIS* GUY TO TAKE YOUR PLACE, WHAT HAPPENED?

HIS NAME'S *DRAKE*... SOME SORT OF *MAD SCIENTIST* TYPE, OBVI-OUSLY, *SOMEONE* TOOK A GREAT *DISLIKE* TO HIS LIVING.

"*SOMEONE*"? GOT ANYTHING *BETTER* THAN THAT TO GO ON?

IF I *DID*, I WOULDN'T BE STANDING HERE TALKING TO *YOU*, PAL! I'D BE OUT ROUNDING HIM UP.

I TOLD YOU *LAST* TIME, SUPERGIRL -- WE'RE NOT *OVERJOYED* HAVING YOU *MEDDLING* IN POLICE BUSINESS IN THIS TOWN!

SORRY, LIEUTENANT, BUT THAT *HAPPENS* TO BE WHAT I *DO*!

MAYBE THAT'S WHAT YOU *DID* IN NEW YORK-- AND ELSE-WHERE-- BUT *NOT* IN CHICAGO! AND *ESPECIALLY* NOT IN A *MURDER* CASE!

I DON'T NEED YOU QUEERING A GOOD BUST BY ACTING *WITHOUT* THE PROPER AUTHORITY!

LISTEN, PETERS, I...

NO! *YOU* LISTEN--

14

--I HAPPEN TO BE THE *LAW* AROUND HERE, AND AS FAR AS *THIS* LAW'S CONCERNED, YOU'RE NOTHING BUT A *VIGILANTE!* WE'VE GOT *PROCEDURES* IN MY DEPARTMENT--

--AND *YOU* SURE *AIN'T* ONE OF 'EM! UNDERSTAND!?

OH, I UNDERSTAND ALL RIGHT! YOU WANT TO BE LEFT *ALONE* TO HANDLE MENACES LIKE *PSI* AND *MATRIX-PRIME*... JUST YOU AND YOUR *.38* HUH?

YOU *GOT* IT, SUPERGIRL! I'M *TIRED* OF HAVING TO PICK THROUGH THE *RUBBLE* EVERY TIME YOU GET FINISHED WITH SOMETHING!

"MATTER OF FACT, THAT SOUNDS LIKE THE *BEST* IDEA I'VE HAD IN A LONG TIME!"

YOU WANNA PLAY COP, *JOIN* THE DEPARTMENT AND GET YOURSELF A *BADGE!* UNTIL THEN, STAY *OUT* OF MY WAY!

YOU NEED A *HINT* AS TO WHAT YOU CAN *DO* WITH *YOUR* BADGE, PETERS?

"GREAT GOING, *KARA!* ANTAGONIZE THE ENTIRE POLICE FORCE WHILE YOU'RE AT IT, WHY DON'T YOU!

"BUT THAT BADGE-HAPPY COP GETS ON MY NERVES--!

"SOUNDS LIKE HE THINKS I'M AFTER HIS *TOUGH* JOB! AHHH, WHY WORRY ABOUT PETERS NOW? ALL I WANT TO DO IS GO SOMEWHERE AND REST--

"--FOR MAYBE ABOUT A WEEK-- A MONTH!

HEY! ISN'T THAT *SUPERGIRL*...?

NEXT: BE WITH US TO *CELEBRATE* THE *FIRST ANNIVERSARY* OF THE *MAID OF MIGHT'S* OWN TITLE IN A SPECIAL *BOOK-LENGTH THRILLER!* NEW COSTUME ... NEW *VILLAIN*... AND ALL KINDS OF NEW STUFF! On sale August 18th! IT'S A DATE!

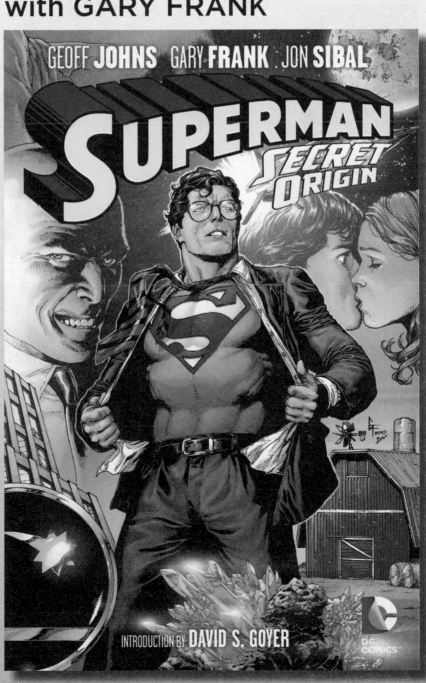